RADIO

A Post Nine-Eleven Strategy for Reaching the World's Poor

Ste ph

Wm. A. Smith

With an introduction by
Muhiuddin Haider, George Washington University

University Press of America,® Inc.
Lanham · Boulder · New York · Toronto · Oxford

Copyright © 2005 by
University Press of America,® Inc.
4501 Forbes Boulevard
Suite 200
Lanham, Maryland 20706
UPA Acquisitions Department (301) 459-3366

PO Box 317
Oxford
OX2 9RU, UK

Library of Congress Control Number: 2005926028
ISBN 0-7618-3254-8 (paperback : alk. ppr.)

DISCLAIMER

The views expressed in this manuscript are solely those of the authors and do not reflect those of the United States Agency for International Development or the Academy for Educational Development nor those of any other organization with which the authors have current or past affiliation.

TABLE OF CONTENTS

Foreword

The tragic events of Nine-Eleven have given a new urgency to reaching the teeming masses of the world's poor. "Why do they hate us?" "What can we tell them about ourselves that might change all that?" "What can we say or do for them that might lift the terrible yoke of poverty which so many of them face?" These are all questions surfacing from the depths of our conscience, demanding immediate answers. The war in Iraq and its aftermath have widened the geographic focus, not changed its immediacy. The urgency to communicate has led the U.S. Congress to focus on the resources of the media. TV, radio, Voice of America, Al-Jazeera have all suddenly become subjects of policy makers' attention.

In spite of the trauma and real sense of urgency, life goes on in many quarters, for better or for worse, in ways not much different from before the tragedy led to this partial awakening. Over eight hundred million people go to bed hungry. Every day more than forty thousand children around the world die of hunger and easily curable childhood diseases. Every five days more children die unnecessarily than in the terrible "tsunami" disaster. With the exception of Communist China, which continues to make great progress against hunger, more people are added to the list of hungry and malnourished each day. The gap between rich nations and poor ones grows apace, conditions of relative wealth and poverty now reaching their greatest disparity in the world's history. Some 4 billion people, or two-thirds of the world's population, survive on less than two dollars a day.

Confronted by the daunting challenges of poverty and the alienation it breeds, international bureaucrats continue their ministry to the world's poor with technologies more often reminiscent of the 19th century than our own era of mass communications. Radio is yesterday's or even yester-year's fad. The logic of promotions and prestige, as cubicle wisdom would have it, dictate adherence to today's fashion over the tried and true. And so, fads come and go in international aid work, their effectiveness never tested, their results irrelevant to all but those they are supposed to help. Trapped in this logic are both the poor and those who are meant to serve them. A brief time tour through the maze of development assistance will discover some of the changing faces on this many-headed hydra. These ever-changing faces are hiding our ability to see the poor, and more im-portantly to reach them.

The four-wheel drive vehicle is the delivery mechanism of choice for foreign assistance, costing upward of one hundred thousand dollars for se-lect vehicles outfitted since nine-eleven with tinted bulletproof glass and armor, marrying 19th century locomotion with 20th century security. The training seminar is the primary point of contact with the poor or "near poor" who are supposed to minister to them but seemingly never do. The conference hall is the preferred proving ground for all this "help." Tucked away safely in a luxurious hotel in London or Paris, development practi-tioners can meet to "discuss" the poor. If the means are somewhat passé, if not downright primitive, and the technology secondhand at its best, then what exactly does the foreign assistance industry deliver? This can change as the direction of a weather vane or as swiftly and directionless as palm leaves in the wind.

As recently as the late 1980s, commodity assistance was the vogue in international aid, but it has disappeared for the most part. Policy and struc-tural reform accompanied it. Increasingly unpopular, these were subsumed recently under the guise of poverty reduction! Private sector support pro-grams followed commodities. Results management then became the new paradigm upon which all these assistance modes would rise or fall. Need-less, to say there were few results and less management. Many results that were achieved were intangible, or only visible with time that the measur-ers often did not have. Schemes continued to replace each other fre-quently. A shift in cape occurred, as the yacht of international develop-ment tacked in yet another windless direction, back to the basics of community empowerment through the agency of private voluntary organi-zations. A democratization and civil society focus followed. After a seem-ingly tacit acknowledgement that all else was failing, "conflict preven-tion" was to become the watchword of the day. The Internet was to have a brief fleeting moment in all this when optimism about the new technology peaked at the turn of the millennium, its usefulness to the poor, however, never really assessed. And the radio? The radio had been out of fashion since at least the late 1970s. Had it been ineffective in reaching the poor?

In spite of this "holy grail" like search for a development "elixir" which resembles more a cat chasing its tail than any attempt "to catch a mouse,"[1] poverty continues to grow around the world. In an era of dwindling funding for development, growing poverty and chaos, can one afford to ignore the ubiquitous tool of human communication that is the radio? Everyday, in the Washington D.C. area, information on personal finances, retirement, health, relationships, gardening, agriculture, automotive care, community and current events comes to us via the radio. With all the resources available to a literate Washingtonian of middle class income, the radio is still one of the best sources of practical information in any of a number of domains. However, strip away the ability to read, strip away a steady supply of electricity, strip away daily newspapers and weekly journals and you are left with the information channels available to most of the world's poor. This is not a situation solely to be lamented though, but an opportunity in disguise. Today's radio is more powerful and less costly— solar or wind-up, digital, satellite or interactive—and enjoys greater political freedom in many parts of the world, than ever before.

In the chapters that follow, we will give a brief history of the use of the radio in development that will highlight some of the most effective uses from experiences around the world. We will talk in particular about interactive programs. Both low and high tech radio, from wind-up to solar powered and digital, will be discussed. Internet use and how the Internet is lowering costs of radio programming and distribution will be the subject of a chapter—the last mile in reaching the poor. We will engage the reader in some discussion of why the use of radio has lapsed and been forgotten in international development work.

Most importantly, we let radio scripts speak for themselves. For many programs, the voice of the radio, even in written form, transmits its power to change and affect lives. A brief introduction to the setting of the scripts places them in their social context, illustrating the interaction between radio and the social problems it is trying to address. A program script in original English, or translated, from some of the very best radio around the world follows. Many chapters have epilogues which tell the story of the impact of the scripts on the local population. The possibilities available from new radio technologies and some excellent current programs will be explored. The world turns.

Notes

1. Deng Xiao Ping, Chinese Premiere, "It doesn't matter if the cat is black or white, as long as it catches the mouse."

Preface

by Dr. Wm. A. Smith

"For the first time in human history we have available to us the ability to communicate simultaneously with millions of our fellowmen, to furnish entertainment, instruction, a widening vision of national problems and national events."

Yes it is true, the Internet is a vast network that allows us to communicate simultaneously, but this quote is not about the Internet. The quote is from Herbert Hoover in 1922, about radio. Radio was the first enfant terrible of the modern communication era. Radio geeks in the 1920s built their own radio receivers and created their own radio networks. Early radio was a free-for-all of ideas and experimentation. Commercialization, the rise of television and now the Internet, have made radio in the West predominately a medium of news, advocacy and music.

This book is a labor of love and respect for radio, particularly radio in the developing world—a world of villages and crowded cities; of wealth, talent, poverty and educational inequality. This is a world of democracies emerging and terrible injustices continuing. It is largely a world pre-Internet and in many cases pre-television and pre-electrification. Unlike the West, this is a world where radio and its ability to reach, teach, advocate and inform are vital today.

I was fortunate to be involved with several of the stories told here, and helped in a small way to foster radio's use in developing countries from the early 1970s to the present day. My work at the Academy for Educational Development, gave me a unique opportunity to see radio at work in Asia, throughout the Middle East and Africa and especially in Latin America. In the 1970s we were constructing radio stations in Guatemala, experimenting with interactive radio in the classroom in Kenya, using radio to train thousands of women to treat infant diarrhea properly and developing radio novellas that often became the most trusted voice in villages which had little or no other contact with the world.

The actual work of radio production was always done by local radio professionals. We provided training, suggested a few new approaches, funded opportunities to experiment and learn new things. We evaluated programs to see if they actually worked to save lives and change public policy. But the creative voice and the control room genius always came from a small group of immensely talented and committed radio journalists, novelists, and educators from countries like Kenya, Honduras, Indonesia, The Gambia and Ecuador.

My co-author, Stephen Sposato's perspective from that of a development economist has allowed him to understand radio's integral importance to the poor and the insufficiency of investment in educational radio today. He has situated radio in its historic context illustrating its power and continuing relevance. We have identified and included some of the best radio scripts from around the world in almost all the chapters. Several were translated for this book and are true works of art. But many other excellent programs went unrecorded. They were live broadcasts. Some that were recorded on audio tapes have long ago been lost; mildewed, scratched and torn by the causal passage of time.

The contribution of the United States Agency for International Development (USAID) to the understanding of how radio works for development has been significant over the many decades I have been involved. If the poor are to be helped meaningfully today, USAID and others must continue to invest in quality educational programming and support local efforts to do so. Radio is the only media with the "reach and frequency" to affect the hundreds of millions of truly impoverished around the world, as we hope to demonstrate in this book. It also happens often to be the best!

If USAID and its contractors made a few mistakes, they are in good company. But the Agency's almost 30-year commitment to experimentation, evaluation and promotion of radio as a means of social change is an enduring legacy, one that must be kept alive and relevant in today's changing world. The role of people like Dr. Anthony Meyer and Dr. Clifford Block who believed in radio when many were skeptical, must be applauded. For people who believe that government can't work, USAID's history of involvement in radio for development is an example of how wrong they can be.

Radio is alive and well. Some of its most important applications have been forgotten, and some of its newest applications are not well known. Despite the rapid adoption of new technologies, radio retains its unique potential to advocate, to train, to instruct, to organize, and to entertain in some of the most desperate, most isolated, and most dangerous places on the earth. There are still millions of radio receivers scattered through the slums of great cities and the mountains of vast rural areas. The story of radio for human development is still being written and our hope is that this book both celebrates the past pioneers and jump-starts a new ear of experimentation and growth.

Acknowledgements

The book belongs to the community. Only its authors have been given the gift of error by the gods. The power to create, to bring to life, is also the power to err. When a mother brings a newborn into the world in all its splendor, she once again rips open the world to the possibility of imperfection, for by bringing life one resurrects all life's inadequacies. If the cardinal sin, as Schopenhauer pretends, is procreation, then an author is the seminal sinner.

Who has joined with us in this immense power to sin on behalf of the community? Who are these mid-wives of the errors hiding in the folds of the creation they have inspired? Those who have helped us arrive on the sill of this communal undertaking, looking wryly out over a world of beauty are many. Picture their chagrin as they discover our imperfections hidden in their otherwise "good works."

The scholarly and earnest Professor of Communication, Dr. Everett M. Rogers was the first to generously help and encourage us, along with Dr. Arvind Singhal his frequent co-author. Together, these two have done more to keep the airwaves within hearing of the poor than the combined prattle of much of the development community. Tom Carter of USAID, Dartmouth philosopher and 18 year denizen of India's Dairy Development Board, had sufficient philosophy to remember the early days of ag-radio in the Indian countryside and exhort us to the Sisyphean task of "getting it going" again. His introduction to Dr. Rogers and Dr. Singhal, and their encouragement, were very much at the origin of a project which at the time seemed bigger and heavier than Sisyphus' rock.

Dr. Tony Meyer of USAID who diligently pursued effective communication solutions for the poor throughout his long career in development shared the early and now hard to find work on the radio found in his personal library and by so doing pointed us down the path which has led us here. Dr. Elizabeth Fox, a prolific author on the history of media in Latin America, where she spent much of her career teaching and doing community broadcasting, has preserved through her writings much of that region's rich history. Dr. Alfonso Gumucio Dagron's own inspired writing on community radio for the Rockefeller Foundation was another invaluable resource.

Sonny Fox of Population Communication International (PCI) had the foresight to understand the value of the present project and to support us with his ample personal "social capital" and that of PCI. In South Africa, doctor of medicine, Garth Japhet's extraordinary work in using the media, both TV and radio, to reach the poor and his tireless and personable efforts in bringing the experience of "Soul City" to communities around the world, merits a special thanks. So too does Anton Schneider of the Academy for Educational Development who helped us apply the fatherly virtue of patience as we guided our creation through its difficult transition to a mature work, enduring as we did the destructive forces which abound in international development work. Acknowledgement also to Michelle Riley, who along with Kristine Pearson, Director of Freeplay Foundation, have so diligently nurtured the growing family of radio listeners worldwide, helping radio's "good works" to spread by providing Freeplay's wind-up and solar radios which "keep on playing" to the world's poor. Kitty Warnock, my first contact at Panos gave us our first readable script, "Woman and War" that convinced us that we could show readers the power of radio through the written word. Kitty and her colleague at Panos, Olivia Bennett, can now wince along with the others.

Romila Sudhir, dedicated development librarian and Krishna Kumar, distinguished author in his own right, believed in the project. They held our hands through the emotional maze that is the labyrinth of the publishing industry, taking a manuscript from inspiration to print. Laura Shelley, diligent editor, and Olivia Marinescu cannot be thanked enough. They put the nails in the book's scaffolding, helping to turn our architecture and the book's *grand design* into reality.

Besides these individuals, there are organizations complicit in this conspiracy of creation. To the Academy for Educational Development, Population Communications International and Panos, a special thanks is in order for the scripts, sometimes translated at their own expense, that have laid bare the beauty and power of the radio. Their tireless radio work around the world has brought information and hope to millions. A special acknowledgement is also due to the Freeplay Foundation and their unflagging support of the project. To these organizations and the continuation of their good works, we would like to donate the proceeds of this book. Like repentant sinners everywhere, this small penitence is our atonement for defiling their good works.

To others who have provided scripts, the incomparable Archers of the BBC, VOA and Soul City, no amount of thanks can suffice. To all those whose diligent research and radio work have made this book possible—one and all—we say "mea culpa."

Stephen Sposato
Wm. A. Smith

A full acknowledgement of rights and permissions for scripts used in whole or in part in this manuscript include: The Academy for Educational Development, the BBC, the estates of Geoffrey Webb and Edward J. Mason, the International Office of Migrations, Panos, Population Communications International, the Soul City Institute for Health and Development Communication, the Voice of America and the United States Agency for International Development.

Introduction

By Dr. Muhiuddin Haider[1]

Health and economic well being are the province of the individual. Like much else in modern society they are also systems with providers and recipients. In order to engage and involve the people who are the targets of our health and economic development programs, we depend on communication to create the essential bridge between our resources and those in need. These connections between programs and people are essential for success. Communication is the key to the good functioning of the health care and development systems. A simple fact of working in international health and development is that development cannot simply be 'done' to a country or population. Resources alone, whether monetary, physical or in personnel, are largely ineffective without the active involvement of the people we are providing assistance to; the vaccinated are as essential as the vaccines, and family planning cannot happen without families. Communication remains the vital component in any program reaching out to the global poor.

I personally find the history and application of development radio to be very compelling, having witnessed radio at work in my native country of Bangladesh. As a young student at the Dhaka University in the late 1960s, I was inspired by seeing development programs using radio communication, often with the still prevalent vacuum tube technology, advance social and technological development, promote behavioral change in family planning, and direct farmers through agricultural transition.

My memories of development radio being used to confront many of the health and development challenges facing my country, fit alongside the experiences presented by Stephen Sposato and Bill Smith, giving this book an added value for me in my work in health communication. My students, too, will be able to profit from some of the first hand radio broadcasts, chosen for their excellence, and set in their context in the manuscript, as well as the compelling story of the radio in development that the authors relate. Radio has come a long way.

Communication in its most basic form is limited; its range extends only as far as the spoken word is heard, and mass communication can be little more than speaking before a gathered audience. However, technological developments allow for great improvements to communication, giving us the chance to reach more listeners, across long distances, and beyond geographic and political boundaries. Broadcast technology, for example, allows for distance communication to happen instantaneously, rather than waiting on the physical delivery of a message or messenger, while newer technologies, such as the Internet and video-conferencing, create opportunities for greater interactivity than the largely one-way exchanges of television and radio broadcasts.

Regrettably, the general rule is that where the needs are greatest, the means tend to be the least, and in poor countries the advances in technology that improve the communication we enjoy go largely unseen. With this in mind, it is important to approach communication technology in health and development from a somewhat different angle. Rather than look at what is possible with technology, we should look at what limitations these technologies face in the environments in which our programs will work. Long distance or mass communication invariably relies on infrastructure for creating and transmitting, as well as receiving, the message. Television and radio require broadcast stations and TVs or radios on the receiving end; the Internet requires server and client computers. While the infrastructure to produce and broadcast a message exists in every country to at least some degree, most of the end-user technologies are far beyond the resources of most individuals, families and often communities among the world's poor.

An alternative view of communications technology makes it possible to develop communication goals that better suit the environment in which development programs are put to the test. The message should be easy and inexpensive to produce and transmit. The technology for receiving the message should be similarly low cost and, ideally, the end-user infrastructure should already be in place. Additionally, it is important that the message be easily understood, and it is in this regard that barriers such as language differences and illiteracy need to be considered. Moreover, the message should be able to overcome obstacles such as distance and physical or political boundaries as needed.

In a simplistic comparison, we can look at several common means of communication—hand billing, an aid team with a four-wheel drive vehicle, and radio. Handbills or flyers are inexpensive to produce, but are limited by the fact that they must be physically delivered to the area and drastically lose their effectiveness in areas with high illiteracy. An aid worker traveling with a four-wheel drive vehicle is similarly hampered by distances and having to make direct person-to-person contact, and carries the expense of both the vehicle, fuel, and personnel support and salary if the worker is not a volunteer. Radio waves, on the other hand, are not limited to ground travel and can cover great distances instantaneously, while requiring comparatively low-cost equipment for both transmitting and receiving. Radio is a uniquely capable technology for reaching the world's poor, marrying many of the strengths of modern broadcast and mass communication with the qualities of being low-cost, comparatively low-tech, and readily usable in the limited technological environment of underdeveloped countries and regions.

In the chapters that follow, Stephen Sposato and Bill Smith take a compelling look at experiences in using radio in health and development. The authors examine in detail the qualities of radio that motivate them to champion its use in aid programs, while also establishing a framework for applying a technology that lacks the richness of many mediums we enjoy in more developed countries. *A priori*, one is challenged to envision uses for radio beyond a passive, marketing-style approach. This book goes beyond that limited role for radio, sharing the rich, yet underreported, experiences of radio-based health and development programs. The innovative models for the use of radio shared in the chapters that follow, illustrated by real world experiences, provide students and professionals with the tools they need to capitalize on a powerful but oft-overlooked technology in reaching the world's poor.

In the first chapter, Sposato and Smith detail the early history of distance communication, as well as the history of radio and the early use of informational radio. Chapter 1 also introduces radio abroad with the development of far reaching radio networks as a part of the expansion of the colonial powers of the early 20th century and the role of radio in post-colonial societies. The authors continue to describe the environment in which radio was used through the second half of the 20th century throughout Latin America, Africa and Asia. Sposato and Smith touch on several of the great successes of development radio in its heyday while sharing the insights of the early proponents of its use before describing the general decline of development radio under various social and economic pressures.

Each of the subsequent chapters serves as a case study for a specific example of radio in international development. The radio programs shared by Sposato and Smith demonstrate innovative uses for radio beyond the simple public service announcement interjected into an otherwise commercial entertainment broadcast. Ranging from provocative 'soap opera' styled series carrying strong social messages to development programs that integrate radio with facilitated meetings at the village level, these examples show the power of radio and creative programming.

Chapter 2 introduces radio programming for social change. It describes the story of a radio drama series in West Africa that utilized provocative storylines to promote changes in family planning, sexual health, and child health. Relying simply on the power of radio and an engaging story, this USAID program successfully reached out to millions of West Africans to promote social change. A similar approach is highlighted in Chapter 3; however, this time the goal of the program is agricultural development and education and the setting is the post-war, ravaged United Kingdom, a setting not unlike many faced in developing countries today. The program, the BBC's "Archers," a pioneer in the creative use of radio for extension, is still on the air today.

In Chapter 4, Sposato and Smith look at an innovative program that use radio as an integral part of a coordinated educational campaign. Chapter 4 examines the success of the Mtu Ni Afya program in Tanzania, in which weekly radio programs facilitated by trained volunteers provided villagers with practical information on issues facing rural Tanzanians and motivated the participants to take action within their communities.

Chapter 5 "'Ama Mas'–Breast-fed by Radio," describes the role of radio as a tool for the broad based training of community leaders. This chapter explores two programs in Latin America that sought to spread breast-feeding education. The first example, "Ama Mas" in Honduras, used radio as a vehicle for instruction supported by printed booklets. This program also used a certificate as an incentive to prod women to complete the program. The second example in this chapter details a similar program in Ecuador. This program built on the experience of "Ama Mas" but sought to provide a greater depth of training for community leaders. This radio-based training would be supplemented by print materials, as in "Ama Mas," and weekly training with local health workers. While the women enrolled in the program were identified by local health clinics and were interested in promoting breast-feeding practices, a lottery was also utilized as an incentive to complete the training.

In Chapter 6, Sposato and Smith look at international radio networks, and specifically the Voice of America. The chapter describes the partnership between the VOA and donors such as USAID, and the challenges donors face in reaching communities through international radio networks. The case cited in this chapter is a program in support of the World Health Organization (WHO) polio vaccination campaign in Nigeria; however, the authors also use this chapter as an opportunity to discuss the broader context of Western broadcast networks in Muslim countries.

Sposato and Smith look at programming centered on the well being of women in Chapter 7, albeit returning to the serial drama format. This chapter looks at the experience of radio programming in confronting the health and social status of women in northern India.

Chapter 8, appropriately titled "Afghanistan—A Missed Opportunity?" looks at the limited role of radio in the international aid effort in that war torn country, and advocates further involvement of international donors in development radio. Sposato and Smith make a persuasive argument for the expanded use of radio in the inhospitable geography and difficult security climate of post-Taliban Afghanistan.

The case examined in Chapter 9 departs from the more overt or narrative approaches highlighted in earlier chapters and shares the experience of "Women and War" on Women's Day, March 8, 1996. Rather than rely on narrative, the program relied solely on the powerfully compelling testimonies of women affected by violent conflict.

Chapter 10 highlights a creative campaign in Gambia that taught women how to administer oral rehydration therapy. Using radio to broadcast the "Happy Baby Lottery," the campaign relied on the inexpensive but far-reaching lottery to provide an incentive for rural mothers to seek out the trained volunteer 'diarrhea experts' in their communities in order to learn how to mix and administer the oral rehydration therapy solution. Both of these programs demonstrate the potential for imaginative applications of radio in educating and empowering people otherwise beyond the reach of health systems, at a lower cost than traditional aid programs.

The authors tackle one of the leading health problems facing the world, HIV and AIDS, in Chapter 11. HIV has increasingly become a disease of the poor and often underserved in much of the world. Where other health services are failing to reach the poor, radio has shown itself to be a cheap and effective route for HIV education. In this chapter, the authors look at the role of radio in HIV education in Africa with radio programming supported by Population Communications International.

Chapter 12 takes on the very typical approach of spot advertising on common radio, essentially the public service announcements, that are often heard on commercial networks. While arguably less provocative than more comprehensive programs are, these "radio nags" can have a meaningful impact. To that end, Sposato and Smith provide a useful analysis of spot messages and the approaches to maximize their effectiveness.

The "Soul Buddyz" program, highlighted in Chapter 13, is an example of radio being used not as a vehicle for promoting change, but rather as the change itself. This chapter presents the use of a radio drama in South Africa to fill a social void and to provide a greater sense of community for young children in poor communities ravaged by HIV, dysentery and other endemic contributors to poor health.

The authors share an experience with radio and the poor from a different angle in Chapter 14. The story of Radio Mineras in Bolivia is one of radio by and for the poor instead of by a government or development group. The network of radio stations established by the miners created strong social connections among the isolated communities spread across mountainous highlands of Bolivia. This chapter examines the relationship between the community and their radio network, and the solidarity demonstrated in the face of violent opposition from nationalist governments.

Interactive radio instruction in elementary education is examined in Chapter 15 "Talking Back to the Radio." This chapter provides a study of a Kenyan program to teach English to young pupils through the use of radio in the classroom. Sposato and Smith look at this case while also bringing to light the experiences of other countries in augmenting their limited teaching resources with interactive radio instruction. This chapter shows that radio can lead to real improvements in educational status when the educational system lacks the resources, sufficiently trained teachers, and materials to achieve those gains through conventional approaches.

The book closes with Chapter 16 providing an analysis of modern radio and its potential for use in international development. Ongoing technological progress has made it possible to do more with radio at less cost than ever before. The technology to broadcast and receive has continued to move forward since its early applications in international development, in much the same way as we see computer technology becoming more powerful while at the same time less expensive. Sposato and Smith conclude the book with a look at the technologies available today and the resources already in place for broadcasting and receiving development radio. At present, radio has the greatest penetration of any media form with low cost radios found nearly universally throughout low and middle-income countries. Beyond the traditional analog networks of radio, the telecommunications revolution has ushered in digital satellite radio with global networks capable of reaching billions of people. While other communications technologies have largely passed over low income countries, radio is continuing to develop a greater capacity to reach virtually anywhere on earth.

The power of radio is the power of voice. Among the most memorable moments in our collective history are the speeches of great leaders like Kennedy, Gandhi, and King. These moments in history were shared not just by loudspeaker or television, but also by radio. Although speech is the most basic form of communication, the spoken word is truly very powerful, whether in the most profound speeches or the most mundane conversations. The spoken word is the way we communicate countless times daily, with friends, family, coworkers, teachers, students, and total strangers. Since the earliest moments of speech, we have tried to extend its reach, if only by simply speaking louder or from higher ground. Today, we benefit from radio, a technology that gives us the ability to speak to communities, to reach across distances, over mountains and rivers, and beyond boundaries, political or social.

Radio, as with any form of communication, relies heavily on the credibility of its source in order to have a meaningful impact. It becomes increasingly difficult or at times impossible to affect change through radio programming when the listeners distrust the broadcaster; what may be intended as helpful information may be perceived as propaganda or deception. This is particularly challenging for practitioners trying to work across cultural or political divides. Long established and generally well-trusted international organizations such as the World Health Organization still face this obstacle in their work, as seen in the 11 month ban on the polio vaccine in Nigeria where Muslim leaders believed the WHO-administered vaccines would cause infertility and spread HIV amongst Muslims.[2] Credibility is especially critical in radio, where dismissing a program is as easy as turning the dial. In order to ensure that our message is well received, we must take into consideration how our assistance is perceived and how we can improve that perception.

There is a great potential for radio in international development. While newer technologies empower us to communicate in bold new ways, it is important not to overlook the significance of a technology within reach of those with the most limited means. The world's poor have largely been passed over by the technological leaps of recent decades. It will be important to close that gap as a part of the continuing efforts in international development but at the same time, we should not ignore what is available, capable and proven. Radio, with a rich history in health and development, is a technology within reach of those with the greatest need. At present, there is no other medium in place with the capacity to extend so far and to reach so many people. The potential listeners among the world's poor are an essential constituency in our work in international health and development. However, while the capacity to reach out is largely in place, it is up to practitioners to create programs that will not only keep listeners tuned in but also prompt them to take action.

Stephen Sposato and Bill Smith make a compelling case through example and analysis for the use of radio, a powerful and comparatively inexpensive tool, in programs aimed at the world's poor. Beyond that, in writing this book, the authors provide students and professionals alike with a valuable history and a practical guide to using this valuable technology in health and development programs.

Notes

1. Dr. Haider is Professor of Communications in the Department of Global Health, The George Washington University School of Public Health and Health Services, Washington, D.C. Dr. Haider had the benefit of assistance from Michael Dávila, an MPH candidate in International Health Policy and Programs at the George Washington University, in reviewing the manuscript and the preparation of this introduction.

2. Fiona Fleck, "Nigerian State of Kano Resumes Polio Vaccination," *British Medical Journal* 329, no. 7457 (July 10 2004), 70.

1
Voice Out —Village In
—The Radio Ushers in Dramatic Change—

Imagine a world where the only sounds were those of nature, the cries of birds on the wing, the rustling of leaves and stalks in the wind, perhaps, occasionally the resonating call of a human voice. You will have recreated the ancestral village, home to humanity and to most of our forbears for the greater part of the millennia that human beings have roamed the planet. Imagine further, the contacts of the village with the external world of city-states, principalities and empire, as later in human evolution these large forms of social organization become more common: the occasional military detail to collect taxes or forcibly conscript young men, the herald at the time of the death of a ruler or the invasion of a hostile horde. Aside from these intrusions, daily life goes on in the village as it had for your grandparents and their grandparents before them. Religious beliefs change little, handed down since time immemorial. Marriage customs and tradition follow suit. News, whatever news there is, is that of the weather, drought, floods or military threat. Culture and language are as constant and repetitive as the seasons; as perhaps, in the retelling by a village storyteller of ancient tales passed down orally from generation to generation.

The advent of radio, a precipitous break in the technology of communication preceded by only a few years by the telegraph, was suddenly and dramatically to put the world in touch, one village with another! Imagine now hearing of customs so different and astonishing that one had never even imagined their possibility, of hearing myriad accents and dialectic variations of ones own language, of machines unknown or dress and weaponry unparalleled. Suddenly the world has become a different place. A place where a beneficial discovery in one place can be quickly transmitted to another, a threat or menace instantaneously conveyed.

Distance Communication, Baby Steps [1]

A cry, a shout, a gesture across a field, the first attempts at distance communication came naturally, later to be enhanced by couriers or messengers from kings. The first attempts at distance communication were primitively fitting to the technology available. In Africa and North America, "talking" drums bridged distances from early times on. The Persian King, Darius I, who set up a relay of men shouting from geographic high points to convey news from the capital to the provinces, enhanced the technologies of simple shouting or couriers for longer distances, in the fourth century BC. The Greek historian, Diodorus Siculus, reports that this type of communication was 30 times faster than couriers, another form of communication at a distance during that time:

> Although some of the Persians were distant a thirty days' journey, they all received the order on that very day, thanks to the skillful arrangement of the posts of the guard, a matter that it is not well to pass over in silence. Persia is cut by many narrow valleys and has many lookout posts that are high and close together, on which those of the inhabitants who had the loudest voices had been stationed. Since these posts were separated from each other by the distance at which a man's voice can be heard, those who received the order passed it on in the same way to the next, and then these in turn to others until the message had been delivered at the border of the satrapy. [2]

Julius Caesar in the *Gallic Wars* writes that the Gauls could call together their warriors in three days through a combination of voice calls, fires, smoke and mirror like reflections from silica and other surfaces. [3] Even the Bible reports the use of fire and smoke by Moses to guide the Jewish tribes fleeing Egypt. Signs and signals for distance communication are also reported in antiquity, but voice continued to be the principal mode of "distance communication" for centuries to come. Lerner comments on the importance of oral communications in sixteenth century Ottoman Empire:

> Oral communication was the rule under the Ottoman dispensation. Public criers, itinerant preachers, and merchant caravans carried the 'news' from one locality to another. It was then orally relayed through the corresponding milieu of each locality, such as the coffee house, the mosque, the market place and caravansary. The contents of 'the news' reflected the utter dependence of the populace upon a remote center. [4]

From Baby Steps to Technology

More than several millennia were to pass for the history of distance communication to evolve from its beginnings in oral communication and sign language to its next steps or rather strides. An optical telegraph, invented by the Frenchman Claude Chappe and his brother Ignace, was first used in 1794 to announce the French victory over the Austrians. The discovery of electric current parallels the work with light and the development of a luminescent alphabet. Many savant names are associated with the discovery and harnessing of electricity: Volta and Ampere in Italy, Wheatstone and Steinel in the United Kingdom and Edison in the United States, but the credit for the telegraph is usually given to Samuel Morse who patented his first device in 1838. On May 24, 1844, Morse sent a telegraph message from the U.S. Capitol to the B70 Railroad depot in Baltimore (now the B&O Railroad Museum) with the now famous citation from the Bible (Book of Numbers, chapter 23 verse. 23) "What hath God Wrought!" A new era in communications was on the cusp.

Voice Becomes Reality

An example of some of the first voice like simulations, sent via electric impulse, was the use of the clicking triggered by the sending of telegraphic code to play musical tunes.[5] In 1876, Alexander Graham Bell consolidated many of the new developments in electricity and communication to develop the first electronic transmission of voice over distance. From this time on the possibilities were enormous, but Bell's invention would only carry a recognizable voice over three to five kilometers. Edison improved Bell's invention to such an extent that in 1878 Edison and his collaborators were able to connect New York City to Philadelphia by telephone![6, 7] The rush was on to fulfill the promise of Bell's invention. A paradigm of telephone based news and entertainment was to yield to a future not yet imagined, as with some of today's internet based technologies. For many years, however, telephone subscription news and music concerts in London and Budapest, Hungary were to precede the radio in distance broadcasting.

Coded Signals Through Space

The next step in the trajectory of communication was to move from wire to the airwaves via Marconi's invention of the wireless telegraph. A self-taught man, in 1895, Marconi was to defy common wisdom and scientific theory of his day by sending a telegraph signal with Morse's code for the letter "S" from his house, near Bologna in northern Italy to a receiver on the other side of a hill three kilometers away. No one prior to Marconi's demonstration believed that telegraph signals could pass from one point to another unobstructed by a solid mass as a hill. Marconi's servant hailed the arrival of the first signal via the wireless by the firing of a single shot, a pre-arranged signal from an earlier day of distance communication. In 1897, Marconi was able to patent his invention in England, birthplace of his mother and home to his financial backers. Within a few years, Marconi had pushed the transmission of the telegraph to over 100 kilometers. In 1901, Marconi succeeded in sending a signal across the ocean from Cornwall to Newfoundland over 3500 kilometers. It would only be a few years until the human voice was transmitted over the airwaves.

War Before Commerce

The first widespread uses of the wireless were telegraphic. The U.S. Navy prior to World War I began equipping its ships with wireless telegraph transmitters. The U.S. Department of Agriculture was also a pioneer in developing applications for the radio. The Department financed early research and USDA in telegraphic code did some of the earliest broadcasts of weather reports.

The public was looking for wireless telephones or radio power and heat transmission to be the next developments in the fast moving science. It took until our day to have commercial wireless telephone service while electric power or heat transmission via radio waves have become tombstones in the graveyard of failed science. Only time will tell if they can be resurrected.

Much of the scientific application of arc-transmitter and vacuum tube technology that would make radio possible came out of southern California in the early 1900s, from some of the same areas that, later in the century, were to give flesh and bones to the Internet communications revolution. In 1913, Charles Herrold experimentally broadcast "The Trail of The Lonesome Pine" 900 miles in the San Jose, California area. In 1916, Lee DeForest, one of the pioneers in trying to adapt arc-technology, inaugurated nightly broadcasts of news and music from an experimental radio station in the Highbridge section of New York City. Five months later, the advent of World War I was to lead to a ban on all private radio broadcasts and listening. Other quasi-amateur broadcasters had also gone on the air prior to World War I in Massachusetts and Southern California.

The first commercial radio station, KDKA in Pittsburgh, began several years after the war's end in 1920. [8, 9] Radio has expanded and grown in a spectacular fashion since. Shortwave gave way to AM followed by FM and beginning in 2002 in the United States digital radio is gradually becoming available.

Development or Informational Radio

As early as the 1930s, radio programming with a decidedly informational, as opposed to commercial or entertainment content, began in earnest. While commercial radio already had informational programming, especially in their news services, lengthier informational magazines or specifically targeted informational programming to suit particular audience needs and interests was a rarity. The U.S. Department of Agriculture (USDA) responding to its mission to educate and assist the U.S. farmer was the first to step into this void with the inauguration of agricultural extension broadcasts in 1926 on KDKA. Over the decades, USDA broadcasting has been one of the seminal factors in informing farmers about advances in crop and livestock science, markets and international trade. To this day, USDA provides daily radio and TV feeds to private stations around the country on a daily basis—reaching a network of 675 affiliated stations, the largest broadcast network in the U.S.—for rebroadcast to the rural and urban populations of America. One can often be surprised stopping in remote rural areas of the U.S. to find that local farmers are better informed about the food and political situation in Cuba or China than their Washington D.C. counterparts are. One explanation of this phenomenon is an avid and motivated listening audience to quality informational programming from USDA.

Development Radio Overseas—The Third World

While radio was taking its first steps in the U.S. and Europe, coming to grips with its possibilities and the needs of its listening audience, radio's development in the third world was truncated by the political situation there. Colonial regimes covered most of what is now the developing world and many of these regimes had little interest in the local population, except as objects of taxation and as military recruits. What radio that did exist there was often in the language of the colonists and out of reach of most of the local population. Native radio, had the financial capital been available, was seen as politically risky and consequently something to be strictly controlled or circumscribed. The situation was to change with the end of the colonial era after World War II.

The Dutch were the pioneers of colonial radio, creating a shortwave radio link between Java and the Netherlands as early as 1918. By 1923, an incredible 2,400 kilowatt arc transmitter was built providing round the clock contact between Amsterdam and Bandung, Java. In 1927, a 25kw station began broadcasting to the Dutch East Indies with this signature "Hello Dutch East Indies, this is PCJJ, the shortwave transmitter of the Philips laboratories in Eindhoven (Holland)."[10] The French (1931), English (1932 "BBC Empire Service"), Italian (1935 Arabic language) and German colonial services were to take several more years before reaching this broadcast level in their colonies.[11]

While colonial broadcasters were not known for their programming for the poor, there were exceptions. In 1950 Malaya—the pre-independence name Malaya was changed in 1963 to Malaysia, six years after the country received independence—was faced with the communist insurgency known as the "Emergency." During the insurgency British controlled Radio Malaya engaged in a deliberate effort to reach poor populations susceptible to the appeal of the communists. The British felt correctly, it turns out, that only by reaching out to the population through development oriented programs could they have any hope of winning their support. They also understood that the radio was the ideal means to do this. Series of broadcasts on health-"village doctor", agriculture- "agricultural forum" and culture-"musical play" organized by village broadcasters were transmitted by Radio Malaya in local languages. A "meet the people" type broadcast portrayed life in new government villages, safe-havens from the insurgency. Indeed one call and write-in broadcaster, the "truth teller," was the most popular radio figure in Malaya, broadcasting twice weekly on the Tamil rural service and discussing development topics. His program stayed on the air for many years. Instruction in the Roman alphabet was another innovative feature of Malay radio of the era. Broadcasts were expanded into a total of seven local dialects in an effort to better reach the poor population. While driven by the "Emergency" and exceptional for its era, Malayan broadcasting towards the end of British colonial rule showed what could be done when resources were matched with an urgency to reach the poor.[12] The story was to shift with the demise of colonial regimes and a newfound interest in the local populations by the newly formed nationalist governments.

Independence

Beginning with the first countries to win independence in the immediate aftermath of the Second World War, nationalist governments replaced colonial rule in India, Africa and South Asia. Radio was to herald the newly discovered optimism of charismatic indigenous leaders who ushered out the decried colonial powers. Emanating from cultures of oral speech and tradition, many of the independence leaders led and inspired their populations, achieving prominence through speeches and discourse. In addition to proclaiming the advent of the nation, the radio was there to carry the speeches of Gandhi (1947), Nehru (1947), Nkrumah (1950), Nasser (1952), Lumumba (1960) and later Kenyatta, Toure and Nyerere. These, as well as other figures who shaped the independence and birth of their nations, were heard over national radio services taken over from colonial powers.

Nationalist leader Tunku Abdul Rahman uttered one word, "independence" or "Merdeka" in local Malay language at midnight on August 31, 1957 and broadcast on Malay radio, which was to be nationalized shortly thereafter. This heralded the birth of a nation via radio for all those within listening distance, as it would around the world, both before and after, in newly independent countries.[13]

It was radio that was first to unite these diverse nations so varied in cultures and languages. But, aside from speeches and news, with a potentially wide audience, broadcasting was to remain an affair of local elites. Radio had not yet penetrated the village to the all-encompassing extent it was to attain over the next twenty years and beyond. Limited language services, scant access of the poor to national language skills, the high cost of radio transmitters and air-time were to limit its scope somewhat. Radio's control was to pass from colonial powers to the post-independence elites. Still, the idea of programming for the poor would slowly penetrate a socialism of urbane elites who had enduring strong ties to the village communities from which they came. These elites dominated the independence movements and their radios.

All India Radio (AIR), which had only six stations at the time of independence in 1947, broadcast mostly news, current affairs, drama and music. Yet, the idea of what was proper culturally was still so entwined with "proper" colonial culture that AIR limited its music broadcasts to "highbrow" Western classical music. In order to hear Indian music listeners turned to shortwave to tune-in Radio Ceylon and Radio Goa, one foreign, the other a non-national broadcaster. There was less than one radio per 1,000 population at the time.[14] All this was to change rapidly.

Emerging post-colonial societies everywhere faced similar constraints. In 1949 Syria, a radio cost on average $165, more than the average annual income of $100. There was one radio available for every sixty

Syrians. While Syria had four broadcast transmitters at the time, a considerably better situation than on the much larger Indian sub-continent, these
had insufficient power to reach more than 30 miles from the capital. Many
educated Syrians preferred the better reception of the BBC or Radio Cyprus and, if they lived outside the capital, had little other choice. [15] Iran
had roughly one radio for every forty inhabitants. At the low end of
broadcast possibilities in the Middle-East, Jordan had but one transmitter
in the early 1950s and one radio per two hundred inhabitants.[16]

The situation in post-colonial Africa was more akin to India with limited broadcast possibilities and low rates of radio penetration, although
given the gregarious social nature of these societies, even a feeble number
of radios reached a large number of individuals. In 1951, Tanzania, or then
Tanganikya, still a German colony, had only one small transmitter broadcasting one hour a week in Swahili with two weekly rebroadcasts. Within
a few years, however, hours had already increased, equipment improved
and service expanded. By the time of independence in 1961, Tanzania was
still estimated to have fewer than 100,000 radios, mostly in and around the
capital, less than one for every 100 inhabitants.[17]

Even in the immediate post-colonial era in Africa, radio was already
being used for developmental purposes and instruction. From the eve of
independence in 1956, Radio Accra began using local Ghanaian languages
and providing programs for rural people. "The Cocoa Family" was broadcast for two years on a weekly basis, discussing problems of rural life and
cocoa cultivation, one of the country's agricultural mainstays.[18] In Benin
in 1960, Radio Dahomey was broadcasting a special program in "Fon"
advising against palm cutting.[19]

Latin American conditions, although varying greatly, were at the upper end of broadcasting possibilities for the period. Uruguay had the
greatest number of radios proportional to its population in the 1950s,
roughly one radio for every five inhabitants with Cuba in second place
with roughly one for every six or seven inhabitants. Within twenty years
of these humble beginnings, villages the world over were to be figura-
tively wired-in.

The broad sweep of the communication revolution that continues to
our day was to affect these societies in dramatic ways. Radios were becoming abundant—the 280,000 radios in India (less than one per thousand
inhabitants) in 1947 had increased to 12.8 million by 1971 (one per 40)—
transmitters had become widespread and programming had begun to take
major strides toward addressing the wants and needs of a broader segment
of the population which included the poor.[20] The discovery of the transis-

tor in 1948 by Bardeen and Brattain at Bell Laboratories in the U.S., replacing the cumbersome vacuum tube, and the progressive manufacture of smaller battery operated radio sets was to vastly accelerate radio's penetration into villages without electricity or telephone wires.[21] By 1970, the declining cost of radio and its availability in poor and rural areas had united the third world in the first or perhaps second step toward globalization. What was previously an hour of scratchy news had become several hours of news, music and alternative programming, some of it developmental in nature. Technology also increased competition and, if airwaves were not yet privatized in most of Asia and Africa, alternative broadcasts from offshore or international services could sometimes be heard through the improved radio technology.

If we advance to the modern era, radios today cost as little as $5 for a Chinese-made transistor widely available in the third world. National statistics show one radio for every 10 Indians, one for every four Iranians, one for every three Tanzanian, Syrian and Jordanian and one for every two Uruguayans—given family and household size, a ratio of only one radio for every five persons means that practically all households will have at least one radio available to its members.[22] Numerous AM and now FM stations span the dial. Shortwave is still another alternative. Hi-fidelity has become an available standard for reception. Digital satellite radio covers the Asian sub-continent and Middle East and will soon be available in Latin America. But, the saga of the radio has many exciting chapters that need to be told before reaching this point.

An Oral Society Extends Its Reach

The oral society that was the village society in the burgeoning ex-colonial states was to become during their first decades after independence, a society increasingly informed through the media. The oral tradition was to marry well to the radio and enhance it. Leadership was based on a number of skills, birthright, physical stature, wealth, clan connections, personality and fortune. The ability to speak well and persuade others was in the forefront of personality traits that could call forth an individual's dominance and ability to lead men and women in traditional societies. As nations formed and social aggregates became larger, speaking well took on the added attribute of speaking at length. In mesmerizing addresses to the nation, leaders turned the art of speech making into one of personal endurance, as they spoke passionately for hours on end, without pause or respite. In an almost hypnotic response, crowds were swayed by their eloquence. Sekou Toure of Guinea, Kwame Nkrumah of Ghana, Gamal Abdel Nasser of Egypt, and Jomo Kenyatta of Kenya were masters of this art. In our own hemisphere, where tradition had given way to the first stages of social development in an earlier period, Fidel Castro remained a master of the art of public discourse. From the very first, the radio was to carry these speeches as in some instances the only national media. The radio was to play a role in the minds of listeners as the unifier of these newly formed nations. Broadcasts in one or even several national languages were also to serve an important unifying role in societies where dozens of dialects were the rule rather than the exception.

Another aspect of the oral tradition that was to change as a result of the radio was the individual model of news diffusion. In village cultures, an individual who had traveled, had a visit from distant relatives, or because of his literacy had access to printed material from elsewhere would often be the source of news from the outside world. This news would then slowly travel in ever widening circles built around this individual's contacts. The radio reduced the importance, though did not eliminate it, of these change agents in village life. Suddenly, what could pass for new or news was instantaneously available to all within listening ear of the radio. In the mild climate of the tropics, and because of the gregarious social structure of the traditional village, the first radios were often played outside for all to hear; this meant ready access to the full import of a broadcast event. One can imagine a village gathered around the broadcast of their first President inaugurating the nation.

The difficulties of the diffusion of information, prior to the penetration of the radio, can be seen in a study by Professor Damle in 1950s India. Professor Damle studied the awareness of different types of information in villages at increasing distances from the central Indian city of Poona in Madaya Pradesh. The nearest village included in the study was on the outskirts of the city, the farthest 80 miles from Poona. Other villages at 11, 20, 24, 26 and 72 miles were examined. Some of the villages were more easily accessible by road; others had differing degrees of social ties to Poona. Classifying the villages as distant, intermediate, and proximate, Damle found marked differences in the three groups. Some of the farthest villages, such as Patan, 72 miles from Poona, were almost devoid of contact with the outside world. Only four people there had ever seen a train, only one was literate, only the headman knew that Nehru was the Indian leader. Knowledge of world affairs, of wars, continents and foreign states was nil, as were cultural concepts other than the traditional village ideas of caste, religion or marriage practices. There were no periodicals or radio in Patan.

Closer to Poona, more information on the outside world was available to more of the inhabitants. In the villages nearest to Poona, some villagers were conversant with the egalitarian anti-caste ideas current in intellectual circles in India since the 19th Century. Awareness of other religious groups, marriage practices and ideas on family and relationships was more common as one neared Poona as was awareness of belonging to a larger political and social organization.[23] The relationship of physical distance to knowledge and customs would change with the simultaneous penetration of radio and the automobile. [24]

Ideas Change Village Life

While the commercial development of the automobile and radio both occurred at the beginning of the 20th century, it was the less costly radio that was to extend its reach further into village life, bringing with it new ideas from distant places. A number of studies from this period attest to the importance of how media availability affects the individual's assimilation of information and adoption of more modern farming techniques, health practices and other changes in village life.[25] Otherwise said, the more people who were exposed to the media, the more they knew about public events and the more informed choices they made in many areas affecting their life and well being. In one of the seminal works of the postcolonial development era, *Mass Media and National Development*, Wilbur Schramm, Director of Communication Research at Stanford University underscored the relationship between the radio, or communications more generally, and economic development. Schramm cited a 1961 UNESCO study finding a correlation of .86 out of 1.00, between per capita radio listenership and income. Schramm's own study found a correlation of .73 for economic development and scales of communication development.[26]

Which comes first the radio, communication, or economic development? This conundrum was something Schramm was unable to sort out. He concludes that they are inexorably entwined.

Propaganda vs. Information

The control of the air waves by post-colonial regimes was a real opportunity to use the state's organizational powers and the resources of the state—albeit meager at the time, still greater than most private individuals could muster— to the benefit of largely illiterate populations dependent on the radio for news and information. It also posed a great temptation to misuse. Many state radios acquitted themselves of the charge with no more blatant distortion or propaganda than one might anticipate from gen-

eral cultural prejudices and the insecurities of the ruling party. The temptation to use the radio for propaganda in service of a cause was, nevertheless, a seismic fault line underneath the prevailing structure of state ownership.

While pro-ruling party propaganda was easy for the public to dis-
count, either through competition from other media, or the test of oral tradition, a broader based propaganda campaign of national unity could be
harder to resist. Such was the seduction of Cairo's "Voice of the Arabs,"
broadcast over short and medium-wave for five hours daily from Algeria
to Uganda, Iraq and the desert kingdoms of Arabia. The "Voice of the Arabs" (Saut al-Arab) carried a pan-Arabist political rhetoric. Observers of
the time credited this political rhetoric with "being little tested by oppos-
ing viewpoints and prone to induce a sort of mob hysteria among illiterate
populations with few sources of alternative information."[27] In judging
these assertions, one should keep in mind that no information is uniquely
objective. It is also difficult to find any information on what other types of
educational programming Radio Cairo may have carried out. What "we"
refer to as "propaganda radio" often resonates with some elements of the
experience of the listener. Nevertheless, the temptation to misuse a dominant control of broadcast rights or informational channels exists. Even private ownership of radio, however, is no guarantee against political distor-
tions, some with the capacity to inflame masses and misdirect popular
energies. The misguided use of the airwaves by private broadcasters was
observed more recently in Rwanda, where anti-Tutsi radio broadcasts over
"Radio et Television Libre Mille Collines" enflamed communal passions,
contributing to the subsequent civil violence,[28] and in Bosnia where TV
and radio broadcasting helped to maintain inter-communal hostility.

Fortunately, for the history of radio, Saut al-Arab's political programming and the hate radio of Rwanda and Bosnia are the exceptions.
State radio in most developing countries has been used judiciously in the
sphere of informational or developmental programming, as we shall see
throughout these chapters, though not always in the more purely political
sphere.[29] The more recent democratization of the airwaves in Africa, parts
of the Middle East and Asia has resulted in greater radio creativity and diversity, much of it providing additional opportunities for the poor as well
as contributing to free speech and multiple points of view.[30]

Community Radio: an Early Start

Free of the colonial legacy since Spanish and Portuguese rule ended
in the 19th century, Latin America was able to move to a diversified

model of broadcast rights and ownership at an early stage. From its very beginnings, radio in Latin America had private and commercial broadcasting alongside that of the state. Church, in the early years almost exclusively Catholic, and community owned radio also had a presence. U.S. investment in radio could also be found. NBC was the first U.S. company to broadcast to Latin America via shortwave in 1934. CBS, Crosley, General Electric, and Westinghouse all broadcast regularly to Latin America either through shortwave broadcasts originating in the U.S. or through locally owned affiliates. The model for commercial radio was news and music, mimicking U.S. commercial models. In the early years, no advertisements were allowed on shortwave.[31]

Community radio was to be a beneficiary of the more liberal and, by comparison, better financed broadcast environment in Latin America. The first reported community station dates from May 1948 in Colombia, Radio Sutatenza. Radio Sutatenza was started in 1948 in Colombia by a Jesuit priest and had as its dual mission the broadcasting of Catholic teaching to poor farmers and their education in skills contributing to community development.[32] Radio Sutatenza grew steadily until bought out in the 1990s by a larger media conglomerate.[33] The Catholic Church, and Jesuits in particular, were to be active in using the radio to reach the poor throughout Latin America and more recently in Tanzania. Other Christian churches also made use of radio in this way.

A more proper example of community owned and operated radio without external mediation was Radio Mineras, the Bolivian miners' community radio. Begun in 1947, Radios Mineras united the poor mining communities of the Bolivian highlands. Entirely community operated, Radio Mineras provided much useful community related information and a rallying point for community discussion.

Radio Mineras or Miners' Radio consisted of a series of loosely affiliated, independent mining community radio stations. In times of political or natural crisis, stations would relay each other's broadcast messages throughout the network keeping communities informed of dangerous developments in neighboring towns. In calmer times, the stations served their own communities, exchanging the occasional program or journalist, sometimes jointly hosting broadcast events.

Periodically over the years, shortly after their inception in 1949, again in 1967, 1975 and 1980, the radio stations were physically attacked by hostile governments, but each time managed to regroup and rebroadcast, sometimes several years later. During the periods in between, lower level hostilities, legal and financial battles not infrequently occurred. Yet by July 1980, when the stations were sacked and once again temporarily forced off the air by a military coup, the Bolivian community radio had grown into a network of 27 stations serving the mining communities with strong support from the powerful miners' unions. They continue, somewhat fewer in number, to this day.

At its simplest, community radio often unites the community with music, greetings and birthday dedications, dating and other social games and community notices. It can be fully participatory or closely directed by a few. At its fullest, it can provide a wide range of informational services, encourage community discussion and forums, unite and lead a community forward into a new era.

While the early community radio experiences began by focusing community energies and attention on solving local problems, many, especially Catholic Church sponsored stations, evolved into dealing with what they felt were political constraints to community development. The rise of "liberation theology" in Latin America was to give a political slant to much of the community radio work of the 1970s and 1980s.

In a later period, main line Protestant Churches sponsored radio stations often with community vocations in addition to their religious ones. The Episcopalian Radio Soleil in Haiti (1980) was followed still later by Evangelical stations throughout Latin America.[34]

Right-wing reaction was to lead to violent attempts to shut some of the early stations down as seen in the successful closure, albeit temporarily, of the Radio Mineras network in Bolivia. Radio Quillabamba, a shortwave community station in Peru, suffered several bomb attacks on its transmitters but managed to stay on the air. As Latin America evolved politically; democracy replacing dictatorship, synthesis replacing struggle and the more conservative Churches taking root, so to have the stations. Today they are finding their role in a less polarized society, but a society in which the struggle against poverty is still one of the principal challenges.

The community radio experience represents a later stage of radio development in many other parts of the world and is having a renaissance today in Africa. Church and community supported until a later period when some donor and NGO assistance flowed to community stations, these early initiatives were largely free from the influence of governments and international aid efforts. While a Rockefeller Foundation Report documents numerous community radio experiences over the several decades since these first efforts, few of these have had the support of the international development banks or their national governments. An exception the report mentions is that of Burkina Faso Radio "Upper Volta" in 1980s West Africa, under the tutelage of Thomas Sankara, the exceedingly popular President.[35] It was perhaps not simply fortuitous for the advantageous use of radio in Burkina Faso that Sankara was Minister of Information before taking over as President. He understood first hand the power of communication in the lives of the poor. While still Information Minister, Sankara initiated a series of six community-based radio stations to serve the country. After President Sankara was assassinated, these radio stations lost national support. Service to the poor, unfortunately, seems like a severe career risk in international politics to judge by these few examples and some we will see later as radio's saga continues.

Development Radio—Programming for the Masses

Within the UN system, UNESCO[36] was to serve as a rallying point for mass communications strategies for developing countries. In 1956, India became the site of the Pune farm radio forum project sponsored by UNESCO, one of the first large scale media projects in the developing world. The project was modeled on the successful Canadian experience with farm radio forums in the 1940s. All India Radio (AIR) broadcast a half hour farm radio program that was followed-up with organized village-level discussion groups. These discussion groups were led by local extension agents and focused on analyzing the AIR program, discussing its relevance to village conditions and developing a plan of action to implement appropriate recommendations. The forums spread beyond the pilot area and were generally considered successful in mobilizing villages and in initiating public works. They continued until 1970 when they died out.[37]

Another pioneering effort of AIR to use radio in agricultural extension was the "package" program. India's agricultural services attempted to compensate for one of the shortcomings of the farm forums by providing follow-up written information and services. Programming and messages focused on a series of related agricultural interactions as cropping, soil fertility and water availability, providing, radio information, brochures and extension advice. The package program was instrumental in spreading the message of new high-yielding seed varieties, paving the way for the "green-revolution."[38]

The relatively early independence achieved in India and the legacy of state service meant an early start to development radio there. Other countries were not far behind, however, in the fields of primary and secondary schooling, teacher training, health, nutrition and agriculture via distance learning over the radio.

Agriculture being the mainstay of African economies, it is not surprising that many developmental radio efforts focused on this sector. Together with the FAO,[39] the newly independent government of Benin, in West Africa, organized programs in 1967. In six local languages, they dealt with planting of palm trees, as well as maize, rice, and cotton cultivation techniques. In Niger, the first programs of the Radio Club Association, which began broadcasting in 1965, covered numerous agricultural production topics (seeds, soil preparation, fertilizers, bovine care), as well as marketing of produce and household concerns of hygiene, potable water and women's household activities. The club also had programs with a civic focus talking about the activities of the National Assembly. Agricultural radio extension began in 1962 in Kenya. In 1966 Cameroon began extension broadcasting in the Fulani and Hausa languages. In the Ivory Coast, "The National Cup for Progress" broadcast, beginning in 1966, gave agricultural information together with music programming and social interaction, organizing producer competitions at the sub-district level. Burkina Faso, Togo and Ghana were also to organize radio clubs.[40]

In West Africa, a French tradition of "animation de groupe" was the foundation for rural radio based on village input. This type of "grassroots" approach has become popular again and although more costly and difficult to execute, is favored by many development practitioners as being more authentic and relevant. In 1977, again with the support of UNESCO, 57 pilot radio clubs were established in Senegalese villages to assist peanut farmers, in growing what was then Senegal's principal export. Even in the 1970s, Senegal evaluators found radio penetration pervasive in rural villages, enumerating a range of two to ten radios for every ten households. The radio programs and follow-up write-in by the clubs, known as "Disso," which means dialog in Woluf, had the full backing of President Senghor, Senegal's charismatic independence leader and first nationally elected President. The letters were distributed to government officials involved with agricultural extension who had the obligation to respond. The President's interventions were to assist in breaking down resistance and turf issues among the various ministries involved, something which has been a continual challenge for media-based learning. Two radio broadcasts per week continued for several years carrying information on not only agriculture, but also health, credit and other aspects of rural life. The program was widely deemed successful and imitated in neighboring West African countries.[41 42]

Diffusion of agricultural technology via the radio was to take hold in the Indonesian archipelago, as well, in both Malaysia and Indonesia. In

Malaysia, Radio Television Malaysia's (RTM) popular Development and Agriculture Service (DAS) has broadcast agricultural extension programs to rural areas since independence in 1957, a continuation of the legacy of colonial era broadcasting. In Indonesia, after the 1969 conference on rural development, a set of directives became the basis for consolidating and expanding Radio Republik Indonesia's (RRI) development outreach to the rural areas. In a more recent development in Indonesia, spontaneous listening clubs have grown up around particular programs and rural development problems reminiscent of the early days of radio clubs. These clubs have provided for group discussion and collective action and have proven advantageous for gathering data on program effectiveness.[43]

Latin America Pioneers Schooling Via Radio
    One of the earliest attempts to use radio for schooling comes from a 1942 experimental radio school in Chile. Remarkable among pioneering efforts, this experimental broadcast was at first supported by advertising on commercial stations. The broadcasts were focused on enriching the then current school curriculum. A number of topical programs of interest to the community were soon added. These included "Knowing Our Children" and "Education from Home," along with programs directed at teachers. Seasoned with time and increased listener-ship, the programs picked up support from the Chilean Ministry of Education, local teachers and the Chilean Broadcasting Association. A total of 26 programs a week were eventually being broadcast by 14 stations covering most of the national territory and enduring for ten years.[44]
    Another of the very early adapters to the possibilities of the radio was Mexico. Only three years after authorizing commercial radio licenses in 1924, Mexico set up a radio station in the Ministry of Education. Ten years later in 1934, in a rather stunning gesture of media savvy that would inculcate a tradition of media-based learning in Mexican culture, President Cardenas donated a radio to every agricultural and workers community to enable them to listen to courses, book reviews and music transmitted by state radio. State radio was later privatized in Mexico. The seeds were planted for other fruits to fall from the tree.[45]
    These early attempts bore additional fruit somewhat later when radio was used to reach rural school districts in the remote Tarahumara region, in Huayacocotla and through "Radioprimaria" in the region near San Luis Potosi. Preceding All India Radio by a year, in 1955, Jesuit missionaries in the remote region of Sierra Tarahumara in Northwest Mexico began a series of "radio schools" broadcasting to participating boarding schools for

the local indigenous population. Ten years later, during an evaluation by the World Bank, the schools were still broadcasting to a new set of radio assisted teachers and students.[46]   In October 1965, Radio Huayacocotla began short wave radio school programs to the rural populations of Veracruz, Querétaro, Hidalgo and Puebla, which in various permutations continue to this day. Some of the challenges radio faces can be seen in the Radio Huayacocotla experience. While successful with its audience and taking place in a Mexican environment favorable to radio schooling, Radio Huyacocotla has continued over the years on the shortwave bands without being able to acquire AM broadcast rights. Students and teachers have been obliged to listen over the static of shortwave reception in the mountains, something they have continued to do, because of the value of their learning experience.

Under the leadership of Paulo Freire, Brazil developed a program of radio schools in the 1960s to reach remote areas of their northeast frontier. Brazil's radio school program featured community organization and development integrally as part of the program.[47]   Freire was exiled from Brazil in 1964 by a military dictatorship, but his work in education continued to be seminal in Latin America. He continued to work on adult education while in exile in Chile, helping to overcome illiteracy there, and internationally through his writings and work as special education adviser to the World Congress of Churches in Geneva.[48]   Freire's philosophy of education can be said to have influenced some of the UNESCO work of the period. He received the UNESCO Prize for Education for Peace in 1986.[49]

In 1970, Mexico "Radioprimaria" began broadcasting lessons for fourth, fifth and sixth graders to rural schools in an area around San Luis Potosi, also in Northwest Mexico. Mexico's Secretariat for Public Education organized the "Radioprimaria" programs as a way of bridging the gap due to a lack of fourth through sixth grade teachers in rural areas. Five years into "Radioprimaria," the program had expanded to 65 schools. It included students in broadcasting roles, making the creation of the programs part of the learning experience and enhancing their relevance to the rest of the student body. While the early Mexican projects demonstrated the possibilities of the radio to achieve classroom level teaching and a rich learning experience, both had problems with equipment maintenance in the distant school districts.[50]

Mexico's nascent tradition of media-based education was also to pioneer exploration of television entertainment-education. The educational television production dramas of Miguel Sabido were both seminal and early in the history of the genre, beginning in 1967 with *"La Tormenta."*

With the assistance of David O. Poindexter, President of the non-profit Population Communications International in New York, Sabido's work was to become known and influential throughout the developing world, inspiring major programming efforts in educational television in India and elsewhere.[51]   In 1974, another effort at radio schooling, the Nicaraguan Radio Mathematics Project done in conjunction with Stanford University, demonstrated that exposure to specially designed mathematics instruction via radio could bring a striking improvement in student math achievement.

Another innovative Mexican experience continues to promote cultural broadcasting. It is the National Indigenous Institute (INI), begun in 1979 and sponsoring upwards of twelve stations reaching 3.2 million indigenous people in 28 native languages. The stations sponsor cultural, educational, news, and entertainment programming with an "open mike" feature allowing direct community access to programming and the airwaves.[52]

Educational Radio and Interactive Radio Instruction Goes Worldwide

While still under British colonial rule in the 1950s, Malaya developed an extensive program of supplemental classroom schooling in Malay, Chinese, English, and later Tamil. History, science, music, hygiene, safety, and current affairs were all taught. Broadcasting of these programs continues to this day, four days a week, ten hours a day in four primary languages over three channels. Primary and secondary school course material is covered with some supplementary material. The programs reinforce classroom teaching and are syllabus based except for the supplementary material.[53]

In Morocco, the School Radio and Television Service of the Ministry of Education broadcasted radio courses to 140,000 pupils in 2,200 classrooms in the early 1960s. In addition, four model lessons, two in Arabic, two in French were broadcast in the evenings for teachers.[54] A teacher training program, "Talking to Teachers," put together by the local Teacher's College was also broadcast via the radio in Sarawak, Indonesia in the early 1960s. Kenya was an early pioneer in radio usage for teacher training (1968) and English as a second language programming (1980). Nepal also offered English as a second language in 1980, and a teacher training program which continues to this day. Mathematics instruction via the radio was also attempted in Thailand and Nepal beginning in 1980 and in the Dominican Republic in 1981.

The problem of inadequate staffing and insufficiently trained rural teachers was to engender a different solution in Kenya than that of "Radioprimaria's" radio schooling in Mexico. In 1968, Kenya estimated that almost a third of its 37,900 primary school teachers had no professional qualifications and that the total number of teachers was woefully inadequate to deal with the widespread illiteracy and low level of scholarship left as a legacy of the colonial period. Kenya chose to address the problem through correspondence courses and radio instruction focused on teacher training, versus the direct classroom broadcasts to students of "Radioprimaria." From 1969 to 1972, 10,000 "unqualified" teachers successfully completed the upgrading courses through radio, correspondence, and residential study and were awarded Kenya's Primary Teacher's Certificate. Many of these newly qualified teachers compared favorably in follow-up studies to those graduating from the regular program of the teachers' training institutes. Ninety percent of supervisors of these teachers reported improvement in student performance after the teacher had completed the qualifications course. Seeking the same goal of enhanced primary education, the Mexican and Kenyan efforts used the radio in creatively different ways to achieve the same end.[55] In Indonesia "Open University" has been supported by both radio and television since 1984 with the participation of 18 stations. Programs are usually magazine, discussion, or feature shows of a half-hour in length supported by written course material.[56]

Reviewers of the period mention four radio development programs noteworthy for their success:[57] the Kenya health broadcasts sponsored by UNICEF since 1975; the nutrition radio campaign in Ecuador sponsored by Richard Manhoff and a New York- based ad firm, which used brief advertisement like spots on nutrition, rather than more lengthy public interest broadcasting; the Guatemalan agricultural information programs sponsored by USAID with the Academy for Educational Development in 1976 and the Tanzanian health campaigns of 1977 undertaken by the national government.

A number of programs based on the Nicaraguan and Kenyan models and referred to as Interactive Radio Instruction (IRI) were created around the world to address differing educational needs. USAID was instrumental in a number of the pilot programs, especially in the 1970s and 1980s after which USAID's interest seems to have inexplicably waned, although programs of this type have seen a small resurgence in the late 1990s and continue to be created up to the present. These efforts and others of the period represented the zenith of development radio.

A Hybrid Model

A hybrid experience in distance learning, development radio and community development was tried in Honduras, spanning several decades beginning in 1960.[58] In that year a young Honduran priest, Father Jose Molina, returned from Colombia where he had studied radio outreach, community awareness and development. In September, he began adult education broadcasts on an experimental basis in the vicinity of Tegucigalpa, the Honduran capital. With support from local pastors and the Catholic Church, his experiment expanded rapidly from 343 schools and 7,240 students in 1962 to 745 schools and 14,624 students in 1964 at the height of the adult literacy program.

A government agency, Popular Cultural Action of Honduras (ACPH) was put in charge of the broadcasts and literacy program. At the same time, the Popular Promotion Movement (PPM), an alliance of village level *campesino* groups, was to work closely with ACPH in an elaboration of its campaign. Radio programs on health, agriculture, and village organization were added to the basic literacy programs. ACPH and the PPM were joined by Church and social action groups in what was referred to as the "Concorde." Government, Church, urban social action, and rural participation gave the target audience of rural campesinos an abundance of social and expert resources upon which to draw, and via the radio and the informal networks of contacts, the means of diffusion. If the model performed less well than could be hoped for, its fault might have been in the very "decentralization" which made it so attractive and "participatory" for many. A lack of strong central leadership made it difficult to focus resources and programming on priority topics with high production values in terms of "social marketing."

Other models can profit from the Honduran's participatory outreach concept while avoiding some of its weaknesses. Models where centralized decision-making is married to a high degree of community feedback will be seen to avoid the pitfalls of the Honduran experience while posing other challenges. Though not resulting in a rural "Camelot," radio did help to unite and instruct the "Honduran" countryside in a manner probably not possible without it.

A National Campaign

One of the seminal events in the history of radio for development was the first nationwide development campaign anchored by radio broadcasts. In 1973, the "Mtu Ni Afya" or "Man is Health" campaign in Tanzania reached two million citizens with health education. The campaign was built based upon several years of experience with nationwide use of the radio. It had its roots in study groups begun in 1967 in the Co-operative Education Center in Moshi, Tanzania and at the Adult Education Center which is part of the then University of Dar es Salaam in the Mbeya region. The program's inspiration also owed much to the Swedish Socialist-labor tradition of study circles, Sweden being the principal foreign aid donor in Tanzania and very active there for some time. Two years of progressive use of the radio for election information and adult education—including literacy, economics and other topics—also preceded the health campaign. As the discussion intimates, "Mtu Ni Afya" relied heavily on organized listening and study groups, as well as the broadcast radio messages.[59] It also represented a considerable increase in scale from the previous campaigns by reaching approximately two million Tanzanians. A total of 75,000 group leaders were trained for the campaign. Concrete actions by the participants were encouraged, as for example the digging of wells or latrines to realize the lessons of the "Man is Health" campaign. Other lessons included covering food, airing bedding in the sun, individual use of drinking containers, boiling and filtering drinking water, along with other practical instruction were widely adopted.

The campaign was largely thought to have been successful. Hall and Dodds, both of whom participated in the campaign as advisers, reported "a dramatic effect on certain health practices among a very large number of people."[60] To examine just one of the program's recommendations, it is estimated that 750,000 latrines were built nationwide. Before and after surveys on health practices emphasized in the program show a 60 percent improvement ratio. Building on this experience, a second phase of the campaign emphasizing nutrition, agriculture and child-care followed.

More Listeners Than Radio Programs?

Table 1.1 lists 22 Interactive Radio Instruction programs around the world from Nicaragua beginning in 1974 to a 1997 program in the Dominican Republic.[61] If one includes with these, the various topical campaigns mentioned above, community radio, and some other smaller campaigns not included in this book, an impressive list of diverse experiences of radio learning can be compiled. Sadly, while numerous in a thirty year inventory from around the world, these less than two dozen IRI activities and sundry developmental programming, hardly scratch the surface of illiteracy and low educational achievement in the third-world. They also represent a laughably small proportion of donor funding for development aid and of developing country investment in education and economic growth, even though most of the activities were considered successful, low cost and effective at raising educational levels and disseminating information—one IRI activity in the Dominican Republic continued for over ten years, many community radios have broadcast for decades.

TABLE 1.1: Inventory of Interactive Radio Instruction (IRI) Experiences

COUNTRY/YEAR	SUBJECT/GRADE	TYPE/STATUS
Nicaragua (1974)	Math/1-3	pilot program,
Kenya(1980)	English	learning gains of 18%
Thailand(1980)	Math 1-2	still aired
Dominican Republic(1981)	Integrated	4 grade primary program
	Programming	
Papua New Guinea (1986)	Science 4-6	science upper primary
Honduras (1987)	Math 1-3	enhanced teacher role
Bolivia (1987)	Math 1-5	part of nat'l. curriculum
Lesotho (1987)	English 1-3	on air
Costa Rica (1988 – 1992)	Math 1-3	continues in El Salvador
Guatemala, El Salvador,		
Dominican Republic		
Cost Rica (1991)	Envmt'l. Education	2 pilot series
Bolivia (1992)	Health 3-4	"radio health'
Honduras (1992)	Adult Basic	3 levels
South Africa (1992)	ESL 1-2	teacher/training,
		continues
Indonesia (1992)	Teacher training	continues
Lusophone Africa(1992)		
	Math 3-4	Dutch/UNESCO financing
Bolivia (1994)	early childhood	for caregivers
Bangladesh (1995)	English	90 lessons developed
Nepal (1996)	early childhood	UNICEF & Radio Nepal
Pakistan	English	grades 3 – 5
Haiti (1996)	Reading, civics, math	in Creole for primary
Ecuador (1996)	Conflict resolution	parents & teachers
Dominican Republic/Costa Rica (1997)		
	English	2 country pilot, World Bank

A frequent issue for educational radio has been the politics of educational activities, not so easily domiciled in Ministries of Education which are more comfortable with traditional teaching methods. Similar institutional issues affect other developmental uses of the radio, where mass communications seems more an institutional threat than opportunity. The donor's loss of support is more paradoxical but seems also to reflect institutional bias and the lack of true vocation to help the poor. Curiously largely absent throughout this rich history is the World Bank, which while the premier financing institution for development and a major financier of education, seems to have yet to discover mass media.

An issue for the broad based use of radio, a "failure to master the medium," according to Theroux and Gunter has been the prevailing philosophy among development radio practitioners that multi-media targeted group strategies are more effective than general broadcasts at transferring information and changing behavior.[62] While there is a good basis for this in common sense and experience, this focus on achieving the best learning has inhibited a broader learning experience for more individuals. Theroux and Gunter cite a survey of 65 development oriented radio projects in the mid-1970s.[63] Only five were "open broadcast," Theroux and Gunter's phrase for general broadcasts to a non-captive mass audience. Less emphasis on the excellence of the project and more on its reach, perhaps a less paternalistic approach, might lead to broader impacts and a more sustainable cost effective use of the radio.

State control of the radio is another issue. State control, often to the exclusion of private operators, has hampered creativity in many places more than it has supported the use of radio to address social problems. There are, nevertheless, many notable exceptions, some of which we have mentioned, where state radio has been used creatively. Where this is the case, a mixed system, a national public radio competing with private stations, seems to offer many advantages.

The state has the resources and vocation to aid the poor by producing quality informational broadcasts, resources that private stations often lack. Multinational organizations and donors, both of which are quasi-state or state affiliated institutions can also play a role in funding developmental programming and contributing to the diversity of information. Few private stations can afford to do this, thus music and "talk" reign where a third party does not provide content.

Democratization movements in Africa, especially West Africa in the 1990s have freed the airwaves and resulted in a treasure trove of community and private stations, thirsty for programming content. Content, which alas, is still largely absent as far as international development organizations are concerned.

One must also be careful to distinguish between private and independent radio. The case of Radio et Television Libre Mille Collines (RTLM) in Rwanda, which broadcast some of the anti-Tutsi programming prior to the civil strife is a case of a private radio closely aligned to the ruling party. RTLM was private, but not necessarily very independent of state and ruling party interests, having been founded by members of President Habyarimana's family.[64] The relationships of the media to elites and their prevailing class interests and ideology is a complex one, especially in developing countries, with shallow economic stratification which does not allow competing voices to be easily financed.

State control has hampered radio development in South East Asia. A notable exception is Radio Tambuli in the Philippines. Its community radio stations have been broadcasting since 1990. Despite existing in a legal limbo that does not yet allow for the proper licensing of community radio, these stations have continued to serve their communities for over a decade. Radio Tambuli grew out of the experience of Father Kiko Magnaye, a Catholic priest. His experience working at Radio Veritas, a Catholic station instrumental in ousting Marcos in 1986, led him to appreciate the power of the radio to aid poor communities. Once again, the struggle for the airwaves seems closely allied to a larger political struggle.[65]

While arguably limiting private initiatives, Radio Television Malaysia (RTM) has been successfully programming in the diverse national languages on educational and other topics of interest to the poor since its inception at independence in 1957. Since independence, in addition to news, entertainment, educational, and cultural programming, a nationalized RTM's popular Development and Agriculture Service (DAS) has broadcast agricultural extension programs to rural areas. This is a continuation of the legacy of colonial era broadcasting during the "Emergency" created to reach the rural poor at a time their allegiance was being tested.[66] National unity and communications were tested again in 1968, this time by ethnic riots. The government responded with national communication policies regulating radio and television programming to promote harmony and national unity. Within this broad mandate, in spite of detailed state regulation under the Minister of Information, the RTM has maintained an excellent record of national service and quality programming of interest and relevance to the Malaysian people.

Around the world, creative uses of the airwaves have found ways to flourish while under the heavy financial and legal hand of the state. Another community radio, Radio Zibonele, in South Africa broadcast surreptitiously for years from a container truck, as part of the struggle against apartheid.[67] Democracy or dictatorship, ethnic or mainstream, political will everywhere is an issue in the constructive use of the radio—the poor and children being last on the list when budgets are increased and international loans sought and the first to be cut when reductions are called for.

In Latin America, unlike Africa and Asia, private control of the airwaves was present almost from radio's inception. Problems of another sort emerged there, as radio struggled to develop broad democratic access to the "airwaves" and public interest broadcasting that went beyond entertainment. A debate of a type about responsible use of the "air" ensued. Such a debate, resolved in the U.S. by the Federal Communications Act that mandated a certain amount of "air time" for public interest broadcasts and guaranteed access, was to characterize the struggle around private ownership in Latin America. Excessive centralization and foreign control, especially North American programming, were issues particular to the situation in Latin American. The debate came to a head at the UNESCO sponsored 1976 San Jose (Costa Rica) Conference attended by twenty Latin American countries. Acclaim at the time for a "New World Information and Communication Order" was reflected at the Conference, which called for governments to enact explicit national communications policies reflecting democratic values and access to the airwaves in the community interest. The Conference proved a watershed for democratization movements in the region. However, political events had already taken a turn away from democratizing popular movements, in some countries even oligarchic ownership gave way to the state under repressive dictatorships, to be replaced again by private ownership, as the cycle of struggle for democracy played out over the Latin American continent. It would be left largely to changing technology to open media channels to greater diversity and competition.[68]

Education-Entertainment and Health Radio

The 1980s saw the further development of education-entertainment in radio and TV, the 1990s an emphasis on health related topics, with a renewed focus on the radio to address the HIV-AIDS problem. The return to favor of the radio in the face of the AIDS epidemic is another demonstration of the latent recognition of its effectiveness when there is a real urgency to deal with poverty and its incumbent causes.

Even in the health sector, however, the record is mixed. While the authors discovered a plurality of scripts and residue of "radio-excitement" reminiscent of the earlier radio days, in the health and family planning sector, including HIV-AIDS radio programming, a careful review of the record here leaves much to be desired. Such sober observers as Drs. Ev Rogers and Arvind Singhal severely criticize the international health organizations' use of the media:

The authors' (Rogers and Singhal) experience, gained over the past 15 years, of advising the Centers for Disease Control and Prevention (CDC, the leading U.S. agency responsible for fighting the epidemic), UNAIDS, and other international health organizations, suggests a major underestimation by such agencies of the role that communication can play in HIV prevention, care, and support. [69]

Ev Rogers and Arvind Singhal fault the well-meaning Centers for Disease Control and Prevention (CDC) and international medical community with focusing too much on science and too little on communicating it, shortchanging prevention and not mastering the communications media when it is used. Excusable, perhaps, except for the fact that we are raised in a society where mass communication is to an educated individual as water is to fish and the AIDS problem is akin to a pollutant spoiling our pond. The experience on which to lean is, nevertheless, indubitably present, especially in the health sector.

In Jamaica, from 1985 to 1989, under the visionary leadership of Elaine Perkins and funding from the Jamaican Family Planning Association, "Naseberry Street" was a popular family drama. It followed the travails and successes of its principal characters from this imaginary Kingstowne working class neighborhood, as they learned the real life consequences of behavioral choices in the arenas of love, contraception and family planning. A question and answer talk show followed each episode and dealt with listeners' real-life questions. [70]

One of the more interesting and successful programs of our era using education-entertainment is "Soul City" in South Africa. It addresses health, HIV-AIDS and a variety of family issues in a soap opera type drama, for radio and TV. In its TV version, "Soul City" is rated as the most popular program in South Africa. Episodes deal with testing positive for HIV-AIDS, spousal abuse, alcoholism and other topical problems in a dramatic setting. While repeating some of the modern shibboleths, the programs are excellent vehicles for community discussion and awareness.

Of course, radio programming and information diffusion can take different forms. In the mid-1980s USAID along with Johns Hopkins University under the direction of Patrick Coleman, a former record marketing executive, organized a competition for Mexican songwriters and performers to produce music videos for teenagers on the topic of saying "no" to sex. A tough sell perhaps, but as it turned out the winning songs were quite popular and were not only distributed as music videos, but also as tapes to radio stations. The songs were followed-up with a campaign of informa-

tion diffusion to newspapers and personal appearances of the artists at
youth clubs and other venues.[71]

Similarly, in Indonesia, inspired by the Mexican experience, in 1987
the Indonesian Family Planning Agency financed, at the cost of $3,000, a
popular song "Wait A While My Love" ("Jangan Dulu") which sold over
100,000 copies and became a popular radio hit. You get the drift. While
perhaps more a consolation to forlorn lovers than an inducement to abstinence, these communication efforts allowed society's elders to dialog with
its youth at low cost and in a broad reaching fashion. Clearly, in Mexico
and Indonesia different voices were being heard via the radio.[72]

Over the years, many of the educational and development radio programs were evaluated thoroughly with differing degrees of positive results. Indeed, the Guatemalan Village Education project was set up to include control villages without radio access and a third group with radio
and extension based follow-up. Radio with extension support was found to
be the most effective method of raising peasant awareness of new technologies. Radio alone also had a positive impact as compared with no services or with extension only. Findings consistently showed the high degree of effectiveness and low cost of the radio in various types of distance
learning. Nevertheless, around the globe, the use of radio as a teaching
tool and supplement has been and continues to be derisively small when
compared to the totality of the working poor, laboring beyond the reach of
information focused on their needs.

Decline of the Radio, Growth of Poverty
In spite of the success of these and other radio programs throughout
the 1970s, there has been a gradual decline in radio and other media programming focused on the problems of a developing country. This is due in
part to competition from other forms of media for business investment,
donor loss of interest and the progressive disenfranchisement of the poor
with the end of the cold war. While access to all forms of the media has
continued to grow, entertainment, pop-music, talk, news and fashion have
supplanted public interest information in the distribution of air time. Nor
did the talk of a "right to information" in some countries (Mexico, Brazil,
and others) or a "New World Information Order" (UNESCO, San Jose
1973) necessarily result in much attention to content and programming.
These ideological forays into the province of the media focused to a
greater extent on ownership and participation than they did on content.
Other criticism of private sector broadcasting as violence prone or value
free, with "little concern for development goals and social needs" (Vene-

zuela) did not often result in increased attention to the provision of pro-gramming.[73] Once again, a debate without issue on ownership and access displaced the real concerns on content.

Other similar clamoring for local cultural content (Peru, Mexico) was also to resolve itself, more often than not, in frustrated debates over access to media, rather than a focus on programming, as again is the case with more recent debates over "community radio." The world has become one when looking at the fashions of speech, dress, and mores displayed on CNN and SKY; but increasingly there are two in terms of the divide be-tween the first world of "haves" and the third world of "have-nots."

The decline in development assistance generally and in media-based development in particular has been mirrored in academic curriculum. Mexico, Brazil, South Korea and Egypt have developed and maintained fairly strong curricula.[74] In the U.S., where the 1970s marked a zenith of development communications, these courses of study have now disap-peared from most faculties. The remaining professors are "lions" of this bygone era with few new teachers or students taking up the gauntlet. In Latin America, where media studies remain popular—more than 300 schools with over 120,000 students—few academic programs focus on anything other than commercial and entertainment media. Programs or even course work teaching communications as an information tool for de-velopment or education are almost non-existent.[75] In India and South Asia, generally the neglect of communications as a pedagogical tool is also typi-cal of current educational curriculum.

China, Radio for the Masses
In 1949, when the Communists took over China, there was one radio for every 580 individuals, considerably fewer per capita than in most of the developing world with the exception of India. The broadcast situation was somewhat better with 83 stations, although these hardly reached be-yond a few major cities.[76]

The Kuomintang Party had established the first "Central Broadcast-ing" station in 1928, in the then capital of Nanking. The station had only 500 kilowatts at its inception, an effective range of a few miles. In four years, its power had increased to a still modest 750 kilowatts. Between 1932 and 1936, sixteen non-commercial stations began broadcasting: three stations under Central Broadcasting Administration; eight under provincial governments, four under municipal government and two under the Minis-try of Communication. Three privately owned stations had also been es-tablished in urban areas.[77]

In 1945, the Communists began broadcasting from their stronghold in Yenan for two hours a day, with 300 kilowatts of power. By 1949, sixteen stations were operating in Communist controlled areas.[78] By 1950, after the Communist takeover there were 83 radio stations: 51 government and 32 private; 22 of the 32 private stations alone were in Shanghai.[79][80] The number of stations was to triple over the next decade while the number of radios grew from one million to seven million sets, roughly one radio set for every one hundred Chinese by 1962.[81]

The Communists were quick to takeover and integrate private broadcasts into national services. They understood the power of the radio medium for both propaganda and mass education. Radio presented the Communists with a unique opportunity to address some of the country's principal development problems. The Party needed to unite the country around its rule. Over eighty percent of the country was illiterate. The country lacked a national language. Mandarin was the language of two-thirds of the population but spoken with numerous dialects and local versions. In addition, there were ten other major language groups spoken by the remaining third of the population. Radio could help unite the country around the Party and help make Mandarin a national language. It could also address the huge educational gap.

"Wire Broadcasting"

Before China could effectively use radio to begin to address these problems, it had to surmount the hurdle of its lack of nationwide availability. The Chinese Communist Party came up with a rather unique solution that it referred to as "wire broadcasting" and group listening. Radios were placed in community centers, schools, hospitals and other central locations where people gathered. "Wire broadcasting" referred to diffusion of radio broadcasts through phone lines and via loudspeakers. Multiplying the reach of radio receivers was to facilitate listening in several locations from one receiver. These loudspeakers were, in a few years, to become so ubiquitous in cities and even villages, on trains, trolleys, and city squares, as to make escaping radio soon more of a challenge than listening to it.

Somewhat later a system of radio monitors was developed. These volunteers and local cadres advertised upcoming programs, assured listening, discussion and assimilation of the Party line. In spite of all the propaganda features with which the Communist Party burdened radio programming, its role as a learning medium was not to be entirely neglected, especially in the less politicized periods during the Party's reign.

During the early period of Communist control from 1949-53 the Party felt it imperative to rally the country around its rule and authority. Their methods seem crude but underscore their intent. "Live broadcasts of mass rallies and trials during each mass campaign became the most prominent programs in the sound (radio) broadcasting system".[82] The broadcast schedule April 1, 1950 on East China People's Broadcasting Station heard in Shanghai and other surrounding areas shows the following program groupings: news and news dictation 35%; music 16%; Russian lessons 12.5%; market news 10%; spoken drama and stories 5%; teaching of singing 4.5%; announcements 4.5%; political broadcasts to Taiwan 6%; other 6.5%.[83] Provincial stations re-broadcast centrally provided radio selections and also had the authority to modify the program, eliminating some selections and adding others where they could provide local news, announcements or programming.

By 1953, the Communist Party seems to have felt that that its position in the country was sufficiently secure to allow it to turn its full attention to the needs of the masses. A shift in broadcast emphasis to include more programming on economic issues and those of the nascent industrialization was to follow. The "Party Line" in Communist ideology was theoretically to emanate from the needs and practices of the masses. In periods when the Chinese Communist system was not turned against itself in struggle, the Party seems to have understood these needs in a way Western donors have not. A glimpse into the Party's proletarian roots is seen from its own organ the *People's Daily*.

On February 6, 1956 the *People's Daily* gave insight into the Party's thinking on the use of the medium:

> If after a day's tensions and labor the masses can turn on their radio and enjoy light and pleasant music, brief news and lectures and easily comprehensible study lessons, then the masses will be greatly interested in sitting around their radio.[84]

This recognition of "study" and the mass education possibilities offered by the radio was to distinguish Chinese radio from most of the Western experience.

By 1958, the radical experiment encompassed in "The Great Leap Forward" had set back radio programming in favor of more politically oriented broadcasting promoting Mao's radical experiment in economic decentralization and rural collectivization. By 1961, however, after the "Great Leap" terminated in economic failure and starvation in the countryside, radio returned to a more diverse set of offerings, including less politically intrusive educational broadcasts. Liu reports: "… programs were oriented more to popular tastes than they had been during the 'Great Leap Forward'. Although propaganda was by no means dropped, it was subtly packaged in entertainment programs." [85]

This situation was to change once again with the advent of political struggle during the "Cultural Revolution," when Mao used the radio's power against his political opponents. Mao's death in 1976 was to offer radio once again the opportunity to become a constructive means of communication for this vast country, consisting of one-fifth of the world's population.

The economic reforms following Mao's death have meant more radios and more broadcast choices for the Chinese masses. Today there is one radio for every five Chinese, slightly less than one per household.[86] Recently China has opened its educational programming to learn from Western experiences and those of the development community. Radio distance learning professionals from the Educational Development Center, a Newton, Massachusetts based private non-profit organization with offices in Washington D.C., have visited China at the behest of broadcasters there to work with them on program development. Digital broadcasting via satellite will in the future provide China with a solution to its physical broadcast problems reaching distant populations over vast and oftentimes formidable terrain. Recently, in preparation for the 2008 Olympics, Beijing began using radio and cassette distance learning to teach English to Beijing cab drivers. The effort is somewhat reminiscent of early radio efforts to standardize Mandarin and later Russian lessons via the radio. A new chapter has just opened in the history of Chinese educational broadcasting, one that continues to retain some of the best of the past.

Other Voices

Most of the history of "development radio" has been through the voices of the developing countries themselves, supported by their institutions at the UN and, especially in the pilot stage, by the donor community. Other voices have been present as well, although somewhat muted until recently. The Voice of America (VOA), British Broadcasting Company (BBC), France Inter (Radio France Internationale) and Deutsche Welle have broadcast to the developing world throughout the period. Radio Moscow and Radio Beijing also maintained active overseas services, especially during the cold war. Broadcast length and programming have varied by broadcaster and region but generally have been heavy on news with some "public interest" broadcasting, with considerably less targeted developmental and educational broadcast programming. Quite recently an economically renascent China has begun to broadcast Chinese news and cultural programming in local languages throughout Asia.

A reawakening has occurred, at least in the United States, regarding our lost dialogue with the developing world. Since 9/11, a new interest in communication is evident among policy leaders, first and foremost, in the sphere of civic messages. Will a renewed interest in development communication follow suit? In the arena of fighting the AIDS epidemic, this already has occurred, to some extent, as the urgency of the problem has led one to look to the most effective tools. Other developmental problems do not yet have the same urgency. However, land and water resources, the environment, and civil strife are problems of the poor that affect all of us. In the ensuing chapters, we will see how the radio is being used to shape answers to these problems.

Notes

`1. Angelo Brunero, "A History of Telegraphy," translated by Andrea Valori, <http://www.acmi.net.au> (28 Dec. 2004). See this excellent history of telegraphy and additional historical material on wireless and the radio.

2. Diodorus Siculus, *Library of World History, Volume X* (Cambridge, Mass.: Harvard University Press, 1939), 19.17.5-6.

3. Caius Julius Caesar, *Caesar: The Gallic War*, trans. H.J. Edwards (Cambridge, Mass.: Harvard University Press, 1917), Book 2, chap. 33. <http://www.earth-history.com/Europe/Wars/ceasar-gallic-2.htm> (18 Jan. 2005).

4. Daniel Lerner, *The Passing of Traditional Society* (Glencoe, Ill.: Free Press, 1958), 113.

5. Thomas White, "United States Early Radio History," <http:// earlyradio-history.us> (28 Dec. 2004).

6. Rachel Sahlman, "Spectrum Biographies - Thomas Alva Edison," <http://www.incwell.com/Biographies/Edison.html.> (29 Dec. 2004).

7. Encarta, "Edison, Thomas Alva," <http://www.Encarta.msn.com/ encyclopedia_761563582/Edison_Thomas_Alva.html> (2 Dec. 2002).

8. J. Miller, "History of American Broadcasting," <http://www.members. aol.com/jeff560/jeff.html> (2 Dec. 2002).

9. Phyllis Stark, "A History of Radio Broadcasting,"*Billboard* (Nov. 1, 1994).

10. Drew O. McDaniel, *Broadcasting in the Malay World, Radio, Television and Video in Brunei, Indonesia, Malaysia and Singapore* (Norwood, NJ: Ablex Publishing, 1994), 26.

11. Philo C. Wasburn, *Broadcasting Propaganda, International Radio Broadcasting and the Construction of Political Reality* (Westport, Conn.: Praeger, 1992), 5.

12. Washburn, *Broadcasting Propaganda*, 63-64.

13. McDaniel, *Broadcasting in the Malay World*, 68.

14. Arvind Singhal and E. M. Rogers, *India's Communication Revolution—From Bullock Carts to Cyber Marts* (New Delhi: Sage Publications, 2001), 68.

15. Lerner, *Passing of Traditional Society*, 268.

16. Lerner, *Passing of Traditional Society*, 309, 395.

17. Don Moore, "Reaching the Villages: Radio in Tanzania", *Journal of the North American Shortwave Association* (1996), <http://swl.net/patepluma/ genbroad/tanzania.html.> (29 Dec. 2004).

18. Jean-Pierre Ilboudo, "Rural Radio: Role and Use Over the Past Three Decades," (paper presented at The First International Workshop on Rural Radio,

Rome, May 2001), http://www.fao.org/documents/show_cdr.asp?url_file=/ do-crep/003/x6721e/x6721e02.htm.>.
19. Ilboudo, "Rural Radio."
20. Singhal and Rogers, *India's Communication Revolution,* 68-69.
21. Richard Fardon, and Graham Furniss, eds., *African Broadcast Cultures* (Westport, Conn.: Praeger, 2000), 23.
22. *Entering the 21st Century, World Development Report 1999/2000* (New York: Published for the World Bank, Oxford University Press, 2000),Table 19 (1996 data), 266.
23. Y.B. Damle, "Communication of Modern Ideas and Knowledge in Indian Villages," *Public Opinion Quarterly* 20 (1956): 257-70.
24. Everett M.Rogers, *The Diffusion of Innovations,* 4th ed. (New York: Free Press, 1995) 86-87.
25. Paul J. Deutschmann, "The Mass Media in an Underdeveloped Village", *Journalism Quarterly* 40 (1963 Winter):27-35. See also: G. K. Hirabayashi and M.F. El Katib, "Communication and Political Awareness in the Villages of Egypt," *Public Opinion Quarterly* 22 (1958): 357-63.
26. Wilbur Schramm, *Mass Media and National Development, The Role of Information in the Developing Countries* (Stanford, Cal.: Stanford Press, 1964) 47; UNESCO, *Mass Media in the Developing Countries* (Paris: Clearing House of the Department of Mass Communication of UNESCO, 1961) 17; W. Schramm, and R.F. Carter, "Scales for Describing National Communication Systems," (unpublished manuscript, Institute for Communications Research, Stanford University, Stanford, Cal.,1959).
27. Lerner, *Passing of Traditional Society,* 255.
28. H. Adelman, A. Suhrke, and B. Jones, *The International Response to Conflict and Genocide: Lessons from the Rwanda Experience,* study #2: *Early Warning and Conflict Management* (Odense, Denmark: Steering Committee of the Joint Committee of Emergency Assistance to Rwanda, March, 1966), 29, <http://www.metafro.be/grandslacs/grandslacsdir500/0742.pdf> (3 Dec. 2002).
29. The ex-Soviet Union, which we do not include in our discussion of developing country experiences, had a much more mixed and contested record. While a pioneer in group learning and distance learning, the politicization of its airwaves was virulently contested. China's record on use of the media, probably equally contested, is reviewed by us briefly in a separate sub-section further on.
30. Some information on media ownership by political parties, the state and influential families with ties to the state in Africa, Indonesia and the former Soviet Union is available from S. Djankov and others, "Media Ownership and Prosperity" in *The Right to Tell: The Role of Mass Media in Economic Development* (Washington D.C.: World Bank Institute 2002), 141-65. <http://www1.worldbank.org/publications/pdfs/15203frontmat.pdf>.
31. Elizabeth Fox, *Latin American Broadcasting: From Tango to Telenovela* (Lutton, U.K.: University of Lutton Press, 1997), 17; See also, Greg-

ory, Bruce N., *The Broadcasting Service, An Administrative History* (Washington D.C.: USIA Special Monograph Series, No. 1, 1970).

32. Daniel Behrman, *When The Mountains Move, Technical Assistance and the Changing Face of Latin America* (Paris: UNESCO, 1954) 32.

33. Alfonso Gumucio Dagron, *Making Waves* (New York: Report to the Rockefeller Foundation, 2001), <http://www.communicationforsocialchange.org/pdf/making_waves.pdf.> (5 March 2003).

34. Joseph Georges and Isabelle Fortin, "A New Dawn for Freedom of Speech Radio: Radio Soleil," in Girard, Bruce, (Ed.), *A Passion for Radio, Radio Waves and Community*, (n.p.: Communica, 2001) chap 9, <http://www.commuinca.org/passion/contents.htm.> (3 March 2003).

35. Girard, *A Passion for Radio,* "Introduction," 18.

36. UNESCO—United Nations Educational, Scientific and Cultural Organization.

37. P.L. Spain, D. T. Jamison, and E. G. McAnany, (Eds.), *Radio for Education and Development: Case Studies*, (Washington D.C.: World Bank, May, 1977); Rogers, E. M., J. R. Braun, and M. A. Vermillion, "Radio Forums: A Strategy for Rural Development", in Spain, Jamison, and McAnany, *Radio for Education and Development*, 361-382.

38. Singhal and Rogers, *India's Communication Revolution.*

39. FAO - Food and Agricultural Organization of the United Nations.

40. Ilboudou, "Rural Radio."

41. Spain, Jamison,and McAnany, *Radio for Education and Development*, 89-90.

42. H.R.Cassirer, "Radio in an African Context: A Description of Senegal's Pilot Project" in Spain, Jamison, and McAnany, *Radio for Education and Development*, 300-338.

43. McDaniel, *Broadcasting in the Malay World*, 120, 224, 239.

44. Schramm, *Mass Media and National Development,* 167-168.

45. Fox, *Latin American Broadcasting*, 30.

46. Sylvia Schmelkes de Sotelo, "The Radio Schools of the Tarahumara, Mexico: An Evaluation" in Spain, Jamison, and McAnany, *Radio for Education and Development*, 33-68.

47. Spain, Jamison, and McAnany, *Radio for Education and Development*, 107.

48. Paulo Freire, *Pedagogy of the Oppressed,* new rev. 20th anniversary ed., trans. Myra Bergman Ramos (New York: Continuum,, 1993).

49. The United States withdrew from UNESCO in 1984 citing "poor management" and political differences with the leftist philosophy of UNESCO's leadership. In September 2002, the Bush administration announced that the U.S. would rejoin UNESCO citing management improvements, doing so a short time later.

50. Sylvia Schmelkes de Sotelo, "The Radio Schools of The Tarahumara" 33-38; Spain, P.L., "The Mexico Radio Primaria Project" 69-114 in Spain, Jamison, and McAnany, *Radio for Education and Development*.

51. Arvind Singhal and Everett M. Rogers, *Entertainment-Education: A Communications Strategy for Social Change* (Mahwah, N.J.: Lawrence Erlbaum Associates, 1999), 50.

52. Eduardo Valenzuela, "New Voices," in Girard, *A Passion for Radio*, ch. 15, 123, 131.

53. McDaniel, *Broadcasting in the Malay World*, 65.

54. UNESCO, *Features*, no. 424 (Sept. 20, 1963): 12-14.

55. P.E. Kinyanjui, "In-Service Training of Teachers through Radio and Correspondence in Kenya," in Spain, Jamison, and McAnany, *Radio for Education and Development*,152-171.

56. McDaniel, *Broadcasting in the Malay World*, 247.

57. Spain, Jamison, and McAnany, *Radio for Education and Development*, 138.

58. Robert A. White, "Mass Communication and the Popular Promotion Strategy of Rural Development in Honduras," in Spain, Jamison, and McAnany, *Radio for Education and Development*, 200-259.

59. P.L. Spain, Jamison, D.T., and McAnany, E.G., "Voices for Development: The Tanzanian National Radio Study Campaigns," in Spain, Jamison, and McAnany, *Radio for Education and Development*,260-299.

60. Spain, Jamison and McAnany, "Voices for Development," 261.

61. Andrea Bosch, "Interactive Radio Instruction: Twenty-three Years of Improving Educational Quality," (working paper in Education Technology Technical Note Series, World Bank, vol. 2, no. 1, 1997); Alan Dock and John Helwig, "Interactive Radio Instruction: Impact, Sustainability, and Future Directions," (working paper in Education Technology Technical Note Series, World Bank, vol. 4, no. 1, 1999) includes an inventory of 21 IRI programs worldwide.

62. J. Theroux and J. Gunter, "Open Broadcast Educational Radio: Three Paradigms," in Spain, Jamison, and McAnany, *Radio for Education and Development*, 338-360, (paraphrased from observations on page 238).

63. Spain, Jamison, and McAnany, *Radio for Education and Development*. p339; Emile McAnany, *Radio's Role in Development: Five Strategies of Use*, Information Bulletin number Four, (Washington D.C.: Clearinghouse on Development Communication, 1976).

64. What News, *Afrik'Netpress*, 29 January 2003. In third-world countries with less than competitive political systems, state and private funds, at least those of the governing elite, are also often mingled inextricably, making it difficult to know where one begins and the other ends.

65. Gumucio Dagron, *Making Waves*, 157-162.

66. McDaniel, *Broadcasting in the Malay World*, 68, 120.

67. McDaniel, *Broadcasting in the Malay World*,199-204.

68. Elizabeth Fox, ed., *Media and Politics in Latin America: The Struggle for Demoncracy* (London: Sage, 1988), 6-7.

69. Arvind Singhal and Everett M. Rogers, *Combating AIDS: Communication Strategies in Action* (London: Sage, 2003), 25-26.

70. Singhal and Rogers, *Combating AIDS*, 127.

71. Singhal and Rogers, *Combating AIDS*, 110-113.

72. Singhal and Rogers, *Combating AIDS*, 113. See also R. Pekerti. and R. Musa, "Wait a While My Love, An Indonesian Popular Song With a Family Planning Message," *JOICFP Integration*, 21 (Oct. 1989): 41-43.

73. Fox, *Latin American Broadcasting*, 73. Quoting from the final report on the state of the media by the Venezuelan Committee on Radio and Television (RATELVE).

74. Rogers, *The Diffusion of Innovations*, 74. Rogers would appear to disagree with the view expressed here that development communications studies have declined in the U.S. His comments were published in 1994, however, prior to what appears to us to be much of the decline.

75. Gumucio Dagron, *Making Waves*, 10. Citing comments of Manuel Calvelo.

76. Aaron Lee, "The Development of Sound Broadcasting in Mainland China During The Mao Era (1949-1976)" (master's thesis, University of California Press, 1971). This section borrows heavily from information in Lee and other English Language sources cited.

77. James W. Markham, *Voices of the Red Giants: Communications in Russia and China* (Ames, Iowa: Iowa University Press, 1967), 341.

78. Markham, *Voices of the Red Giants*, 360.

79. Frederick T.C. Yu, *Mass Persuasion in Communist China* (New York: Praeger, 1964), 124.

80. Wen Chi-tse, "People's Broadcasting during the Last 10 Years", *New China Monthly,* no. 72, (Sept. 1955): 232, in Chinese, cited in Lee, *The Development of Sound Broadcasting*.

81. Alan P.L. Liu, *Radio Broadcasting in Communist China*, 2nd.ed. (Cambridge UNESCO, 1964), cited in: Markham, *Voices of the Red Giants,* 362.

82. Alan P.L. Liu, *Communication and National Integration in Communist China* (Berkeley, California: University of California Press, 1971), 33.

83. Yu, *Mass Persuasion in Communist China,* 132.

84. Lee, *The Development of Sound Broadcasting*.

85. Liu, *Communication and National Integration in Communist China,* 123.

86. *Entering the 21st Century,* 1996 figures.

2
Family Values
—Health and Family Planning Radio in West Africa—

Burkina Faso, Cameroon, Togo and the Cote d'Ivoire are poor countries in West Africa. Average income ranges from $300 to $600 per year. This buys basic food, little in the way of goods, adequate clothing— occasionally quite magnificent embroidered cloth garments for weddings and other important occasions—but leaves little for a rainy day. Most families have a radio and some have television, although the electricity to watch it is at best intermittent. Health services are cheap, can generally be afforded with some skimping, but medications are expensive when they can be found at all. Otherwise said, a medical diagnosis, often a very good one from a trained Doctor, is generally available, the treatment or cure often inaccessible. Of course, traditional local medicine is also available whether herbal or totem.

French is the language of schooling and spoken by those who have done a few years of primary school or live in the urban areas. African languages, quite numerous, even over small geographic areas, are spoken by all. Accessibility of French as a common language to large segments of the population facilitates the use of the radio, although the use of French by the rural poor is more circumscribed.

There are several different religious affiliations in the region: Muslim, Christian and animist or traditional native religions. In addition to the problems of poverty and development, the region has been confronted with the HIV-AIDS epidemic. While polygamous, the stricter Muslim culture has sheltered some communities from the inroads the disease has made in other parts of Africa. This, however, has begun to change and the incidence of the disease is beginning to spread rapidly within the region. The HIV-AIDS problem comes in addition to the region's other severe problems, as two of the four countries have suffered from civil strife in recent years.

In general, it can be said that as communities grow and change, family values and cultural practices often are confronted with realities that challenge people's beliefs and practices. In some cases, practices are questioned yet endure because they are grounded in well-established values that persevere, often over millennia, and form the bedrock of community cohesion and human society. The biblical prohibition against taking another's life is one such value, which while violated in time of war and by the state persists in governing our behavior toward our fellow man. Marriage, as an institution, is another that is currently subjected to assault by the many changes that have affected our societies. Yet, it is difficult for us to imagine doing without it.

Sexual promiscuity, on the other hand, while certainly part of social life throughout the ages, is more frequently challenged and seen as inappropriate social behavior. The relationship of positive social values and the practices that accompany them: marital fidelity, inheritance, sexual abstinence, respect for law and communal arbitration of disputes, proscriptions on teen sex or reluctance to countenance public displays of violence, along with many others, constitute the fabric of our societies. West Africa is no different and along with the ever-present change that is part of the human condition, these cultural practices will evolve, sometimes rationally in response to new threats as HIV-AIDs, sometimes irrationally in response to fear and superstition.

Western nations and the development community, in particular, have been noticeably aggressive in promoting their own "values" at the expense of indigenous ones. It is doubtful that countries and societies with high rates of divorce, teen pregnancy, alcoholism and drug use, and numerous forms of inequality can effectively preach the superiority of "monogamous" marriage, western family values and male/female equality with a high degree of credibility. Many listeners are offended and unconvinced by our assumption of the superiority of our ways. These societies, in the absence of state funded welfare and safety nets, have found caring ways to deal with the poorest members of their communities and are rightly skeptical of wealthy societies which leave many of their own behind, without even a tear, or backward look, in their direction. The Muslim religion is stern in its admonition to aid the poor, something that most Muslims practice. African Muslims, Christians and animists alike, adhere to the concept of extended family, protecting the weakest of its members and obliging every family member to use his or her success to the benefit of the whole family.

Yet while these values have worked for better or worse for African societies throughout the ages, they too are subject to change and challenge from an ever-changing environment and from the many incursions, some positive some negative from the modern world.

Oral societies especially will discuss the relevance of values intruding from the modern world. Given this, well mediated radio generated by the local population and providing information and reflection, rather than propaganda and prejudice, can serve to inform the debate that will in any case take place.

"THE KEY TO LIFE" is one such program. This 26-episode radio series was developed as a means of provoking such reflection and informed discussion. The series, set in the West-Central Africa region, seeks to include relevant reproductive and child health information within the context of a dramatic, entertaining story of a young man's quest to find his father. The series was produced by the Academy for Educational Development, a Washington based educational non-profit organization, in collaboration with the *Atelier Theatre Burkinabe* and based on the work of a team of dramatists from all the focus countries. It was funded by USAID's Health Office, one of the bright spots in the U.S. assistance program in terms of its understanding of the importance of communication to development and improving the condition of the poor. The program aired from April to December 1997 in the four focus countries and on Africa Number 1, a regional station which broadcasts widely throughout the region. The broadcast stations had a combined capacity to reach more than 55 million people. Here are several gripping episodes from "THE KEY TO LIFE".

The Key to Life (Yamba Songo)

Narrator: Day one, episode 1.

In Yaoundé (Cameroon), while Songo comforts his mother Matalina, who is crying over the death of her husband Ateba, the family, who has gathered together, divides up the deceased's possessions.

Radio: Tears, cries, glasses knocked together and noise of drinks being served.

Matalina: Why have you left, why now? What will become of me without you, Ateba? You were all my hope.

(The Patriach demands silence raising his voice. The family responds with silence.)

Patriarch: Matalina, you've cried enough now. You need to stop. God's will has been done and no one can change that. Here. My brothers, as is our custom, we have come to divide Ateba's belongings.

Radio: General surprise.

Matalina: What! I won't.

Patriarch: How's that?

Matalina: I refuse. It's not the time, after my husband's death to go poking around in his things. While he was sick, which one of you stuck your feet in the door? No sooner is Ateba dead than we discover his relatives. How's that! It won't happen the way you think. Ateba has left his possessions to his children and me.

Patriarch: (laughing) Whatever Ateba has earned he earned it himself, by the sweat of his brow. We supported his efforts. Morally, his possessions belong to all his family.

Voice: I don't believe it.

Matalina: In laws, you're all the same. One of your family dies and all you can think about is getting a hold of his things. This time, I swear, you won't succeed; my husband has left this will leaving his possessions to us.

Patriarch: Ha, Matalina, that's how you did it. You took advantage of his illness. So, no longer in control of himself, he signed this document under pressure from you.

Matalina: Look at the date when it was signed.

Patriarch: (Interrupts Matalina) This was signed?

Second Voice : (Interrupts the Chief) He was sound of mind and body.

Patriarch: What? Sound of mind and body. Give me these papers; I'll tear them up (tearing). See where you'll find another set.

Matalina: That's criminal.

Patriarch: It's the law of the family.

Matalina: You're criminals, but I won't stop here, I'll go to court.

(The Patriarch once again calls for silence in the crowded room raising his voice. The entire family obeys and silence reigns.)

Patriarch: As Chief of this family, I want to thank you for your presence here. We are going to begin the disposition. Iwana, you . . .

Iwana: Yes.

Patriarch: You get the television. You, Eboua, you will get Ateba's five jackets. As for you Antagana, you've got a driver's license, right? You get the Renault and the four chairs. Then! As for me, I get the radio, the hunting rifle and the two bamboo chairs. As for you N'nama, the bed and mattress and his wife go to you!

Radio: *(Joyous cries)*

Patriarch: Listen to me, the disposition continues. Aateba's clothes will be parceled out among his cousins in the village. And, as for his house, we're going to sell it to pay back the debts we incurred for his funeral.

(Multiple voices, the Patriarch reaffirms order among the attendance.)

Antagana: Uncle, I want to speak. No, I can't take the car. Ateba left it for his son, Songo, whose finishing up his studies. You understand, don't you?

Third Voice: We decide here.

Songo: You're people without a heart. My father is not even dead a month. Already you're after his possessions, forgetting about his family. Have you thought about his children's welfare for even a minute? If he were alive, would he have thought about giving you all his possessions disinheriting his family? Think about it and you'll understand that this would not have been his wish.

Patriarch: Quiet Songo, quiet or I'll have more to say to you.

Fourth Voice: It's the truth.

Patriarch: But what are you talking about? It's the truth? How? Besides, you're only a child. This is family business. You're too little to participate. What's the matter with this child? Did someone make somebody of you or *what? Besides, we don't even consider you Ateba's child. Ask your mother if you want to know?*

Matalina: Hold on, don't talk about that now!

Patriarch: We're going to talk.

Women's Voice: Enough said Matalina; it's not worth the trouble to have him ask you now.

Matalina: I didn't ask you. If need be, we'll settle this now.

Patriarch: Really, you're getting out of hand.

Women's Voice: It's not necessary for him to ask for explanations from his Mom. Tell him simply that he's not a family member and this doesn't concern him.

(laughing)

Songo: You can laugh if you want. I'll defend my mother as well as my little sister and brother's rights. I swear to you. You've torn up a copy of the will but we've got the original. If you continue, I'll call the police.

Patriarch: Police? What police Songo? We've acted according to our customs.

Songo: Whose customs?

Patriarch: The customs of our tribe.

Voice: If you don't want the family name tarnished you better leave the widow and her children Ateba's inheritance.

Patriarch: We'll talk about this in a family counsel.

Assembly: Yes!

Patriarch: So much for our traditions.

Assembly: Huh?

Patriarch: This isn't normal.

Assembly: It's not normal?

Patriarch: Let's just go and leave the bastards to themselves. We won't tell people like this what to do.

Songo: Me, a bastard?

Matalina: Who are you calling bastard? You won't get even a sewing pin from this inheritance.

Patriarch: We'll see about that.

Matalina: You won't get anything.

(Everyone exits, voices continue the discussion, voices heard calming Matalina.)

Musical Interlude

Narrator During this same time in Ouagadougou (Burkina Faso), the oldest girl of Yamba and Poko is in labor.

Radio: Rain beating on tin roof, utensils being sorted out.

Yamba: Norago, the poor thing has been going at it since six o'clock. What can we do to help her?

Norago: It's two in the morning. Eight hours of work. But say, Yamba, who's in there with your daughter and wife Poko?

Yamba: I asked the neighbor, Tenin, to come.

Norago: Oh, why not take her to the maternity?

Yamba: Oh no, it's not possible. Since the beginning of her pregnancy until today, she hasn't put a foot in the pre-natal ward.

Norago: What!!!!!

(Koumbou continues to suffer and moan.)

Tenin: Push, push harder!

Poko: Tenin, know what, run and call the mid-wife, Talato. Go quick!

Yamba: Oh, it's Talato who's come.

Talato: Yes, yes.

Yamba: Hello, Talato.

Talato: Hello, Yamba.

Yamba: Everything o.k?

Talato: Yes, fine.

Yamba: Hurry, they're inside.

Talato: Look how pale she is. How long has she been suffering like that?

Poko: Since nightfall.

Talato: Poko

Poko: Yes.

Talato: bring me some water and soap.

Poko: O.K.

(Koumbou continues to suffer, Tenin comforts her.)

Talato: I'm washing my hands and I'll be there. Koumbou open your legs. Let yourself go. Don't hurry me. The day you did this, you didn't pray? Sit down, let me see. The day you give birth, there is nothing shameful, toss me a cloth and let me see.

Poko: Wait, wait we'll see.

Talato: Poko, come touch and see for yourself. Hey Poko, really, I don't want to discourage you but this is serious.

Poko: Serious?

Talato: The child is facing the wrong way. Back first. I can do something, but you'll need to give me a razor blade.

Poko: A razor blade, why?

Talato: To open her up.

Koumbou: No! No! No! You can't cut me open.

Poko: Cut my daughter open? I won't agree to that.

Talato: O.k. but it's you that called me. Either you bring me a razor blade, I cut her open and do a caesarean or you take care of your daughter yourself.

Poko: I can't agree to this. Tenin, isn't it better to bring her to the maternity ward?

Tenin: That's better.

Radio: Poko leaves the room and joins the other men outside.

Poko: Father

Yamba: Hey, what's the matter?

Poko: Her condition is serious.

Yamba and Noraogo: Really?

Poko: The child is not coming out properly.

Yamba and Noraogo: No!

Poko: And Talato wants to cut her open, but I won't agree.

Yamba: No, but, listen if all you need is a 15 Francs blade to take the baby out, there's no reason to say no. Go get a blade now.

Poko: Not on your life.

Yamba: Really.

Poko: I want to take my daughter to the maternity ward.

Noraogo: Hey, Yamba, run and call a taxi.

Yamba: Who me? A taxi, where do you think to find a taxi at this time of night?

Noraogo: But Yamba, your neighbor has a car, we can ask him to help.

Yamba: No, it's out of the question. I won't do it.

Noraogo: So, o.k. then I'll go and ask him. (Turning to Poko) Go get her ready to leave.

Yamba: That's your affair.

Radio: (With great difficulty Poko and Tenin carry Koumbou outside.)

Radio: (Car arrives)

Noraogo: Your neighbor is here. Let's go, quick.

Poko: Courage, make an effort; we're going to make it.

Radio: (Vroom)

Yamba: Get going. Bye!!

Radio: (The car restarts and drives away.)

Musical Interlude

Yamba: Noraogo, look more than three hours have passed and we don't have any news. What do you think is going on there?

Noraogo: The medical situation is complicated by the young age of your daughter. One should let a girl become a woman before becoming a mother.

Yamba: Oh that. Kids today. She brings home a child without even know-ing who got her pregnant. That's something else!

Noraogo: Is it really the children's fault. Your not taking your responsibil-ity. God blessed you with children and you do nothing but complain about having daughters.

Yamba: There you go again. Another of your disagreeable asides.

Noraogo: It's whose fault? The Doctor says that the sperm determines the baby's gender? The woman doesn't play a role. Whose fault is it then?

Yamba: Another reason to see the village doctor. With his traditional products, I can finally have boys.

Noraogo: Did you ask your wife her point of view?

Yamba: Well! Well!

Noraogo: After all she'll have to carry the baby nine months.

Radio: (Car noise approaching.)

Noraogo: Hey! It's a car coming?

Yamba: Yes.

Noraogo: Ah, it's Tenin.

Tenin: Ah, God have mercy. She's given birth.

Yamba and Noraogo: Yeah!

Tenin: All the midwives were really kind, your daughter is too young to give birth. They gave her a cesarean. It's o.k., the child is alive. They told us, really, that one hour more and we would have lost the girl and the child. They said that a pregnant woman should visit the center from her third month until giving birth, if you want to avoid this kind of thing.

Yamba: Understood.

Tenin: Here's a prescription.

Yamba: A prescription? O.K.! Fine. But, Tenin, tell me what did she have?

Tenin: She had a child.

Yamba: (smiling) Yes, but what gender?

Tenin: She had a girl.

Yamba: What? A girl? Another? In my yard? Not on your life. Then, I refuse to buy these things.

Tenin: A girl isn't a person then?

Yamba: I don't want any more girls in my house.

Noraogo: Listen, give me the prescription, I'll buy the drugs.

Yamba: That's your problem.

Noraogo: Go get the new mother's things. Yamba, calm down, calm down. Come along, we're going to see your daughter and her child.

Yamba: Who?

Noraogo: This will serve as example in the future.

Fade away.

End of First Episode.

   The level of listener exposure to "The Key to Life" varied from city to city, ranging from 11% of those in the listening area in Douala, Cameroon to 32% in Ouagadougou, Burkina Faso. Over 90 % of the listeners said they found the series interesting (somewhat or very). Evaluations found that those exposed to the series reported positive behavior changes as a result of listening to the series. It had an effect! On average, those who listened heard six out of the twenty-six episodes. Listeners reported having discussed the program content with an average 3.5 individuals and recommending the program to an average 3.1 people who had not yet heard it.

Fully 52 % of listeners reported taking positive action with regard to family planning. Specifically mentioned were speaking to a partner about family planning, deciding to limit or space births, going for family planning information from a clinic or other source and using a family planning method. Some 16 % reported taking an action with regard to diarrheal disease and 73% reported taking some action with regard to ST disease or HIV-AIDS. Using a condom, having fewer partners or speaking with a partner about the risk of disease were the most frequent actions mentioned. Being tested for AIDS or seeking treatment were mentioned less frequently.

3
"Grace Dies In Barn Fire"
—Agricultural Extension Via the Radio—

Many agricultural development specialists claim that agriculture is too location specific for agricultural knowledge to be spread via the radio. In their minds, the only viable method for progress in agricultural knowledge and cultivation is a visit to the yeoman farmer by an extension agent under the tutelage of the development worker. Such agents, perfectly trained, possessing the correct diagnosis of the farmer's problem and armed with the scientific and affordable solution are the development specialist's answer to low agricultural yields in peasant farming and reducing hunger and malnutrition worldwide.

It is best not to mention, even discreetly, to these specialists that even if all the development money available were consecrated to agriculture, at the expense of health assistance, vaccinations, HIV-Aids information, even primary education or micro-lending; all this money would not be sufficient to reach the roughly 3 billion rural farmers worldwide. Such an indiscretion would hardly pose a challenge to their reasoning as their mission seems less a ministry to poor farmers worldwide than an effort to control the flow of meager resources now allotted to development.

One need only do some simple calculations to understand the magnitude of the problem. The United States Agency for International Development (USAID), in the face of increasing problems of hunger and malnutrition worldwide, recently discussed nearly doubling its development assistance to the agricultural sector in poor countries from slightly more than $200 million to $400 million. If the cost to reach a poor farmer with agricultural information that might improve his lot were only $1 a visit per year, the increased USAID program would reach only 400 million, considerably less than half of the world's rural poor. Of course using extension agents, in the manner being proposed, $1 per year would buy few farm visits. At a cost of $10 per annum the USAID program would reach 40 million at a more realistic $100 per year the population of farmers helped would be only 4 million. Recommended extension frequencies are hardly a visit a year, but rather once every two-weeks to a month. A major USAID agricultural productivity project in Guatemala the REAP project spent approximately $3,000 per farmer reached. Compare this to the fraction of a cent per listener hour attributed as the only cost of many radio programs.

Of course, USAID is not the only international donor to invest in agriculture, although outside of the World Bank, it is the largest. Moreover, it would hardly be necessary to reach every farmer worldwide for progress to occur because of spillover demonstration effects. Nevertheless, these figures give some idea of the gap between the resources and the challenge of rural poverty given the backward and costly methods that the international community has chosen.

Since at least the 1930s and, if one counts the telegraph, significantly earlier, other means than personal journey on foot, horse and buggy or the automobile have facilitated communication between rural and urban areas. This is especially so when cost and the informative content of the message are the principal concerns. To reach the large number of poor in rural China, India, South Asia and Africa where roads are poor or non-existent, banditry and civil war make travel prohibitive, and overnight facilities, provisions and fuel are rare, only mass communication presents a feasible solution, on a regular basis.

Yet mass communication via the radio is hardly a second best. It is frequently the case that a poorly trained extension worker arrives in a village after the farmers have left for the fields and leaves before they return in order to be back in the district capital before nightfall. Unlike that situation, the radio can be beamed to the village during peak listening hours, after farmers have returned from their fields and while they are sitting around eager for some external communication and information. Quality control, when there is only one source of transmission, is infinitely easier than it is with the diffusion of a worker trained extension model. Unlike the frequent developmental problem where workers give farmers conflicting recommendations, radio messages are part of the public domain, subject to the scrutiny of all.

The radio has been and is successful in rural development. U.S. farming grew through the 1930's with the help of radio extension from the United States Department of Agriculture (USDA). Freely syndicated USDA radio and television programming is still distributed and played daily by stations all over the U.S., helping farmers with current problems and keeping them informed of issues affecting them. The "green revolu-tion" in the 1970's encouraged farmers to plant newly developed dwarf varieties of wheat and rice and explained the increased requirements of these varieties for fertilizer and water. Radio forums and farmer discussion groups organized around the debate and the adoption of radio-transmitted farming recommendations helped diffuse the "green revolution" to the In-dian peasantry. In a later stage and on a wider scale, similar advances were obtained through the "packaged" information campaign whereby All India Radio (AIR) broadcast a bundled package of farming techniques supple-mented with written material distributed at rural centers. In Guatemala, the "Basic Village Education Project" tested the radio against non-radio and augmented radio extension with positive result.

The longest running radio program "The Archers," on the air from Monday, January 1, 1951 when it first aired on the BBC, to this day, started as an agricultural extension program to teach UK farmers how to increase productivity after the devastation of World War II. The aftermath of the war confronted England with many problems, not the least of these being, hunger and the ravages of war on the countryside. Soldiers came back to the farm; many of them farming as adults for the first time. They desperately needed training on how to deal with widespread bottlenecks to production with limited means. After trying a number of methods, includ-ing more formal radio presentations, the farm radio drama "The Archers" was born.

Godfrey Baseley, a BBC producer of agricultural programs, had un-successfully tried programming using agricultural ministry experts "talk-ing heads." This was a bit like our development "chief of party" agricultu-ralist whose twice-yearly interview on local radio passes for "use of the radio" in development circles. Baseley's more formal interviewing at-tempts at radio broadcasting did not reach farmers effectively. But, he was devoted and interested enough to understand the power of the medium to solve real problems. In a series of client interviews, Harry Burt, a Lincoln-shire farmer, suggested that what farmers really needed was a popular program, a farming version of the hit radio soap of the day "Dick Barton," private eye. The farming program created from farmer Burt's suggestion and Baseley's acumen would eventually surpass its soap rival in popular-ity and live on long after.

Baseley went on to create a gripping radio drama of a contemporary rural English farm family, "The Archers," who faced many of the prob-lems their listening neighbors were confronting. By 1955, "The Archers" had achieved a regular listening audience of 20 million. Somewhat aston-ishingly, early Archer episodes were regularly heard by over a third of

English households, a figure difficult to match in broadcast annals. Over the years, the program has treated many important British agricultural issues. According to a BBC highlight on the program, foot-and-mouth disease, TB, mad-cow disease, rights of way and rural poverty were some of the major topics explored in the series. While the BBC's "Archers" lost its educational vocation in 1972, as other means of providing farm information became available in the UK, the program continues to this day as a widely popular serial on English farm life. Many of the issues confronted on today's dramas are still relevant.

The "Archer" episode that follows, from March 1952, was so emotionally engaging to its listeners that its story line was picked-up as a headline in the English tabloids the next day:

"GRACE DIES IN BARN FIRE"

Because the "Archers" were so real to their listeners, this headline shocked many who wrote and called the papers. Many of those who asked about Grace were "Archer" listeners who should have known that Grace was a fictional character. Such is the power of radio.

The farm message in this episode will probably never be lost to any of the listeners to the original airing of the drama. It was the need for ample water supplies on rural farms—a pond was recommended—to fight eventual fires. Promoted by rural fire departments, this bit of social marketing to rural listeners was sure to have its effect when they contemplated the fate of Grace. Wind carried sparks from autumn leaf burning leading to a barn fire was a second message inserted to inspire reflection on the causes of farm fires. This same reflection will not be lost on the modern reader who will note that burning leaves is now forbidden in many urban and peri-urban settings because buildings are in the vicinity.

Here is an excerpt from the "Archer" episode, "Grace Dies in Barn Fire". [1]

Announcer: "The Archers", an everyday story of country folk.

THEME MUSIC {Reminiscent of yeoman and English countryside}

Phil and Grace are having a drink before dinner at the country club with Reggie Trentham, Carol Grey and John Treggoran when Grace, in going to the car to find an earring she has dropped, finds the stables on fire.

*The loft above the boxes is burning furiously. Between them, they man-
age to get all the horses out, but Midnight makes for the stables again.*

Grace: *(off) Whoa! Midnight!*

John: *What's up?*

Carol: *Midnight couldn't have been tied and—(gasps) Look!
She's going back to the stable.*

Reggie: *What! No Grace, don't do it!*

John: *Oh my God!*

Carol: *She's going in after Midnight! Grace!*

Phil: *Grace! Grace! Come back! The roof's collapsing! For God's sake,
Grace come back.*

John: *She'd gone in!*

Reggie: *Look at that roof!*

(Rumble of roof collapsing)

It's caving.

Carol: *Horrible!*

John: *Phil! Phil, you fool!*

Phil: *Let me go! Grace is in there! Let me go, blast you, John!*

John: *It's suicide! If you—(smack: John reacts)*

Phil: *(going off fast) Grace! Grace!*

Reggie: *Phil, you madman!*

Carol: *Don't let him!*

*(Running footsteps on gravel. Crackle of fire, louder. Hooves
approaching at the gallop.)*

Phil: *(Coughing: Offline)*

John: *(Yelling) Phil! Phil!*

Phil: *(Off) Look out! Midnight's gone away!*

> *(Horse to peak and off, Galloping on gravel.)*

John: *Where are you?*

Phil: *(Coughing, Coming Nearer) Near the tack . . . can't see . . . Grace! Grace! Oh my God! Grace! Where is she?*

John: *No. She must have . . . There! Look! Under that beam! (smoked gasp)*

Phil: *(coughing beside himself) Get it off her! Help me! Get it off! (Strains) Heave!*

John: *(Grunts and strains) Can't budge it!*

Phil: *Harder! Harder! (Strains) Heave, blast you! Pull your guts out!*

Reggie: *Off, coughing) John! Phil!*

John: *(Yelling) Here! . . . Here . . . (Strains) Buck up!*

Reggie: *(Coming on) See you . . . strength!*

Phil: *(Straining) The straw under her's catching alight! Stamp on it! Don't let the fire touch her!*

Reggie: *All right!*

John: *(Straining) Get on this beam and heave, Reggie! Quick!*

> *(All grunt and strain)*

Reggie: *(Gritting) It's coming . . . bit more . . . all together . . . heave.*

John: *Phil—get her out while Reggie and I are holding it up.*

Phil: Grace—Grace . . .

John: Buck up! Can't (coughs)—can't hold it much longer.

Phil: All right. Got her!

John: Get out! Quick!

Phil: (Goes off coughing)

Reggie: Okay, John. Drop it.

> *(Thud, clatter, crackle of flame)*

John: Did he get her out all right?

Reggie: Yes, I think so! Look out, John! Mind your head! Burning hay showering down!

> *(Crackle up and down)*

John: Shan't get through that way now!

Reggie: The tack room window! Come on!

> *(Scrambling, grunts, etc.)*

> *Dash your elbow through it!*

> *(Crash of glass)*

> *Bit more! We'll cut ourselves to ribbons if we go through there!*

> *(Crash of glass, glass tinkles, etc.)*

John: Okay Reggie! Out of it!

> *(Clumps, bumps, grunts, etc.)*

John: Nothing'll stop it now! Place'll be gutted!

Reggie: Yes. Thank heaven the wind's not blowing toward the house.

John: *Come on. Round the other side and see if Grace is all right.*

> *(Fade crackles to background of car approaching fast and pulling up, car door slams.)*

Dan: *(Coming on) Anything we can do? Anybody called the brigade?*

Reggie: *Oh, hello Mr. Archer.*

Tom: *(Coming on) Saw the blaze from down the village and come straight up.*

Walter: *Anybody called the brigade?*

Reggie: *Yes, I did.*

Dan: *By George, its going, isn't it? Take more than us to put that lot out.*

Tom: *We'd better do something.*

John: *We can run our hoses out—*

Reggie: *And the horses'll have to be attended to. Where the devil are Phil and Grace? They got out did they?*

Dan: *Eh? What do you mean?*

John: *Grace went back in there after Midnight. Phil followed her.*

Reggie: *They got out surely!*

Tom: *You mean to say they're—*

John: *No, they must have got out.*

Reggie: *Walter—*

Walter: *Ay, Reggie, lad?*

Reggie: *Be a good scout and go across to the house. See if Phil's taken Grace there and make sure somebody's called an ambulance—*

Walter: *(Going off) Ay, right'o—*

Dan: *Ambulance! What the devil—*

Tom: *Are they hurt? What happened, John?*

John: *Part of the roof collapsed as she went in. One of the old beams must have struck her as it fell. It was sort of wedged against the wall and she was under it.*

Dan: *Hurt bad?*

Reggie: *Not so far as we could see. Probably just knocked cold.*

Tom: *But, the fire—was she..?*

John: *No, didn't touch her.*

Dan: *Thank heaven for that. (Going) Well, come on, Tom. Let's do some thing.*

Tom: *It's got a dickens of a hold.*

Reggie: *(Climbing After) Our domestic housepipes won't touch it. Better to use them to stop it from spreading.*

Dan: *(Off) Ay, right.*

John: *We'd better see to the horses. No knowing where Midnight'll be by now. Went off at a tearing gallop—terrified.*

Carol: *(Coming on) Reggie! Reggie!*

John: *Carol—are Phil and Grace—?*

Carol: *(Coming on) Across at the house. But, I think you better go into Valerie.*

Reggie: *Val? Why—what's the matter?*

Carol: *She came out here just as you and John went into the stable. She saw you go. The shock was too much for her.*

Reggie: *Whaaat! You mean she's . . . ?*

Carol: *Yes, I'm afraid so. I—I'm terribly sorry.*

Reggie: *(Going off) Oh, my sainted aunt!*

Carol: *They were both so looking forward to it.*

John: *Will she be all right?*

Carol: *Yes. I've sent for the Doctor.*

John: *What about Grace?*

Carol: *Don't know about her. Had Val on my hands.*

                    (Boom and crackle of flames)
        More roof fallen in.

                        (Whinny off)

        Those horses are getting restive, tugging at their ropes.

John: *Yes. Come on. Come and give me a hand to question'em.*

                        (Fade down)

            *(Fade up general fighting activity and crackle of flames.
            Unintelligble shouted instructions etc. in background)*

Tom: *Any more hose, Walter?*

Walter: *(Off) No, Tom! Can't find none!*

Dan: *There's a stand pipe over there, but the blasted hose won't reach!*

Walter: *(Coming on) How much of the tackle did you manage to get out?*

Tom: *Not a lot. We hooked a bit out through the broken window with a
        hay rake then the flames drove us back.*

                (Fire engine bell faintly in the background)

Dan: *Listen a minute! (Pause)*

(Fire engine bell in background)

That's the fire engine!

Tom: *Can't have took'em above fifteen minutes to come from Hallerton. That's darn good goin'.*

> *(Fire engine and bell approaches. Ambulance bell approaching)*

Walter: *Ambulance, too, by the sound of it.*

Dan: *Keep out of their road and let them get at it. Tom—*

Tom: *Ay, Dan.*

Dan: *Show 'em where the water is.*

Tom: *Right'o. Water's over here you chaps!*

Voice: *(Off) Righto! Thanks!*

> *(Ambulance pulls up)*

Dan: *Stay here, Walter! Do what you can to help'em.*

Walter: *Ay, Right'o.*

> *(Ambulance door opens)*

Dan: *Will you take the ambulance on up to the house? I'll come with you and show you.*

Voice II: *Right. Jump in.*

> *(Ambulance door closes and moves off.)*
> *Fade up ambulance ticking over)*

John: *I'd better give Christine a ring, hadn't I, Mr. Archer?*

Dan: *Ay, p'rhaps you had better.*

Carol: Where's Grace?

Dan: They're jus bringing her out on a stretcher.

John: (Aside) Still out, isn't she?

Carol: (Aside) Looks like it, poor thing.

> *(Footsteps pause. Slithering effect of stretcher put
> into ambulance)*

John: Phil—are you all right?

Phil: (Down) Yes, I'm all right. Thanks for helping me, John.

John: That's okay. Couldn't do much else.

Dan: You'll be going in with her, oh, lad?

Phil: Yes.

Voice II: (Slightly off) All right, sir, if you're ready to get aboard.

Phil: Thanks.

*(Ambulance door closes. Mike in the ambulance with Phil & Grace. Driver's
door slams and ambulance with bell ringing gets away behind.)*

> *Can I sit here by her?*

Voice II: Yes.

Phil: (Rousing) I think she's stirring . . . Grace . . . Grace.

Grace: (Weakly) Phil?

Grace: (Relieved) Phil . . . Phil . . .

Voice II: (Quietly) Scuse me, sir. I'd better just have a look at her.

Phil: It's all right Grace. Nothing to worry about.

Grace: Phil . . . I love you, Phil . . .

(FADE)

(Fade up sounds of badminton being played)

Chris: *(Petty shriek) Oh, curse the thing!*

Paul: *(Slightly off) Keep it up, Chris! You're doing all right.*

Chris: *It just won't go where I want it to.*

Paul: *No, but you're getting the swing.*

Chris: *Badminton! Tacha!*

Paul: *Come on. Knock up again. Don't be discouraged.*

Chris: *Oh, all right Paul.*

(Renewed play)

Now lob—lob high!

Chris: *I can't control the thing! (Grunt of effort) Hopeless!*

(Play stops)

Paul: *That wasn't at all bad—really. You've shown a tremendous improvement.*

Chris: *Shall we stop now?*

Paul: *Had enough?*

Chris: *More than enough.*

Paul: *(Coming on) Okay, Chris. You'll find the game more interesting as
you get on -*

Chris: *I don't think I will.*

Paul: *Mm.*

Chris: I'm just not going to take to badminton, Paul. It's not a game I'll enjoy. I know it.

Paul: You're just discouraged, at the moment, because you can't do everything you want to.

Chris: I'll never learn. I'm not very interested in learning. And as long as I feel like that there's not very much point in my joining the badminton club, is there?

Girl: (Coming on) Miss Archer?

Chris: Yes?

Girl: There's a telephone message for you.

Chris: Oh, thanks. Where—over there?

Girl: Yes, that's right.

Chris: Wonder who it is? Mum, perhaps.

Paul: Everybody knew you were coming here, didn't they?

Chris: Yes.

(Phone up)

Hello, Christine Archer speaking. Oh, hello John. What . . . (Taking it) What!

When? Oh good golly! But how did it? . . . Yes . . . yes, of course. Immediately.

We'll come straight away!
(Phone down)

Paul: What's wrong?

Chris: We must go. Fire at the stables. Almost burnt down.

Paul: Good gosh! Are the horses all right?

Chris: It isn't so much the horses. Its Grace!

Paul: Grace!

Chris: Yes, She was injured. Quickly—get your things and let's go . . . toh, doh! Why did I play badminton tonight of all nights?

(Fade down. Fade up general clear up background)

Dan: We'd better get this tack into the back of my car, Walter. I'll take it down to Brookfield with me.

Walter: Ay, right'o, Dan, me old beauty.

Dan: Sure you don't mind having two or three of the horses?

Walter: No, course not.

Dan: John!

John: (Off) Yes, Mr. Archer?

Dan: Will you lead one of 'em down? Better for us to have 'em down there where we can keep an eye on 'em.

John: (Coming on) Yes, of course I will.

Walter: Where's Tom?

Dan: Gone to try and fetch Midnight. Somebody said she was seen straying down by Ramsden's place.

Carol: (Coming on) Shall I lead one of the horses?

Dan: If you don't mind, Carol.

John: Chris said she'd be along.

Dan: We can probably get all of 'em down to Brookfield before she gets here from Borchester.

Walter: Eh, there ain't much left of the stable, Dan, is there? Must have bin dry as a tinder box.

Carol: Yes. There was no stopping it once it got started.

Dan: What did start it?

John: Yes. Haven't really had time to think of that, have we? It was going like the dickens up in the loft when we got out here. Must have started up there somehow.

Dan: Well, I expect the fire brigade chap'll have a good look round now they can get in.

      (Diffidently) Er Carol.

Carol: Yes?

Dan: What did you think of Grace?

Carol: It was a crazy thing to do, but it was wonderfully brave, dashing in there like that-

Dan: I mean, how did you think she was when they took her away?

Carol: *(With difficulty) Well . . . its hard to say, but . . .*

John: *(Quietly) I didn't like the look of her very much.*

Dan: *(A long thoughtful inhale) Just what I was thinking myself. (Change of mood)* Well, we'd better get these horses put away somewhere. I expect Reggie's got some head-collars we can borrow. We didn't manage to save many out of the tack room. Carol, if you can manage Cavalier, and Walter and John start out with Flash and Isabella—

      (Music link into door opening and closing)

Dan: Well, that's got 'em settled, Chris. They'll be all right till morning, now.

Chris: Thanks for all your help, Dad.

Dan: That's all right love.

Chris: *It must have burnt like fury.*

Dan: *Quite a blaze I can tell you. Seen Midnight?*

Chris: *Yes. I've put a blanket over her for tonight.*

Dan: *I had a quick look at her. She didn't seem to have done any damage to herself. Lucky, considering the way she bolted.*

Chris: *Yes, I—I feel all sort of edgy, as though there's something I ought to have done but haven't.*

Dan: *Just unsettled with the night's happening, I expect. I didn't water Judy. Did you? Is that what's worrying you?*

Chris: *No, Dad. I did her.*

Dan: *Here—you're insured up at the stables, aren't you? Premiums paid up and that?*

Chris: *Yes . . . I think p'raps its Cavalier. Played up a bit in strange surroundings. I'd better go out and have another look at him a bit later . . . and there's the tack.*

Dan: *That'll be all right in the barn till the morning. You can sort it out then.*

Chris: *(Sighs) Shall I make a cup of tea?*

Dan: *Not a bad idea.*

(Tap and kettle filled)

Chris: *Did Mum go to the pictures with Mrs. P. after all?*

Dan: *Ay, she's missed it all.*

Chris: *(Pause) I—I'm still a bit dazed by the whole thing, Dad.*

Dan: *Ay.*

Chris: *Oh, why did it have to be Midnight that went back in? If Grace hadn't gone back after her—*

Dan: *Probably slipped her collar after they tied her up. She hadn't got it on when your Uncle Tom found her.*

Chris: *P'rhaps.*

Dan: *Don't suppose they had much time to tie 'em all up properly when they fetched 'em out, Chris. They had to work pretty fast, y'know.*

Chris: *Yes I'll never play badminton again. What a fool I was to go out.—*

Dan: *Oh, don't be daft love. Nobody knew the place was going to catch fire, now did they?*

Chris: *I just don't understand how it happened. The loft went up first you say?*

Dan: *Ay, so I believe . . . I heard one of the firemen saying something about a bonfire somewhere near—*

Chris: *A bonfire!*

Dan: *Ay, Reggie's chaps were sweeping up the leaves all yesterday. A bit of wind got up. I'm not saying that's how it happened, but if this wind had taken a spark upinto the hayloft . . .*

Chris: *Yes . . . it could quite easily happen.*

Dan: *Yes, easily done.*

(Door opens and closes in background)

Chris: *That somebody just come in? Not him surely. Too early for her to be back.*

Dan: *Might be your Uncle Tom or Phil p'raps -*

(Inner door opens)

Chris: *It's Phil.*

(Slow footsteps approach)

Dan: Didn't expect you back quite so soon. Chris and I were.. .. (Sudden realization)

Phil . . . Phil lad . . . What's gone wrong.

Phil: (Dazed, helpless, unable to believe it himself) She's dead. In my arms . . . on the way to the hospital . . .

The message of "Grace" is subliminal. Nowhere is it specifically said that leaves should not be burned in the vicinity of hay or buildings or that water needs to be available to fight fires and feed animals. Yet these messages probably reached an "Archer" audience of farmers in a very real and lasting way. Other agricultural information "bits" from the early "Archers" were more explicit. In some of the early episodes, "Archers" characters would actually read "Ag Ministry" bulletins on certain subjects. In one episode, a farmer reminded his neighbor not to forget to submit his form by the date required. The two approaches cohabited, side by side, without the BBC really taking a strong position in favor of one or the other. Episodes on the economics of pig farming were strung out over more than a year as one of the Archer characters sought to make his fortune to be able to "marry-up" and feel worthy in his own eyes of his bride's family. "Archer" listeners tuned in avidly and not only for the economics of pig farming.

There are probably almost as many ways to transmit radio messages as there are radio stations and programs. Would a more explicit or expostulatory program reach farmers more effectively? Would it reach as large an audience as a more dramatic or subliminal message? Will other targeted populations: youth, urban, the aged, etc., react similarly to rural listeners? Answers to these questions will vary by culture and epoch and be resolved by producers and listeners. One thing is sure, however, and that is that someone who has not heard the "news" cannot react or adapt to it.

Though the "Archers" lost its teaching vocation as its principal goal in 1972, in favor of entertainment, it continues to focus on rural life and retains an agricultural advisor. Topical issues of agriculture continue to be accurately discussed. In a throwback to the earlier days, Tony Archer was tried and found not guilty of destroying experimental GMO crops. An actual case, concerning destruction of genetic crops by Lord Peter Melchett, head of Greenpeace UK, came before an English magistrate recently. The judge had to admonish the jury not to compare the case to that of Tony Archer. The *London Times* reporting on the Lord's acquittal stated that "Tony Archer" had been through this before. Lord Melchett's defense, fear of imminent harm to property from the crops, mimicked the defense used by the fictional "Archers" in another merger of English reality and Archer fiction reminiscent of "Grace." Competition from TV has diminished "The Archers" reach but the program still commands an audience of over 5 million listeners weekly.

Notes

1. This early "Archers" episode was written by Geoffrey Webb and Edwin J. Mason for the BBC. Use of the script comes to us courtesy of the BBC and the authors' estate.

4
Tanzania's Fireside Chat
—The Story of Radio's Role in Nation Building—

In Washington D.C. there is a bronze monument to the power of radio. The monument consists of a woman knitting while her husband stands behind his chair. Both are intently listening to the radio sitting on the modest table placed between them. The Franklin Delano Roosevelt (FDR) monument celebrates one of FDR's most powerful and one of his best remembered contributions to America—his fireside chats. In the depths of the depression with millions of Americans unemployed, the resolute calming voice of a master politician was heard thirty times during his twelve years in office.

On May 26, 1940, Roosevelt delivered his "getting ready for war" fireside chat. 65 million Americans—70% of the total home audience—heard the broadcast. By comparison, the next most popular broadcast, the Louis-Schmeling fight in 1938 had a 57.2% rating. The country's most popular comedy shows, Jack Benny, Bob Hope, etc., were getting fabulous ratings of 30-35%.[1]

The 1930's and 40's were the glory days of radio with commensurate social impact around the world. While FDR was calming America, Joseph Goebbels was exciting the German people on the wonders of the Third Reich. Radio carried both the first breath and the last-gasp of Nazis vitriol into the homes of millions of Germans. At the same time, Winston Churchill was using radio to sustain the British people through the darkest hours of World War II. What better examples do we have of how the same technology can be used for both good and consummate evil?

The story of Rwanda's hate radio is also well known. It shows that malevolent uses of the media are still alive. Some bad ideas never die. On the other hand, there is Tanzania's fireside chat; mobilizing tens of thousands of people in villages all across one of Africa's poorest countries—not for ill, but to listen, to discuss, to decide, and to build.

The story of "Mtu Ni Afya" (Man is Health) is one of great forgotten successes of development radio. It is a story more relevant today than ever. It is the story of 2 million villagers who constructed, in one-year, 750,000 pit latrines. Latrines built not by forced labor but as the result of new knowledge, community debate, and volunteer action. As you read about Tanzania's great experiments of the 1970's ask yourself, don't we need a "Mtu Ni Afya" against AIDS in Africa today?

It is May 1973 and we are in an isolated village in rural Tanzania. There is no electricity, no running water, no sewage system, no latrine, no post office. For the past half hour, villagers have been gathering outside the home of a young local leader. They talk about what everyone talks about—the day's work, whether it will rain tomorrow, and the price of grain. Suddenly, there is familiar music from the radio—a single battery powered radio for all 85 villagers. The music is a cue to get organized, to sit down, and to begin listening. There was a booklet for everyone and a radio trainer's guide for the group leader. The printed materials didn't always make it to the villages on time, but the group settles in to listen to the program anyway.

Each radio program lasted 20 minutes. It covered a specific health problem—diarrhea, tuberculosis, malaria, etc. The programs themselves are not what we would call exciting today—really just straightforward stuff. It was information about disease.

"Mtu Ni Afya" was the voice of a trusted and admired government. It was supported by the national political party TANU that had only recently assumed power after years of British colonial rule. TANU was not hated and feared. TANU was the father of the country and it was led by one of Africa's most beloved and charismatic leaders, Julius Nyerere. This fact will turn out to be more important than anyone anticipated.

"Mtu Ni Afya" (Man is Health) tells villagers about the most common, basic diseases that kill, cripple, and disable tens of thousands of Tanzanians every year. It talks about clean water and latrines. It teaches thousands of Tanzanians for the first time that mosquito bites pass on malaria. Villagers learn that mosquitoes like to breed in standing water—in the tiny puddles of water collected in broken pottery or festering in old barrels. It talks about the dangers of sharing cigarettes. It is not because tobacco is thought to cause cancer—but because tuberculosis can be spread by sharing spittle on cigarette butts.

For twelve weeks, groups of villagers, ranging in size from 12 to 100, met in the evening around the radio to hear new information and to discuss what to do about it. Group composition included both men and women, young and old. Participation was voluntary—whoever came was welcome.

A "trained" leader guided the discussion. Training was given to 75,000 teachers, co-op leaders, and adult education volunteers—an amazing accomplishment by itself. The training focused on techniques for participation and on actions that communities could take in response to specific programs.

One million booklets were printed, most of them distributed and used as discussion guides after the radio programs were broadcast. They were read aloud by literate members of the community in order to reach those less able to read. After a group of 30-100 individuals listened to the broadcast, the larger group was broken into smaller subgroups. The formal model was:

➢ Radio gives information.
➢ Printed guides give discussion questions and suggested actions.
➢ Trained leaders ensure participation by everyone.

In one group, the subject of tuberculosis was the week's topic. The symptoms of tuberculosis were presented—persistent cough, phlegm, headaches, etc. As they discussed TB, it became clear that one member of their group had all the symptoms of TB. TB is scary. It was already well-known to be highly contagious. The natural reaction would be to ostracize the fellow. However, the group reflected on the new facts they had learned, that TB can be controlled and that to isolate someone would be to keep the disease in the village. Then, they decided to take up a collection and send him for treatment.[2]

Every program ended with an exhortation to talk and to act. This, it turns out, was the real genius behind the success of this startlingly simple but powerful radio program. Talk, think, decide, but then act. "Mtu Ni Afya" did not emerge full-blown from the head of some foreign advisor or local radio star. It was the result of two years of hard work, experimentation, and nation building.

Radio was first used in nation building in Tanzania as the best means to reach election officials in Tanzania's successful election experiment "Uchaguzi Ni Wako" in 1970. It taught citizens what an election was, where to vote, what a political party was, and how local councils governed. All this may sound suspicious to us in 2003—elections run by a national government with instructions given out by radio? However, in 1973, with Tanzania under the leadership of a man as distinguished as Julius Nyerere, it was African democracy at work.

In 1970 President Nyerere declared a national literacy year. Not a bad idea when you consider that 90% of Tanzanian adults were functionally illiterate. The Ministry of Education was then charged with educating millions of adults and children. Pilot campaigns were planned in six villages to eliminate illiteracy by 1971.

"Uchaguzi Ni Wako" (The Choice Is Yours) was the first major stepping-stone towards "Mtu Ni Afya". Many lessons were learned from it and from the literacy campaign of 1971. Both of the early campaigns combined radio, study guides, and group leaders. However, the early study guides were too complicated and didactic. There were no exhortations to action on the radio. And finally, both the political and the literacy campaigns had been pulled together too quickly. There was no local buy-in from key officials and community leaders.

By 1973, "Mtu Ni Afya" was able to correct these mistakes. Organizers placed emphasis on the "curriculum" and the "trainers." Radio was still considered an important call to community. Many were still critical of the dearth of materials reaching villages and of the sometimes excessively large number of villagers who thronged to the radio listening groups. This popularity endangered the goal of one trainer to thirty villagers.

Today, we can look back and see the real genius of the program was not testing or student-teacher ratios. It was not the entertainment quality of the radio program, the curriculum of the printed guides, or even the charisma of group leaders. It was the power of one simple idea—don't just tell people things, ask them to do something about it. Every program and every group was to include a discussion of what individuals and communities could do to improve the health conditions of their village. Evaluators of the program reported the results in terms of the most common activities and the percentage of groups in the test sample of 2,131 groups as follows:

TABLE 4.1: "Mtu Ni Afya" CAMPAIGN RESULTS

Removing close vegetation around each house	28%
Digging, repairing or rebuilding latrines	20%
Destroying containers of stagnant water	19%

Boiling and/or filtering water	12%
Cleaning areas around water sources	11%
Draining pools and ponds	5%
Using malaria tablets and/or insecticides	5%
Digging rubbish pits	4%
Digging wells	3%
Building racks for cooking utensils	3%
Avoiding sharing cigarettes and drinking containers	3%
Putting bedding in the sun	2 %
Covering food	1%
Collecting construction materials	1%

Twenty-eight percent, 28%, that's a success? Yes, because it was 28% of thousands of groups of listeners. This is the power of radio to reach and affect what in Tanzania amounted to millions. We are talking about mass media and mass action. Two million Tanzanians took part in "Mtu Ni Afya,"—twice the number anticipated. Under the program, 750,000 latrines were repaired or newly built. A latrine takes about 50 man-hours to build. Fifty times 750,000 equals 37.5 million man-hours of donated volunteer labor. The Ministry of Labor in Tanzania set one shilling as the standard hourly wage—that is 37.5 million shillings of free labor from a campaign that cost only 1.5 million shillings.

The most expensive part of the campaign was printing the brochures and many of these never arrived or arrived too late. In an earlier campaign, the printing cost of posters alone had accounted for almost 40% of the total costs. Radio was the cheapest, the most listened to and the most powerful single channel of communication.

In the past thirty years, we have seen enormous progress in making radio more fun, more entertaining, and more available. This book documents a few of the hundreds of radio experiments that have fostered human development around the world. But, the lesson of Tanzania's "Mtu Ni Afya" program is still lost to many of radio's new advocates.

Radio can *act* people into change more easily than it can *teach* people into change. Unfortunately, too much of our basic program model remains the same whether it be entertainment or news. We identify some important information, for example, use a condom. We make it fun, dramatic, even compelling. We broadcast it to millions and watch as this new knowledge changes their lives. Yet, most information does not change our lives. Most information—in a crowded marketplace of cluttered, confusing and contradictory ideas—organizes itself in a way to meet the preconceptions of what we already believed to be true. "Use a condom?" one might ask. "I don't have AIDS!" is a frequent reply. Yes, information is useful. Information can prod us to think in an informed way about our problems; it can tell us about new disease and new products. We remember many radio programs. We report they "affected" us. However, what do most people do about them?

Radio often asks us to do nothing, or asks for so little that it is not truly motivating.

"AIDS kills!" a program tells us.

This is a common health message and perhaps one of Africa's most important. Hearing that AIDS kills, what is the listener supposed to do? Worry? Don't they already have enough to worry about?

"AIDS is transmitted by sexual contact."

Some of the listeners may know this critical fact. Perhaps they thought mosquitoes carried AIDS. Now that they know this, what should they do? Have less sex? Perhaps.

"Condoms protect against AIDS. Use a condom."

People should use condoms. After hearing this message repeated thousands of times, more Africans are using condoms today than ever before. This is a call to action, but are enough people using condoms to stop the epidemic? Obviously not. If calls to action are what are needed, why isn't this one resulting in as much action as the one resulting in construction, of 750,000 latrines after only one year, in 1973 Tanzania?

One answer is that "Mtu Ni Afya" was not *just* a call to action; it was a call to *group* action. It was a call to action *delivered in a group.* It was a call to action *to think together, talk together, and decide together*; not just to obey some alien radio voice and then act individually. It was also a call to action by a *respected voice in national life, TANU and its leader, Julius Nyerere.*

"Mtu Ni Afya" was a *supersized* fireside chat compressed into a campaign that lasted 12 weeks and not twelve years. It was a fireside chat in times of trouble, from a beloved leader (TANU) coupled with a call to think and act together. That is the great lesson that has been lost from this magnificent early African effort at social change. Radio can change the world if the voice is trusted, if the people are asked to think as a community, and if they are told to act and solve a problem, not just be "aware" of the problem.

Notes

1. Doris Kearns Goodwin, *No Ordinary Time* (New York: Simon & Schuster, 1994), 240.
2. Budd L. Hall and C. Zikambona, *Mtu Ni Afya: An Evaluation* (Dar es Salaam, Tanzania: Institute of Adult Education Studies, No. 12, 1974).

5
AMA MAS
–Breast-fed by Radio–

joyful music . . .

Woman: Your son is a boy now Doña Chela, he is very good looking!
Chela: Aiiiii, it's that I have always breast-fed him.
Woman: Breast-fed?!
*Chela: Yes, because maternal milk has always the best elements I could
    ever give my kids.*
Woman: And why is it the best milk?
*Chela: For various reasons, because it is more nutritive, because the kids
    do not get sick that easily. it helps them grow up healthier and
    stronger. . . All my kids love me.*
Woman: Of course Doña Chela, if you are a breast feeder!
Chela: Yes, yes . . .
*Very Serious Speaker with strong voice: We work towards a healthy com
    munity, Ministry of Public Health . . .*

In the 1980s, Honduras was a rapidly urbanizing country. As thousands poured into the cities, they left behind long-held traditional practices
to adopt "modern" ones. Breast-feeding was one of the first causalities of
modernization. Breast-feeding is critical in developing countries because it
is the child's best protection against infant diarrhea, one of the primary
causes of infant death. In countries where water is contaminated and re-
frigeration is largely unavailable, food and water are deadly. However, as
mothers turned to an urban life suddenly "breast was no longer best."

Urban women were often heard to say: "breast-feeding is for unedu-
cated women," . . . "any way I don't have enough milk," . . . or "breast-
feeding makes my breasts sag, I want to be attractive for my husband."

Formula feeding had been promoted by formula companies in hospitals and after only a few years, formula was considered the "modern" way to feed a child.

Thousands of women needed to get the facts and to believe them. Spot announcements about breast-feeding would not be enough. There were thousands of women abandoning breast-feeding and there was no money for mass training, even if you could get women to leave the home or the workplace for training. The solution was radio—it had to be *radio training* in the home and on-the-job.

AMA MAS was an on-air full-scale breast-feeding course. Mothers had to sign up at their local health centers, which were widely available in the urban areas of Honduras. To participate, they had to listen to nine 20-minute radio programs, obtain a simple brochure then follow along and pass a test. After completion, they would then receive a certification as an AMA MAS mother. It sounds complicated. And it was. Women are busy. Where would they find the time to get all this done? The programs were 20 minutes long at scheduled times, not short spot announcements. Women had to get the pamphlet, follow it, and take a test.

The motivation turned out to be the desire of these upwardly mobile women for education. Many of them had only lived in an urban setting for a few years and had little or no schooling, but had a strong desire to be educated. The symbol of education was a graduation certificate. Many women were willing to do it all, if they could get a certificate of graduation. Indeed, 85% of the women who signed up for the course completed the test and got a certificate. This is an unprecedented response until you realize how much these women desired an education.

They were hungry for education, but they did not want a college degree in nutrition. They needed simple clear instructions on how to breast-feed properly. How could they ensure an adequate milk supply and how could they learn why breast-feeding is so much better than bottle? The nine courses were organized around nine simple but little known facts about breast-feeding:

• The more the baby sucks the breast, the more breast-milk "comes down".
• Start giving the baby soft food (not bottle milk) after the fourth month.
• As soon as the baby is born, the faster he/she sucks the breast, the faster the breast-milk will come down.

- If the baby empties both breasts in each breast-feeding session, there will be more milk available for the next session.
- Hunger is the best breast-feeding schedule for the baby. Breastfeed him on demand.
- The Mom that breast-feeds the child in a hurry, or under pressure, will leave him hungry.
- Babies behave like grownups; some times they are hungry and breast-feed a lot, sometimes they are not, and breast-feed little.
- A breast-feeding woman should drink more than 6 glasses of liquid a day (milk, fresh fruit juices, soups etc.)
- The breast-feeding woman needs to eat for two. The radio programs were constructed to follow the pamphlet. The radio characters posed the questions in the pamphlets, and then helped listeners answer the questions properly reinforcing learning through conversation.

Some of these guidelines have changed since the 1980's. We know now, for example, that children should breast-feed exclusively for the first six months. But the core knowledge was right on target.

The AMA-MAS booklet was another key to the education process. Radio plus print have big payoffs when actually teaching skills. Mothers who were going to change such a critical behavior needed to see, as well as hear, the message. Remember, this was in an environment where the trend was dramatically towards formula and against breast-feeding.

In fact, the course was on-line training, just the first dramatic phase in a decade long campaign to make breast-feeding the standard of care for newborns in Honduras. The women it reached hung their certificates on the wall. They practiced breast-feeding and were successful. They became advocates for a return to the old ways. And they opened the way for dozens of other campaigns to be successful.

Ecuador—1987

Five years after the Honduras experience, radio was once again confronted with a mass education problem. This time it was not a single, simple behavior like breast-feeding. Radio needed to create a core of intelligent, trained advocates for three complicated child health behaviors. And, it had to do this job with a speed and scale that had never been done before.

As in Honduras, the targets were literate women. They were easier to reach, easier to motivate, and were more able to help, lead and promote change in their communities. However, this time the motivation had to be more than simply a desire for education and a certificate. The design was as follows:

> ➤ Use health centers to identify female community leaders
> ➤ Target women who were literate and had children less than 5 years old and
> ➤ Target women who volunteered.

The targets were 7,000 women spread throughout the country. They would receive a brochure, modeled after the one in Honduras. However, because the content of this program was so much more complicated than breast-feeding, they would also meet weekly with local health staff to actually practice the tough skills of managing child health.

The content of the radio program combined entertainment with education. The typical program began with a short musical introduction to give mothers time to get to their radios. This was followed, not by a radio "lecture," but by a radio soap opera that depicted characters who became well known all over Ecuador. *Don Sebastian* was an elder carpenter and worked in the church. He acted as the community's memory, while *Miguel,* a fictitious health worker, and *Rosita,* the radio drama's rural mother, asked questions and learned from each other. *El Motas* was the strangest character—a cotton-headed figure who was the "Sancho Panza" of the drama; making jokes, keeping the program lively, and often asking the "dumb" questions that no one else would ask.

In Ecuador, every woman who finished the radio course and every health staff member who assisted with the radio course would be eligible for a lottery prize. The prize for mothers was a year's scholarship for their child to cover all their school expenses. The winning health workers received a grant to continue their health training. Both prizes were highly valued.

Eighty percent of the mothers who signed up graduated from the course—36 radio programs, 20 minutes each, plus weekly meetings with health workers over the seven week duration of the course. Graduation became a village event, with the whole community running out to congratulate their neighbors and see them receive their certificate and their lottery entry card.

Actually the card itself was kind of sexy. It was designed to simulate credit cards, which at that time only rich people could afford. The bright yellow plastic card was printed with the program logo and a lottery number. The graduates name was written on each card during the graduation ceremony.

The first set of programs was so successful that a second set had to be created. Ninety radio stations across the country were involved in programming and the number of women who participated far exceeded the goal of 7,000. These programs became a part of a large national mobilization against infant mortality. Radio training targeted the creation of local leaders on a mass scale and on a tight time frame. No other medium could reach and affect so many rural leaders in such a short time.

This chapter illustrated two ways radio can "train" community leaders on a large scale and in a short time frame. In these examples, radio reached community leaders in the home and on the job. Radio overcame strongly held beliefs that led to high infant mortality and costly medical care. These two stories demonstrate clearly that radio can be a powerful "on-air" trainer—teaching life-saving health content and creating a cadre of well-informed and experienced advocates for change. Both stories are the result of government investment in radio programming through USAID during the 1980s. They were conducted by teams of local Ministry of Health staff in Honduras and Ecuador, along with local radio professionals in both countries and with the technical support from the Academy for Educational Development. The two stories are told together, because they illustrate how one program built on the other to address ever more complex mass training needs.

Radio, as this book shows in one example after another, is not just news and music. In Honduras and Ecuador, it was the teacher in an adult education course that reached tens of thousands of women, motivated them to join in, taught them complex skills and saved millions of children from disease.

6
The VOA
—VOICE OF AMERICA—

Between the U.S. Capitol and the "Air and Space Museum" of the Smithsonian Institute in downtown Washington D.C., lie about four city blocks. This mall is open, tended grass with wide, hard-sanded pedestrian walkways, which gradually give way to a hilly rise before the nation's capitol. Here the lush green grass of the Capitol lawn, interspersed with massive selections of magnolia, elms, southern oaks and poplars, thrives in the rich soil of what was once the swampy flood plain of the Potomac.

Just off to the South, lying between the mall and the Potomac River, hidden from sight only by the constant distraction of the beauty of the mall and the vista of the Nation's Capitol is a large vintage building.[1] The 1938 built Cohen building, originally home to the Social Security and Railroad Retirement Administration, mixes semi-art deco elements with Egyptian motifs and the federal area's ubiquitous stone columns. Its façade is attractive, if unremarkable, for this city furnished with costly federal edifices. Remarkable, however, to the errant eye that may wander there, are the massive three story satellite dishes on the roof of the building.

The building now houses the Voice of America (VOA) and the Department of Health and Human Services (HHS). The satellite dishes, however, have little to do with Health and Human Services, at least as far as the Agency is concerned. They are literally the "Voice of America." Like a large set of the nation's vocal chords, they broadcast 22 hours a day, via satellite to receivers around the world, as they have done since the Agency's inception in 1941.[2] Perhaps they are more startling in their conquest of "air and space" than anything in the nearby museum, including the space shuttle and equipment from the first walk on the moon. These satellite dishes and the associated infrastructure around the world, literally cover the planet with "the Voice of America's" world news and public events broadcasting.

It is somewhat remarkable, as well, that an agency with only 1,000 employees, less than the number of building security guards in several Federal agencies, succeeds in programming daily, virtually around the clock, in 53 languages with an estimated 94 million weekly listeners. Together with grantee broadcasters Radio Free Europe, Radio Free Asia, Radio Sawa, World Television and Radio and TV Marti the budget for the Voice of America and affiliated broadcasters under the Broadcasting Board of Governors is $265 million annually.[3]

Congress, after the tragic events of 9/11, augmented broadcasting funds significantly, turning the Voice of America Arabic Service into a full time radio network, Radio Sawa, to reach the populations of the Middle East.[4] Congress fully understood the importance of reaching potentially hostile masses of the world with information about America, our values, interests and vision for the world. The recent discussion about Radio Freedom's Persian language broadcasts and their resonance with Iranian dissidents illustrates this vividly.[5]

In 1996, Voice of America saw an opportunity to expand its traditional news and public interest broadcasting into areas affecting more directly the lives of their listeners and in ways that might provide them with information and solutions to problems they faced. Beginning with the World Health Organization's vaccination campaign to eradicate polio and more recently extending to HIV-AIDS and other health issues, the Voice of America undertook to use limited amounts of its funding to broadcast a sustained information campaign with listener feedback in these areas.

This was not the first venture of Voice of America beyond the "news" broadcast to a more informational and listener oriented programming. Shows on the use of appropriate technology in conjunction with the Volunteers in International Technology Application (VITA) as well as call in and write in shows on listener health problems had been done in the past. However, the 1996 initiatives represented a concerted effort to add programming dealing with the problems and concerns of the common man rather than that addressed to an elite news-consuming public. Most VOA listeners are currently found in developing countries. There, the "common man" is poor, earning less than two dollars a day, illiterate and hungry for information on the outside world, especially as it relates to him, not to mention hungry for food and a better livelihood. Many of the grantee broadcasters under the Board of Governors have expressed interest in adding informational development broadcasting to their programming, but lack the funding.

Radio Sawa

Indicative of the radio's power when all else fails, within a few short weeks of the events of 9/11, Congress was talking about putting-up additional VOA transmitters throughout the Middle East. This would be done to reach an audience of the Arab masses with public interest broadcasting about America, telling people who we are and what we represent. The gap of cultures and lack of knowledge of each other was causing misunderstanding and resentment. What better way to bridge that gap, than the radio?

One of the initial and most creative efforts to expand VOA's audience reach was "Radio Sawa," a 24/7 broadcast effort, with better transmission, enhanced program values and more audience targeting than traditional VOA broadcasting. Enhancing the transmission possibilities to include FM, AM, digital satellite and Internet alongside the VOA shortwave staple certainly gave Sawa a leg up. But Sawa's real innovation came from the experience of American popular broadcasting. Audience surveys and targeting market segments were to be important techniques for Sawa to connect to a wide and reliable listenership. Sawa did just that. Trying to reach the burgeoning Middle Eastern youth segment of the population—fully 60% percent of the population of the Middle East, an estimated 300 million, is under 30 years of age—Sawa hit on a "fast-paced" formula of American pop music, Arab music and short public interest spots and news. With FM bands in seven Middle Eastern countries and broadcasting via AM, shortwave satellite and Internet radio channels to the region as a whole, Sawa quickly found a broad and responsive listenership. With 86% of respondents having listened to Radio Sawa FM Amman, Jordan within the week of a survey taken there, Sawa had the highest listenership of any FM station in Jordan's capital, fully 26% higher than radio FM Amman, and 66% higher than the BBC.

In addition to Jordan, there are Sawa broadcasts on the FM band to Kuwait City, Kuwait, Abu Dhabi and Dubai in the United Arab Emirates, as well as AM broadcasts out of Kuwait covering Iraq and Rhodes. Plans exist to increase this coverage using transmitters in Cyprus to Egypt, Lebanon and Syria. Via satellite and digital transmission dishes, listeners in Saudi Arabia and other areas can hear Sawa. Broadcasts are done in six Arab dialects, especially tailored for different markets and cultural environments.

Surveys put total Sawa listenership in the several millions. While surveys are still anecdotal in some markets, like Iraq where access is difficult, Sawa is said to be the most popular radio channel there![6] In Iran, the Sawa sound alike, Radio Farda, which only recently began operations, though not able to broadcast on AM or FM bands but via a more limited Internet connection, registered 460,000 hits per day, 52,000 pager per view daily and 280 e-mails a day, 20 an hour, on its Internet radio feed.

Sawa's fast paced format does not include development magazines, but it does do short public interest spots on HIV-AIDS, drunk driving, female societal issues ("Women Make Good Bosses?" is one such program) and other often provocative topics for a Muslim Arab audience on "Sawa Chat". Many of these spots are interactive and include audience feedback or questions. After all Sawa's motto is "You listen to us, we listen to you!" Sawa would like to do more. It is doing all this for several tens of millions of dollars compared to a total VOA budget of less than $140 million, less than the cost of a jet fighter. What is missing? The Broadcast Board of Governors, responsible for Sawa and all USG broadcasting, inaugurated a TV programming schedule the Mid-East Television network in 2003. More money for radio journalists, programming and transmission would allow Sawa along with the TV broadcasters, to expand its Radio journalism. Instead, with the war for hearts and minds barely engaged, Sawa's funding is going down.

International Broadcast Services

In the sphere of informational and developmental broadcasting, BBC services have always done a considerably greater amount of programming than the VOA and related U.S. broadcasters. The BBC World Service listening audience is estimated at 150 million worldwide. In agriculture, health, small business, education and many of the domains discussed in previous chapters, the BBC has done excellent work over many years. Unfortunately, the collapse of development funding in the 1990's and the competition faced by radio and public service generally have also affected the BBC which has cut back dramatically on its overseas programming. France Inter, to the French speaking world, and Deutsche Welle, in German and English, continue an active international broadcast program. Chinese radio, a newcomer, has an increasingly active international broadcast outreach throughout the Asian region.

Non-Governmental Organizations (NGO's)

Contributions from other organizations have also assisted local broadcasters to fill their program day with useful content in addition to the all-present music and "talk" broadcasts. Panos is a development funded private voluntary organization (PVO) which does remarkably good work and is discussed in a subsequent chapter. Population Communication International (PCI) along with the much larger Academy for Educational Development (AED) have participated in the emergence of development communication. They continue to be two of the principal practitioners preparing developmental programming, the former specializing in population, family planning and health issues. Both are covered in chapters focused on their programs.

A large Newton, Massachusetts based NGO, the Educational Development Center (EDC), focusing largely on education in the United States, also provides distance learning programming internationally notably, distance learning, in Zambia, Tanzania and Ethiopia, as well as its nascent work in China, part of the on-going liberalization there. EDC was one of the early pioneers of distance learning in Latin America. The Developing Countries Farm Radio Network (DCFN), a small Canadian PVO, provides open source radio scripts over the Internet for developing country farmers. The University of Florida's specialists in tropical agriculture prepare the scripts. Although the Farm Radio Network's government funding has declined with the overall reduction in development funds in Canada and more generally among the G-8, the PVO draws on a rich tradition of Canadian rural farm broadcasting which it attempts to keep alive for developing country farmers.

U.S. Agency for International Development (USAID)

USAID has provided a small amount of funding for some excellent pilot programming in distance learning for adult and primary education as well as agriculture and health. This has taken place largely in Latin America, but health programming has been on a more worldwide basis. Unfortunately, as we point out in other chapters, there has been little follow-up to the pilot media programs and there has been an absence of focus on media in most of USAID programming. With little media work done in democracy and conflict or transition, USAID's focus is largely on trying to build local media through support for journalist training and to a lesser extent on infrastructure rather than on programming. USAID would maintain that the difficult undertaking of building an independent local media is undoubtedly important. However, even if these efforts were to succeed, which they often do not, the stations would still need quality programs that they can ill afford.

Other National and International Donors

    National donors such as the British, the Dutch, the French and the Canadians have all shown a greater relative interest in media than has been the case in the U.S. The British through their Department for International Development (DFID) have given particular support to Panos as have the Dutch. The French underwrite the World Association of Community Radio Broadcasters (AMARC) and the Canadians have had long experience in rural radio and support the Farm Radio Network.

    Among the International Organizations, UNICEF has been a pioneer in using WorldSpace Satellite Radio[7] in Sudan where its civil war makes traditional development type activities even more onerous than is ordinarily the case. Sudan is one of many countries especially apt for radio services. UNESCO has supported the development of community radio infrastructure and in the more distant past was a major promoter of mass-media campaigns on health, agriculture and in primary and adult education. The World Bank has, unfortunately, been largely absent from the use of communications technology to reach masses of the poor with perhaps several minor exceptions.

    While it might seem to many readers that the above activities argue that donors are not oblivious to the media, this would largely be a misimpression. Many of the activities, especially those in distance learning and agriculture are old, dating back to the 1970s and 1980s. With the exception of the health sector where communications is understood to be an important part of every activity extending health treatment or information to a population, communication and communication experts are not a part of the mainstream for most development activities.

    In agriculture, there is great, unexplained resistance to any communication oriented activity that is not a person-to-person model or based on the Internet. Small business services have generally not used mass communications to facilitate their reach. Our primary, secondary and adult education efforts no longer use these very successful media and mass communication tools. Conflict resolution and democracy efforts are largely not media focused. Those that are generally invest largely in building local media at the expense of programming that might have a more immediate impact. This lack of focus on media based solutions must further be understood in an increasingly media-centric world where globalization and fashions learned on CNN or SKY are reaching into every corner of the world. In the revolution that is our times, the donors remain wedded to the past to the detriment of their only real clients, the poor of the world.

VOA "Hausa" Programming in Nigeria.
    In this morass of indifference and lost opportunity, some heroic efforts of VOA programmers to reach the poor with useful development information stand out. In a Nigeria torn by civil strife between Muslim and Christian communities, VOA programming about the World Health Organization (WHO) polio eradication campaign ran headlong into community and religious prejudices that were opposed to modern day science and the world wide campaign to eradicate polio. The following excerpts from VOA broadcasts in Nigeria and some community reactions illustrate the powerful possibilities of media to initiate community discussion and awareness and begin a process of change.
    When WHO sponsored vaccinators began to first reach rural areas in the Muslim north, one of the initial reactions was that this was another attempt by Westerners to impose their values on Muslims. Indeed, in a context where the divorced and promiscuous West is preaching the superiority of its family values and treatment of women, this might not have appeared too far-fetched to the average Muslim listener. Yet children were still dying of polio in Nigeria, a disease practically eliminated in the rest of the world. VOA broadcasts tried to address some of the lack of information and move the debate from the realm of suspicion to that of information. A VOA broadcast from November heard in Nigeria follows:

November 9, 2002
Rosanne Skirble

This week's radio script of Our World:

MD: TK 1: "OUR WORLD" THEME, in full for:06, then under . . .

HOST: Welcome to Our World on VOA . . .

Kick-off ceremony for National Immunization Days, Rogo, Nigeria
MD: TK1: Theme up full briefly, then under, hold throughout . . .

HOST: I'm Rosanne Skirble sitting in for Rob Sivak. Today—the global campaign to rid the world of polio, a crippling, highly infectious and some-

times deadly virus that strikes young children. We travel to Nigeria in West Africa, where polio remains endemic, and join National Immunization Days, a nation-wide effort to vaccinate every Nigerian child against polio. We follow a surveillance team, talk with polio survivors and explore the possibilities of a polio-free world.

CUT 1: DR. A. AWOSIKA "I see a sense of mission. I see a sense of calling. I see a responsibility to the people, and all this inculcated in service. It has brought people to feel that (they) can do something for other people."

HOST: The global campaign to eradicate polio—the largest public health initiative in history—today on "Our World."

CUT 2: AMBIENT CROWD SFX IN ROGO, ESTABLISH BRIEFLY AND HOLD UNDER HOST:

HOST: Polio Eradication in Nigeria starts here, at a ceremony in a large, dusty lot at the Community Islamic Center in Rogo, Nigeria. Banners and posters announce the latest campaign. Men in long-flowing white robes and women in bold African prints take their seats under the shade of circus tents. Islamic religious leaders from nearby villages are here with government officials, health workers, international aid advisors and dozens of women with babies in their laps.

CUT 3: SFX OF MUSIC

HOST: They have come to Rogo—a small community of mostly Muslim residents in Northern Nigeria—to celebrate the kick-off of National Immunization Days, a weeklong campaign that promises to deliver the oral polio vaccine, village-by-village, door-to-door, to the more than 40 million Nigerian children under the age of five. There are speeches and songs. A roving group of musicians carrying instruments made from dried gourds, chants an important message: "Please madam, immunize your children, because if you don't, you have cheated them, and you have cheated yourself."

MUSIC UP BRIEFLY AND FADE UNDER HOST

HOST: Polio is a highly infectious viral disease that invades the nervous system and can cause paralysis, even death. It commonly attacks young children and is spread by food or water contaminated with feces. An epidemic of polio caused panic in industrialized nations in the 1940s and 1950s. Fifty-eight thousand cases of poliomyelitis were reported in the United States alone in 1952. Polio is not curable, but it is preventable with vaccines. And new vaccines—finally brought into wide use by the mid-1950s—are credited with halting the epidemic in much of the world. But the disease persisted in many developing countries, which during the 1980s accounted for 95 percent of the polio cases worldwide.

Stephen Cochi is director of the Global Immunization Division of the U.S. Centers for Disease Control and Prevention in Atlanta. He says that on average in a susceptible population, one in 200 polio-infected children develops an irreversible paralysis. The others become carriers of the virus and are contagious for about two weeks.

Cut 4: STEPHEN COCHI "But it spreads silently and that makes it difficult to stop the spread of the virus, because it is already widespread in a community when you first get this signal of paralyzed children manifesting the fact that they have the virus."

HOST: That is why one case is considered an epidemic. Mr. Cochi adds that without a human host, polio cannot survive—a major reason that effective immunization has sped the eradication effort.

CUT 5: STEPHEN COCHI "The polio virus is, as we say, on the ropes. It is making its last stand in the world. Before the vaccine era, polio had conquered the world. Polio existed everywhere in the world. We've come a long way in a very short time since then."

HOST: The global initiative to eradicate polio began in 1988. The United Nation's World Health Organization, UNICEF, Rotary Club International and the Centers for Disease Control and Prevention in Atlanta spearheaded the campaign.

The assault on polio has yielded results. The number of cases has fallen 99.8 percent since 1988 from 350,000 to 480 in 2001. But the wild polio virus remains endemic in ten countries. The largest reservoirs of the disease are in India, Pakistan and Nigeria. These nations share conditions that support polio transmission—low rates of immunization, poor sanitation, a dense population and a weak public health network.

Still, experts say global polio eradication is doable. World Health Organization officials expect to reach that goal by 2005.

Nigeria—the focus of our program today—has the largest population in Africa—more than 120 million people. Public sanitation is a serious problem across the country and routine immunization is low. A 2001 UNICEF study says 54 percent of the children between 1 and 2 (years of age) are routinely immunized. That figure drops to 4 percent in the northwest part of the country where polio is most problematic.

Even so, the number of new polio cases in Nigeria between 2000 and 2001 fell from 2000 to 57. What might explain the trend is the National Program on Immunization. In the late 1990s, Dr. A. Awosika was brought into Nigeria's newly elected democratic government to develop the program. She says the administration—then and now—places a high priority on public health services, especially for children.

Dr. A. Awosika, director of Nigeria's National Program on Immunization

CUT 6: DR. A. AWOSIKA "To me, it's a success and an encouraging one. It started from nowhere and with nothing in late 1998. We had no data to work with and now we have a strong database in Nigeria and immunization can build on that. We have brought the child into focus in Nigeria because we have placed so much premium on what it means to give the child its rights."

HOST: Since 1999, the National Program on Immunization in Nigeria has mobilized 200,000 people for National Immunization Days, held two or three times a year for house-to-house campaigns.

The massive exercise includes a strong support staff of international aid workers from dozens of international agencies. But most of the vaccinators, field guides, surveillance officers, team supervisors, trainers and managers are Nigerian. Two-person teams—a vaccinator and a town guide—are assigned to knock on every door in the country.

CUT 7: TRAINER'S VOICE, ESTABLISH BRIEFLY AND UNDER HOST THAT FOLLOWS "I would like to get a volunteer to be a vaccinator, a volunteer to be a local guide, a volunteer to be a father, a volunteer to be a mother, a volunteer to be two or three children.

HOST: Just days prior to the National Immunization Days, training sessions like this one take place in community centers, clinics, hospitals and schools across the country. Housewives, health workers, civil servants and unemployed citizens are hired for the campaign. The women work as vaccinators, the men as local guides. They practice their parts, take tests on polio facts and are coached by the trainer to "leave no child behind."

CUT 8: MRS. SALOME S. TOR "You are not going to have problems. If you explain very well, no one is going to refuse you. Everyone is moving together. Your ward head knows every corner of the village and he is leading to show you the children below five years. Just exercise patience and try to explain and they will accept you. Thank you." (Applause)

HOST: The entire country is mapped—every district, every local government, every ward, every settlement, every house, every footpath, every landmark. AMBIENT SFX OF CAR AND SETTLEMENT

HOST: We turn off the main highway onto a dirt road into Kibiya, a district with dozens of small settlements where goats and sheep roam freely. We stop along a street of crumbling concrete houses and watch as a crowd gathers around a town crier who shouts, "The District Head is calling on members of the community to cooperate on immunization teams who are making house to house visits. This is to immunize children under the age of five against poliomyelitis."

Village scene, Kibiya

CUT 9: TOWN CRIER, ESTABLISH BRIEFLY AND FADE UNDER HOST

HOST: Here in Kibiya, Colonel Anna Odey—a squat and lively 63-year-old retired army nurse and grandmother—is clearly in command of the immunization operation. She imposes stern, but kind, military discipline on her 54 two-person teams. Wearing green aprons—and carrying Styrofoam coolers with vaccines and ice packs over their shoulders—the teams must reach every child in 129 settlements. Having worked on polio campaigns over the last several years, Colonel Odey says what has changed is that the Islamic religious leaders now endorse the initiative. They are father figures, she explains, that men and women in Northern Nigeria look to for spiritual guidance.

Rosanne Skirble with traditional Islamic leader and ward head in Kibiya

CUT 10: ANNA ODEY/SKIRBLE ANNA ODEY: "And we have ward heads and village leaders who uphold the traditional institution and authority.

And, with them backing us, we get the inhabitants to accept this immunization for their wards without problem."

HOST: "This is such a remote area. How do you know that no child has been missed?"

Street scene, Kano

ANNA ODEY: "That is the work of using the villagers themselves, who know the nooks and corners of each settlement and the village and ward heads (who) know all of their inhabitants that even if I should go back to one of them and say, "In a house in this corner or this corner the man refused," without even telling him, (the ward head) might even know the person, and he would call and ask, "why have you rejected (the immunization). That is, if there is a rejection."

HOST: "Do you feel confident that you can wipe polio out of Nigeria?"
ANNA ODEY: "By the grace of God and the tempo we are going, we will wipe polio out of Nigeria."

Cut 11: SFX—BABY CRYING AS CHILD IS IMMUNIZED, SFX OF VOICES: FADE UNDER HOST . . .

Vaccinator marks finger of a child after administering the oral polio vaccine

HOST: On this day, no one refuses the vaccine. Houses are marked with chalk symbols to show where children have been vaccinated or where vaccinators must return.

Workers also check for symptoms of new cases. This is how surveillance teams track the virus. And this is also how Nigeria—after three polio-free years—will eventually be certified by the World Health Organization as polio-free.

Village child immunized against polio

World Health Organization epidemiologist, Ali Takai, is one of two surveillance officers in the northern state of Kano, a high-risk area. Alerted by an observant local informant, he hurries to the countryside to examine a child. Based on what he sees, he will order laboratory tests that either confirm the presence of the wild polio virus, or show a case of acute flac-

cid paralysis, an adverse reaction to the oral polio vaccine. The latter occurs in only one out of every three million doses of the oral vaccine and the condition is not contagious.

Vaccination worker walks to remote settlement

CUT 12: SFX CORNFIELD/GIRL'S CRYING

HOST: A two-hour drive and a walk through a dense field of guinea corn put Dr. Takai at the feet of a tiny little girl. She lives in a small farming hamlet of mud huts nestled in the shade of ancient trees. Dr. Takai gently bends down to examine the naked child who is frightened and crying.

CUT 13: DR. ALI TAKAI/SKIRBLE ALI TAKAI: "The left hand is weak. Likewise, the left leg. The weakness is flaccid, not spastic therefore consistent with an acute flaccid paralysis case. So, this case is based on the clinical presentation of an acute flaccid paralysis, or polio for which we now have to collect the stool sample and send it to the laboratory to see whether we are going to isolate wild polio virus or not."

HOST: How old is this child?

ALI TAKAI: "Two years old."

HOST: "And has she been immunized before?"

ALI TAKAI: "She was immunized twice and only yesterday she had the second dose of O-P-V (oral polio vaccine)."

HOST: Should the stool specimen prove to contain the wild virus, it will be sent to a special polio reference laboratory like the one Olen Kew directs at the Centers for Disease Control and Prevention in the United States. The CDC laboratory in Atlanta genetically sequences the virus and tracks its transmission. Mr. Kew says the information helps answer some important questions about the spread of the disease.

CUT 14: OLEN KEW "Where are the communities sustaining continuous circulation of the wild polio virus? Where should the immunization team put their best efforts? So helping the WHO and immunization teams where you can shut the tap off at the source is a key function of the laboratory network."

HOST: Since the global polio eradication initiative began in 1988, 2 billion children in 94 countries have been vaccinated against the disease. Last year alone, the vaccine reached 575 million children. The World Health Organization puts the price tag for these efforts at three billion dollars through 2005. The money isn't guaranteed. W-H-O is currently trying to bridge a 275-million-dollar-funding gap.

HOST: Support for the polio eradication campaign has come from national governments, international agencies, and other major partners. Rotary International—through its clubs in 163 countries—is the largest private donor, contributing 493 million dollars, with promises to raise another 80 million more by the end of 2003.

The way Ellen Thompson sees it, that's a small price to pay for a polio-free world. Ms. Thompson—crippled by polio at age five—is a leading advocate for the disabled in Nigeria, many of whom are polio victims.

She says people with disabilities face hostility and rejection. Many are unemployed and resort to street begging. Their children, she says, become able-bodied beggars.

CUT 15: ELLEN THOMPSON "And me as a person with disabilities, I interact with them, talk to them, and (work on) how we can get assistance to train these children because they don't know anything. In the morning they take their mom and dad to the street and then back again the next morning."

HOST: Ellen Thompson—who has walked with arm braces her whole life— has a university degree and a good job as a training officer in Abuja, the Nigerian capital. She says disabled people deserve equal rights and equal access and works to make that happen.

Today she visits an open-air repair shop located on the side of a busy highway in Kano, a major city in the northern part of the country.

CUT 16: MIX INTRODUCTIONS WITH STREET AMBIANCE, SNEAK ABOVE

HOST: About 30 men and boys—all polio victims—meet here regularly to adapt vehicles for people with disabilities. They install hand pedals on tricycles and retrofit cars and motor bikes with hand controls. Ellen Thompson says by doing this they help themselves, and they help others.

CUT 17: ELLEN THOMPSON/SKIRBLE ELLEN THOMPSON: "They are people who want to do something for the disabled, who must start something for themselves. And, that is why they are bringing their talents together here on their own. They manufacture these things to alleviate their own plight."

HOST: This is the post-polio world for Ellen Thompson—a world with less poverty, where children are routinely immunized for preventable diseases, and where the disabled are judged by what they can do.

CUT 18: ELLEN THOMPSON "There is ability in disability. And what a person with disabilities needs to do is accept your disability and improve on your abilities. Don't allow your disability to wear you down. I can not walk like other people, but I have got a lot of things I can do!"

MUSIC—ESTABLISH BRIEFLY AND HOLD UNDER HOST

HOST: Health officials in Nigeria are determined to stop transmission of the polio virus by the end of the year. The program has involved an entire nation—from government ministers, religious leaders, and health workers to local officials, grassroots organizers and citizens in villages.

National Immunization Program director, Dr. A. Awosika, says the combination of good surveillance techniques and door-to-door campaigns—carefully synchronized with neighboring African states—have proved to be an effective strategy over the past year. She says the campaign has fostered a powerful sense of purpose among all those involved.

CUT 19: DR. A. AWOSIKA "I see a sense of mission. I see a sense of calling. I see a responsibility to the people, and all this inculcated in service. It has brought people to feel that (they) can do something for other people."

HOST: Leaders in the global polio eradication initiative—officials at World Health Organization, UNICEF, Rotary International and the Centers for Disease Control and Prevention—often remark that the program has gone beyond the eradication of a major disease. They say the program has developed new international partnerships, created a disease surveillance system, established a global laboratory network, strengthened routine immunization and set the stage to tackle other diseases.

Stephen Cochi is the director of the Global Immunization Division at the Centers for Disease Control and Prevention in Atlanta.

CUT 20: STEPHEN COCHI "We have taken some new steps in improving primary health care worldwide regardless of whether they live in an industrialized country or in the poorest countries of the world."

CUT 21: ROBERT STEINGLASS "I certainly think that polio needs to be eradicated. I think polio has a lot to teach us, but I think that many people are completely overstating the case in terms of what polio eradication will leave behind in terms of a legacy that will be useful for further development efforts."

HOST: Robert Steinglass directs a child survival project for the U.S. Agency for International Development (USAID). He believes that where the global polio initiative has missed the mark has been its failure to improve routine immunization programs.

CUT 22: STEINGLASS/SKIRBLE STEINGLASS: "For a long time and even now there has been a lack of finance to finish the job on polio eradication. Polio needs to be eradicated. The finance needs to be found for it. Part of the marketing strategy that has been used is to say that we have to eradicate polio, and by the way, by investing in polio we are going to benefit the entire routine immunization program. But it is so clearly not the case for people who work in the field who understand what the routine program requires. Throughout the 1990s, despite the existence of new vaccines, none of these new vaccines were being introduced in routine immunization programs, and they couldn't be introduced through a polio platform. Are you going to directly solve injection safety issues through a polio platform? Polio, as you know, is an oral vaccine."

HOST: "What is it going to take to strengthen routine immunization programs?"

STEINGLASS: "It will take the commitment of all the partners, including the ministries of health. It requires skilled staff and manpower. In many countries that had successful routine immunization programs, the staff had been recruited to work on polio in other countries on international assignments. So it will require the redirection of resources and the commitment of ministries and their partner agencies to working on routine immunization."

HOST: *The USAID program that operates in Nigeria is training men and women in villages to play a greater role as advocates for their own health care needs. They learn grassroots organization and problem solving.*

In Yargunda (PRON: AIR-GUNDA)—a small farming hamlet—five women have been designated as child health promoters (CHPs). They have taken a USAID seminar on breastfeeding. Their job is to teach others in the village what they have learned. On this day one of the CHPs takes her file of large picture cards to show a neighbor.

Women in this program gain status among their peers. They feel empowered and want more training. They promote the National Immunization Days and vaccinate their children against polio. But, these mothers say they also worry about more widespread diseases and conditions like AIDS, measles, malaria, malnutrition, respiratory infections and diarrhea. They wonder, how can they protect their children?

They start by educating each other. Seated on straw mats in a courtyard in front of their home, they begin to sing a song written for them by one of their husbands. He joins them to plead, "Listen people. Listen to the preaching!"

CUT 23: MUSIC—"LISTEN PEOPLE. LISTEN TO THE PREACHING" ESTABLISH, FADE UNDER HOST

HOST: *Our guide, Salamatu Bako, a USAID health and nutrition officer, translates the words of the song . . .*

CUT 24: SALAMATU BAKO "He talks about diet during pregnancy, about exclusive breast feeding. He even talks about developmental milestones of a child and advantages of breastfeeding, then the importance of immunizations and then the chorus is saying, "Listen brothers and sisters, listen!"

HOST: *The women are forming a drama group. They want to spread their health message at weddings, at festivals and naming ceremonies. Just how well they practice the lessons they preach may determine the future well-being of their community and their nation.*

SNEAK UP ON CHORUS . . . MD: CLOSING THEME (sneak for :06 under prev spot, then up full for :05, then under:

HOST: And that wraps up another edition of Our World. If you have any comments on the program please write to us at Our World, Voice of America, Washington, DC, 20237 USA, or e-mail us at our-world@voanews.com. A special thankyou goes to all the men and women in Nigeria working on polio eradication who assisted my reporting. Also many thanks to editor Rob Sivak and technical director Eva Nenicka. Rob Sivak will be back at this same time next week, for another radio expedition into . . . Our World.

MD: CLOSING THEME (up full, hold for fill to 26:00)

The VOA encounters two distinct problems in trying to increase its development programming to help the poor. VOA's primary mission is to report news and public interest broadcasts. Therefore, programming specifically addressed to improve the lot of the poor must be financed from surplus revenues or funds raised separately from regular VOA appropriations. USAID funding "passed through" to the VOA is helpful in this regard. It has allowed the VOA to finance partially, or fully, a number of creative programs for the poor. Provision of additional Nigerian VOA "stringers" or reporters, trained in health and community broadcasting, is one example of this. Another is the Nigeria Project through which USAID financed additional stringers, training and community forums organized around issues of communal conflict. The Nigeria Project, though widely considered successful within the VOA and USAID, was not continued because USAID moved on to other priorities with its own limited funds. As we know, the communal strife in Nigeria has not been appeased by these two years of USAID and VOA effort. With USAID funding, the VOA also took on a major effort to reach urban and rural populations in strife torn Angola providing health and other public interest messages.

As important as funding constraints are, an equally important problem for increasing developmental programming is VOA broadcast policy. As all VOA broadcasts emanate from Washington, the 52 language services of the VOA must vie for studio and transmitter times, which are severely limited. This is especially true on the shortwave spectrum. Adding both studios and transmission facilities might partially address this bottleneck, but costly satellite and receiver facilities would need to be expanded commensurately. Obtaining local AM and FM broadcast rights and access to nascent digital satellite broadcast technology are other possibilities.

An exception to current VOA broadcast practice has already been made for the urgently needed Radio Sawa. In addition to broadcasting on the shortwave bands, Sawa was able to obtain AM and FM frequencies from a number of Arab countries. Sawa also broadcasts digitally via satellite and over the Internet on Radio Farda. Sawa has also been given unique authority and broadcasts will shortly begin emanating from Dubai in the United Arab Emirates rather than from Washington.

Simple solutions are available if the U.S. government were really committed to development in the same way as it has shown it can be through the public interest broadcasting to the Middle East via Sawa. Regional broadcast studios and facilities for developmental programming would mitigate many of the cost problems and enhance listener-ship if weak short-wave signals were bypassed. Such broadcast solutions could also provide for better and more relevant programming. Since VOA is a public domain service, it could provide local stations with hours of creative and useful material. This could replace some of the music and outrageous talk, which as in much else, developing countries offer in order to imitate us.

The Future of USG Broadcasting

With the advent of Sawa, Radio Farda, the recent BBG purchase of an AM station in Pakistan and the advent of the Mid-East Television network Al Hurra, U.S. government broadcasting appears embarked on a new era of expansion. Yet there remain important challenges. Not only are independent local media like Al-Jazeera popping-up to challenge a "U.S. point of view" but the issue of credibility of U.S. government sponsored media has been raised from within. In the late summer of 2004 a remarkable petition signed by a third of VOA's staff questioned Sawa's mission in terms of what VOA staffers claimed was a lack of an "objectivity" guarantee in its Charter similar to the one granted the VOA. Sawa management rejected the charge. VOA staff also challenged the shift in funding from VOA type news and public affairs programming to Sawa's lighter fare. Clearly age old journalistic challenges of fair and objective reporting and its relevancy have not gone away.

Notes

1. Since this chapter was first written the new American Indian Museum has come to partially and attractively block the view to the mall.

2. In December 1941, the Foreign Information Service (FIS) predecessor to the Voice of America made its first direct broadcast to Asia from a studio in San Francisco. According to the Voice of America official history, "On February 24, 1942—79 days after the U.S. entered WWII—FIS beamed its first broadcast to Europe via BBC medium and long wave transmitters. Harlan Hale opened the German language program with the words: 'Here speaks a voice from America'. The name stuck, becoming the signature opening on all FIS broadcasts of the era, and becoming the future moniker for all U.S. Information Agency radio services." http://www.voanews.com/english/portal.cfm. (28 Jan, 2005).

3. Fiscal year 2002 appropriation broke down as follows: Radio Free Europe/Radio Liberty $71.006 million, Radio Free Asia $25.779 million, VOA $143.546 million, Radio and TV Marti $24.872 million.

4. The effort was conceived under the Clinton Administration by Norman Pattiz, founder of Westwood One, America's largest radio network and Clinton appointee to the Broadcasting Board of Governors (BBG). Sawa's launch date was accelerated and received increased attention after 9/11.

5. In December of 2002, a series of op-ed pieces in the *Washington Post* argued about the International Board of Broadcasters (IBB) policy to revamp Radio Freedom's Persian language service to Iran so that in addition to its politically focused programming it might reach a wider, less political audience. In January 2003, Radio Farda, a Sawa type broad-based broadcast format, was launched.

6. This was the situation prior to the U.S. invasion of Iraq.

7. WorldSpace Foundation, the non-profit partner of WorldSpace Corp. and principal UNICEF collaborator for distance learning radio in Sudan is now called First Voice International (1st Voice).

7
Female Infanticide, Bride Burning, Sutee
—The Paper Thin Sari in Flames—[1]

India is a hugely diverse country. Over 1 billion Indians, a sixth of the world's total population, live in the sub-continent, a land mass three times the size of the United States. Teeming poverty is everywhere. Whereas people in Africa are poor, they often appear robust and healthy. Emaciation among India's masses has reached the point of becoming generational, according to nutritionists, stunting and malnutrition are visible to the casual observer on the overcrowded streets. Average per capita income is $430, not the lowest in the world but when multiplied 1 billion times in crowded conditions—seven cities exceeding 3 million in population—suffering of all sorts abounds.

India is one of the oldest and culturally evolved civilizations in the world; the Upanishads are the oldest religious and philosophical texts in the world and undoubtedly still the richest. The Hindu religion is a direct descendant of these early teachings, its ancient reflections and stories shaping today's religious practices. India also gave birth to Buddhism and, while the religion has migrated, many of its traditions and teachings have been absorbed. Layer upon layer of diverse cultures color the Indian patina. In such a place, change comes slowly and with difficulty.

However, change must come, if the challenge of Indian poverty is to be met, and it is coming. A nuclear power and an international force in the computer software industry, India's intellectual centers are first world in their science and technology. Ancient beliefs and practices co-exist alongside the most modern. Maharajahs brush coattails with computer executives. University trained software engineers, doing contract work for Microsoft and reading *The Economist*, have their marriages arranged. Affirmative action has more to do with caste than race, but can still be the cause of tension and ostracism. Religious traditions determine what can be eaten, how it is to be prepared; astrology determines the time and date for major life events as weddings; and politics is everywhere and nowhere at the same time, democratic yet hopelessly dysfunctional. Such is the poverty, richness, diversity, as well as hope that is India.

One of the decidedly more arcane and less modern practices, inherited by India from its past, is the sometimes extreme treatment to which some Indian women are subjected. While male dominance is a characteristic inherited from many warrior and agricultural societies—though not all, as evidenced by the matriarchal society found among the Dravidians, as close as South India—it has not always evolved to take on the extreme forms of female infanticide and immolation found on the sub-continent.

Male heirs have been thought advantageous in many rural societies, for their ability to work and insure their parents' well being in old age. For similar reasons in less secure societies, male descendants were thought to provide some measure of protection from external violence. The dimorphism of the human species also leads more readily to physical domination by the larger male.

In many societies, these quasi-rational predilections were also enshrined into laws and social practices reinforcing them. As these constraints began to lessen in modern societies, sexual roles evolved. Though this represents a general pattern, there have also been numerous variants and exceptions. Preference for male heirs has not always evolved to the point of female infanticide, nor male dominance to social pressures for female immolation. Reasons for these evolving in India are probably unknowable, but could include the possibility that the impoverished conditions of India magnified tensions prevalent in many societies; the layering of peoples from invasion and partial assimilation exaggerated social responses; or, something simply went awry in a particular sub-sector of Indian society. Whatever the reasons, these practices are perceived as wrong by most Indians and in fact are illegal, but, nevertheless, persist.

One social practice in India perpetuating ancient roles is that of female dowry due the groom at marriage. In traditional households since the groom became responsible for the bride's well-being after marriage, a dowry was thought appropriate to assist in this process. Though roles have changed as society modernizes, the practice persists. It has led to perverse and unintended consequences. Poor families, giving birth to daughters fear the burden of the costs of the eventual marriages. Spouses seeking to divorce are reluctant or sometimes do not have the means to repay a dowry which would normally be returned with the divorced women.

Another ancient practice that of female immolation in order to accompany a deceased spouse into the afterlife, or "sutee", is now forbidden by law. Sutee has also contributed to aberrant behavior, leading some to devalue female life as it is weighed against other social obligations. Female infanticide, spousal immolation and accidental death are all outlawed social practices. Yet, they persist on the margin of Indian society with regrettable frequency and can enjoy a resurgence in periods of increased economic and social tensions. How can change be brought to the Indian masses?

Population Communications International (PCI), a U.S. based non-profit organization, with offices around the world, was created in 1970 as a division of the Population Institute under the leadership of David O. Poindexter, its first President. PCI's work has been one of the major influences in media based diffusion of information on family health and fertility over the decades. David Poindexter, personally, brought the rich Mexican experiences with telenovelas to the attention of India's Prime Minister, Indira Gandhi, and as a result began a now lengthy history of Indian use of education-entertainment for health and population messages.

"Taru" was a social content serial drama sponsored by PCI and its Indian partners. It premiered in the Indian States of Bihar, Jharkhand, Madhya Pradesh and Chhattisgarh in February 2002 on All India Radio (AIR). In May, it expanded to Uttar Pradesh, Uttaranchal, Rajasthan, Himachal Pradesh, Haryana and Delhi. At its height "Taru" reached over 60 million listeners in the very densely populated North of India in the national language of Hindii. Fifty-two episodes of "Taru" were aired on topics ranging from HIV-AIDS, immolation, infanticide, female education family planning, reproductive health and other health and social issues related to the family. PCI worked with a local NGO, Janani, and AIR in preparing the dramas. Researchers from Ohio University have helped design monitoring and evaluation studies of the program's impact. Here is an episode dealing with female infanticide. Judge its impact for yourself:

"TARU"—EPISODE 11

Compere: In the last episode of Taru, you listened to how Phirki Chachi provokes Raj Rani against Neha, blaming her because of her social work. Even this does not satisfy her and so she goes to Kapileshwar also telling him lies to make him turn against Neha. But, with Neha's good luck, Aloni Baba and Rasik Guruji come there and try to pacify the situation. Raj Rani is not convinced, but she doesn't dare say it openly to Aloni Baba and Guruji. And the matter ends there. Now, let us move to Suhagpur village, where Taru and Shashikant are trying hard to solve the problems of the village people.

Theme Song

Music

Earth, water and sky Sun, moon and stars . . . Their all encompassing glow, spreads over the universe . . . My nimble feet see a light, for a life better and brighter . . . Turning dreams into reality, that marks my per- sonality . . . Meeting companions on the way to empowerment, together, we march to enlightenment . . . Now, the targets are no longer difficult.

Scene-I

(Taru is sitting in the village Primary Health Center named "Sheetal Cen- ter" performing her day–to-day work. Shashikant enters)

Shashikant: Taru, did you go to Naresh's house—?

Taru: Yes, I have just come back.

Shashikant: How is the old lady now—?

Taru: You will be surprised to know, Shashi, that her fracture has proved a blessing for her. She is now a completely changed person. . . . (Smiles) She is now all love and affection to her daughter- in-law and her grand- daughters. (smiles again) You could never have expected this from her earlier.

Shashikant: Yes, Taru . . . the old lady is completely changed now. And this has brought a happy change in the life of her son Naresh and his wife also . . .

Taru: Yes, of course . . .

Shashikant: Earlier, the poor husband and wife were feeling terribly guilty that they had to cajole Aloni Baba, the holyman, to tell a lie to pacify their mother. They felt so bad that they had to tell lies to her to change her mind.

Taru: Yes, Shashi. Sometimes a difficulty in life becomes a blessing for us and changes the course of our life. By the way, how is Neha now? Did you go to her place?

Shashikant (in a disappointed tone): Yes, Taru. Myself, Naresh, Atoni Baba—the holyman and his disciple, Guruji—all of us went there. Neha is going through a bad time (pause) The old aunt, Phirki, never misses a chance to provoke her mother-in-law against her. And then, the mother-in-law takes it out on Neha—She does not miss a chance to heap insult, humiliation upon hapless Neha.

Taru (in a shocked tone): Didn't you people try to put some sense into that old lady's mind?

Sahshikant (taking a deep breath): We tried to reason with Neha's husband, Kapileshwar. It was no use trying with older members . . . Only the village holyman—Aloni Baba could do it. He spoke to Neha's mother-in-law.

Taru: What did Kapil have to say?

Shashikant (furiously): He is a clever guy. Knows how to evade straight talk. He doesn't like Neha's knack for social work.

Taru (surprisingly): But, what is wrong in that, Shashi?

Shashikant (sarcastically): This is what you feel . . . But, you know, they are a family of landlords. They can't even think of their daughter-in-law going to the low caste, poor people's colony to make their girls literate. (Sound of somebody coming running towards them)

(startled) Look there, Taru. That boy, rushing towards the centre, seems to be Mange Ram's son, Deenu.

Taru: Yes, it is Deenu. What is wrong with him?

(A boy aged 8-10 years panting, with deep breaths, enters the health centre)

Boy (panting): Come quickly, Sir. There, in our colony, Kalua is creating a scene in front of his house. He says he will kill his new-born daughter. Come, do something or he will surely kill her.

Taru and Shashikant (together): What . . .

Shashikant (shocked): What! Kalua is killing his baby girl?

Boy: Yes, Yes, his wife gave birth to a baby girl this morning. He was away. at work in the fields, then. He returned just now and says he will kill this girl.

Taru (in a worried tone): Who sent you here?

Boy (in a sad tone): Kalua's wife asked me to rush and request that you to come soon. Please hurry up before it's too late.

Taru (gets up): Let's go, Shashi

Shashikant (hurriedly): Come, let's rush. We will inform the village holy-man - Aloni Baba and his disciple, Guruji, on the way.

(Sad Music) (Change of Scene)

Scene-2

(Kalua's house. Noise of crowd gathered outside his house. Kalua is shout-ing. Sound of his wife crying.)

Kalua (Shouting): I will kill all of them. I will kill them. I will kill all the daughters you give birth to.

(Shashi, Taro and the Boy enter the Scene)

A Man (hurriedly): Shashikant, sir, you came at the right time. Please do something. We have tried every trick with him. But, he has gone mad. Please stop him.

Shashikant (furiously): Kalua, what is this? Have you gone mad? I say, stop this nonsense.

Kalua (agitated): Please sir, keep away from this. Now, no one can save her from my hands.

Taru (shaking with anger): Kalua, don't be mad. Why do you want to kill your own child? Even the wild animals don't behave like this.

Kalua (sarcastically): Madam, I say, you keep away from this. I know you upper class rich people very well.

Taru (angrily): You know nothing. . . .

Shashikant (in a furious tone): Do you know, Kalua, what you are doing? You can be thrown into prison if you do this. It is a crime, do you know?

Kalua (sarcastically): This talk of prison and a crime is all bullshit. Damn, if I care about all this. You big, rich people, you are all hypocrites. If you go for a test and abortion, it is alright. If we do it, it is crime. Why? (pause) Don't you know, girls are a big burden, a curse for us poor people. With their education, dowry, and what not, 'it is better not to have them. . . This is my family . . . I will do what I like . . . Now please, leave me alone.

Taru (shouting with anger): Kalua, don't you dare go into the house, I wam you . . .

Kalua (shouts): I will kill her . . . I will kill them all.

Taru (to Shashikant): Shashi, you take him away. I will go inside to his wife.

(She goes into the house. Kalua's wife is crying inconsolably. Seeing Taru, she comes running to her.)

Kalua's wife (crying): Please, madam, for God's sake, save us. Save my child from this butcher. I will not live to see my child dead.

Taru (in a consoling tone): Don't worry. Shashikant will not let him enter the house.

Kalua (shouting outside and cursing his wife): You bloody woman. Hand over that girl to me or, I will throw both of you out of my house You go to hell. I don't care . . .

Kalua's wife (crying inside the house): I will not stay here now. I will go away. I will beg work anywhere, but will not let you touch my baby.

(The village holyman Baba and his disciple Guruji enter)

Aloni Baba: God is great, God is great. . . .

Guruji: May God bless all. Shashikant, what is all this? What is the matter?

Aloni Baba (to Kalua in raging tone): You cursed soul! You will perish.

> *(Sound effect of loud music)*

Here . . . I invoke my invisible power (Sound effect)

Kalua (nervously): My holy lord, why are you angry with me?

Aloni Baba (to Gumji): Rasik, warn him to behave. Tell him not to incur God's wrath or God will destroy his entire family. . . warn him, ask him to behave . . . ave.

> *(loud background music)*

Guruji (trying to reason with Kalua): Kalua, don't torture your wife and children or you will also suffer . . .

Kalua (stammers and murmurs): Me, me . . .

Guruji: You will be thrown in prison for this sin in this life. After this life, you will go to hell. So, behave yourself.

Kalua (to Baba hesitatingly): But, my holy lord, you know, girls are a big curse in our society . . .

Guruji: It is only because of men like you . . .

Aloni Baba (furiously): You fool, sinners and foul-headed men like you are responsible for the miseries of women. If men change their ways, women would be automatically free from all troubles.

Kalua (hesitates): But, Baba, how would it help? Even if I change myself, how will you change others?

Aloni Baba: First, you change yourself. Then we will change others also. Come, let's go inside. (Chanting God is great. . . .)

(They all go into the house. Sound of an infant crying and Kalua's wife weeping.)

Guruji: Aha . . . What a beautiful child . . . like an angle . . . like Laxmi— the goddess of wealth.

Kalua's wife (hysterical): No, no, I will not let anyone touch my child . . . No, never . . .

Shashikant(consoling her): Don't worry, sister, your baby is quite safe . . .

Taru (reassuringly): And as for her future, I promise that Sheetal Center will give her full care till she is able to support herself.

Aloni Baba: What else do you want Kalua? Come now, take your daughter in your arms and kiss her. But, I warn you . . . no mischief . . . or else this crowd will punish you or throw you out of the village.

Kalua (to his wife): Give me my child . . . give her to me . . .

Kalua's wife: No, never

Kalua (to his wife): I am sorry, dear. I am very sorry . . . I will not harm her. Please, give her to me. (Takes the child in his arms affectionately)

Guruji (with a sigh of relief): Kalua, a day will come, when this girl will be the dearest to you and you will stand against all odds to shield her..

Aloni Baba: You are the mother of this baby . . . take care of her, be brave and face the world . . . and you will see that this girl will become your most potent strength.

(to Taru) Taru dear, I am very happy today. Let's go to your, what do you call it?

Taru (laughs): Sheetal Center.

Aloni Baba: Yes, yes, the Center. Let's go there. We will sit and relax there for a while.

(Guruji and Aloni Baba leave from there singing joyously. The crowd follows them)

[SONG]

0 Lord, you are residing on that high snow clad mountain. Please look after the world and its creatures.

[Change of Scene]

Scene-3

(Taru, Shashikant, Aloni Baba, Guruji are present at the health centere talking to each other)

Taru (affectionately): We are grateful to you Baba. You have come here after a long time.

Guruji: My holy lord was busy with other things. But, did you notice? Naresh's mother now does not harp on having a grandson. Everyone is so pleased to see this change in her.

Taru (hesitating): That's right, sir. But, I am still not sure about Kalua. I am afraid he might still cause harm to his infant daughter. I don't trust that man at all.

Guruji(with full confidence): Don't worry. He dare not do anything now. . . Now, that the child is care of Sheetal Center, why should he be feeling any burden. She will be brought up with other children at the Center.

Aloni Baba (with a smile): Our great culture, you know, is meant to serve the society. If someone refuses to see reason, he has to be tackled by other means then . . . you know that, Rasik (laughs)

(Nisha enters the Center)

Nisha (calling from outside): Taru, Taru, where are you?

Taru: I am here . . .

Guruji: Is it Nisha?

Taru: yes, Sir . . .

Nisha (entering the room): Good afternoon, my holy lord.

Aloni Baba (lovingly): God bless you, my dear . . .

Compere: Listeners, you have just listened to this episode on how Taro and her colleague Shashikant, with their sheer perseverance and undeterred courage, saved a baby girl from the heinous crime of infant killing. Terrified ,due to the supernatural threat of harm by the holyman Aloni Baba, Kalua was transformed into a chastened man. This change of heart and mind on his part brings relief to all. Just around that point of time, Nisha comes with an urgent message from Neha that they should rush to her village to help stop a child- marriage. To know what happens there, please listen to our next episode of "TARU".

And now our address -

Serial 'TARU'
Post Box No. 73,
All India Radio,
Parliament Street,
New Delhi - 110 001

Please do send us your response. Your letters are awaited eagerly

(Music)

(Title Song)

[EPISODE]

Nisha (to Guruji): Good afternoon to you, Sir.

Guruji: Lord bless you with happiness

Shashikant (to Nisha): Come Nisha, Why you are here today?

Nisha: Shashikant, I have brought a message from Neha. She has requested you all to come to her village immediately . . .

Taru (nervously): Why, what is the problem? I hope she is alright?

Nisha (assuring): Oh yes, she is fine, but her family is bent upon a child marriage.

Guruji (with a sigh of relief): Don't worry, dear. Now that we have re-ceived the message, you don't have to worry.

Taru (to Guruji happily): O.K. Sir, now, how about a good song to us?

Shashikant (laughs): Yes Sir, before going on another assignment, let us re-energize ourselves with more strength and vigor .

Aloni Baba (to Guruji): Yes, Rasik, I am also eager to hear a good song from you.

Guruji: Now, that you say so, I have to sing.

(Guruji sings a folk song and everybody joins him by singing and playing instruments merrily)

My heart swings like a leaf in the wind, The easterly wind has a message in it, My homeland beckons me to return . . .

Theme Song

Music

Earth, water and sky. Sun, moon and stars . . . Their all encompassing glow, spreads over the universe . . . My nimble feet see a light, for a life better and brighter . . . Turning dreams into reality, that marks my per-sonality . . . Meeting companions on the way to empowerment, Together we march to enlightenment . . Now our goals are no longer out of reach.

Music

Closing: Announcement:

You were listening to the eleventh episode of Radio Soap Opera 'TARU'. This episode was written by Dr. Anita M. Kumar, directed by Ms. Karuna

Srivastava, assisted in production by Mr. Mukesh Shukla and produced by Mr. Kamal Dutt.

The participating actors were Banwari Taneja, Ash Narayan Mishra, Brij Bhushan Shukla, Sanjay Verma, Pallavi Bharati, Deepa Nainwala, Surendra Sagar, AIka Ameen and Asheesh.

Headquartered in New York, Population Communications International (PCI), producer of "Taru", develops educational-entertainment programming for radio and TV in Asia, Africa, Latin America, the Caribbean and the United States. PCI has recently strengthened its HIV-AIDS programming in China, the Caribbean, Kenya, Mexico, Pakistan, South India and Tanzania. In the U.S., PCI hosts an annual "soap summit", a gathering of "soap opera" professionals to sensitize them to social issues like HIV-AIDS, which they can then incorporate into their dramas.[2]

Notes

1. "Sutee" is a Hindu word referring to the practice of a wife's immolation upon the death of a spouse. Outlawed in India, it's practice is increasingly rare but continues on the margins of Indian society. The "Sari"is a wrapped dress worn commonly by Indian women.

2. Singhal and Rogers, *Combating AIDS*, 331.

8
Afghanistan
—A Missed Opportunity?—

The United States Agency for International Development (USAID) had already been active in Afghanistan trying to relieve the devastating effects of a prolonged drought when war broke out with the Afghan Taliban and Al Qaeda after the terrorist attacks of 9/11. With the dislocations of war adding to growing hunger, food was airdropped into the country alongside the war's military ordinance. With the exception of a small flap over the color of the food packets, which made them undistinguishable from anti-personnel mines, the relief operation went well. It allowed the U.S. government to claim credibly, that their efforts were aimed not against the Afghan people, but against the Taliban and its leadership. By December, opposition on the ground to U.S. forces had largely collapsed and relief efforts were to shift to a more exclusively overland operation, supplies coming up through Pakistan, via truck convoy.

In February, the USAID Administrator, Andrew Natsios, addressed the Washington press corps ostensibly on the effectiveness of the relief operation. His entire opening remarks, however, except for a few minutes at the end, focused instead on USAID's featured use of radio as a tool for humanitarian assistance. Mr. Natsios advanced this use of the radio as an innovation in humanitarian assistance. It allowed recipients to become aware of the availability of aid, when and where rations could be obtained, their individual and family entitlements to food rations, type of identification required, food preparation and ancillary health messages. The AID Administrator spoke of the numerous advantages incumbent in the broadcast of these aid messages via the radio, not the least of which, according to his C-SPAN presentation, was the empowerment that accurate information would give the population. For the first time, people in remote areas who needed help would be empowered to receive assistance without fear of theft or extortion.

   USAID funded a modest four-month program through an intergovernmental organization the International Office of Migrations (IOM) and the Voice of America (VOA). They broadcast several brief radio messages a week, in Dari and Pashto, the principal Afghan languages, on the availability of aid and its uses. Broadcast by the VOA on several shortwave bands, the 10 - 15 minute spots could be heard throughout most of the mountainous country. In many villages, it remains a major point of contact with the outside world and foreign reconstruction assistance. One of the broadcast segments from February follows:

Voice A: (A female voice) (With opening sig under voice) a verse about Eid (Pashto/Dari). e.g. A Pashto verse (Tapa) says: Akhtar de kalee tha ra na wur matha de jur karal da hamzulu Peghoroona.
(Translation): You didn't come to the village to celebrate Eid (Akhtar) together. So I am ashamed in front of my mates.

(Opening sig rises for another 2-3 secs, then gradually fades out)

Voice B: (A male voice) Hello and welcome to our program. It's good that you tuned to us. Make sure you listen to our program Monday through Friday (At the same time), on the same station.

Voice A: Don't tell us you don't know who we are, we are:

Voice B: (Introducing themselves, only by naming himself and his colleague).

Voice A: And you know that this is a program to tell you about the activities of international aid agencies and Afghan NGO's and also to tell you what they do for you and what you can do to help them and so help yourselves.

Voice B: This program is brought to you by Humanitarian Emergency Afghan Radio project, run by International Organization for Migration or IOM. IOM is an intergovernmental body, serving displaced people around the World.

Voice A: In today's program we have a brief bulletin of news regarding aid activities and a report about the Eid celebrations in Kabul.

(Music Srting)

Voice B: And here is the news:

• *Crime, banditry and looting continue to be a problem in many areas of Afghanistan. The World Food Program (WFP) reports that in the district of Dilaram in Nimroz Province, 500 tons of wheat, barley and maize seeds have been taken from an NGO warehouse. The seeds were needed for distribution to needy farmers for winter planting, but now they have been stolen.*

• *And in another incident, in Jaji, Paktia Province, on the night of 16 December, armed men robbed an NGO working on mine clearance activities. Among other goods, the criminals stole a quantity of explosives.*

• *The continuing danger of mines and unexploded ordnance (UXOs) was further highlighted by a tragic incident that occurred near the Maslakh IDP camp near Herat on 18 December. Two children, aged 9 and 10 years were killed, and two others injured, by a yellow B.L.U. 97 bomblet. They had been out collecting firewood.*

The Herat Regional Manager of the Mine Action Program, Mr Siddiqui, helped rescue the injured children and recovered the bodies of the two dead children. Speaking with great emotion, Mr Siddiqui had this to say: "Today is Eid for all Afghans, but it's a tragic day for those Afghans who lose their children while trying to provide for their survival."

Mr Dan Kelly, the Mine Action Program Manager, told journalists in Islamabad today that there are some 5,000 Afghan de-miners. He said they are all committed to working to stop the suffering caused by mines and UXOs. Dan Kelly also urged Afghan people to understand clearly two new dangers of UXOs that have appeared since the end of the coalition bombing campaign.

First, there are the bright yellow bomblets that tragically killed the two children near Herat. Coalition forces have provided the Mine Action Program with full information on 103 sites where these yellow bomblets were dropped.

The danger is that about one in ten of these bomblets failed to explode. And that means they are still active, highly unstable, and likely to explode if they are touched. So if you live near any of these 103 sites, please take care and remind your children of the basic mine awareness message:

If you see a UXO or any strange object, don't touch it.

That message remains true for any place in Afghanistan. And for people who live near any of the 103 sites where the yellow bomblets were dropped, the message is especially important.

The two children in Herat are not the only casualties from new UXO dangers. The bombs dropped on ammunition stores caused thousands of rockets, mortars, missiles, mines and other explosives to be spewed out over fields and roads and even villages up to 5 kms away. This has occurred mainly in areas close to frontline fighting. So, if you live within 5 kms of a bombed ammunition store, once again the message is the same:

If you see a strange object, don't touch it!

• *On a brighter note, some 750 children at the Tahiya Masqan orphanage in Kabul are today receiving a somewhat unusual visit—from a group of New York City firefighters and police officers on a humanitarian aid mission to Afghanistan. The New Yorkers are bringing food, powdered milk, and blankets for the children at the orphanage.*

And another 750 Kabuli children who are also living in difficult circumstances—either because they have to go out to work, or because they have disabilities—have also received warm clothing and extra food. This has been provided by Save the Children and distributed among the needy children by their local Afghan NGO partners.

• *Save the Children has also distributed wheat and some other foods to over 8,000 households in Maimana district of Faryab Province.*

• *But, a less happy tale comes from the Sar Shahi camp in Jalalabad. The camp is temporary home to about 3,000 families, or around 18,000 people, mostly from Kunduz, Baghlan and Tarkhar provinces. However, over 1,000 of these people are still living without shelter, according to an NGO who visited the camp recently. This was reported by UNOCHA at their press briefing in Islamabad on Thursday.*

• *The NGO, Refuges International (RI), on Thursday made several recommendations for effective reconstruction efforts in Afghanistan. The* agency urges NGOs and UN agencies not to base themselves only in Kabul, but to open regional offices throughout the country. That way, says the agency, they can ensure that aid reaches rural communities and embraces all ethnic groups, including the people who do not have influence in the capital.

However, the agency also acknowledges that the challenge will be to find genuine civilian partners and not just give more power to the warlords.

RI also advises donors to be careful to avoid inviting corruption. This could happen if they flood the new government departments and NGOs with large grants that they cannot manage effectively. Instead, RI recommends a focus on funding small community-based projects. This should help ensure that aid reaches the people who really need it.

RI stresses the important value of the expertise and experience of Afghan NGOs, and also those international NGOs who have strong networks of Afghan staff. Many Afghan NGOs, including those headed by women, told RI that they were capable of managing projects themselves. They said they already had valuable experience at community level. They felt that with training and capacity building, they would soon be able to operate to international standards.

RI, therefore, urges that reconstruction be de-centralized, utilize Afghan skills and experience, and focus on community-based projects.

They also recommend that NGOs work with communities to form advisory committees which include women as well as men.

[News Bulletin Ends, followed by music Sting 3-5 Secs]

Voice A: The lazy silence of the few quiet hours that always follow Iftaree was broken by the sound of firing on the 30th Day of Ramadan. (If wanted - actuality of firing sound gradually rises, Maintains and then gradually fade out. (Duration about three secs). The firing sounds continued for an hour.

Voice B: And this is how the news of Eid was announced in Kabul.

Voice A: In the morning, Eid prayers were offered in different Mosques (Grand Mosques or Jame Masjids). All prayed for peace, unity and brotherhood. Hatred was condemned and love towards each other was praised.

Voice B: After Eid prayers, people greeted each other, and the celebrations started. Children had already come out on to the streets and playgrounds. They were wearing their new clothes.

Voice A: Street sellers, selling food and soft drinks had opened their stalls, and in the playground the swings were erected.

Voice B: As the day passed, the business was booming on the streets. "I am very glad today, I have already earned more than two hundred thousand Afghanis," said Akhtar Mohammad, a swing owner in the Microrian area of Kabul. He was charging (500) Afghanis per one full turn on the swing per child.

Voice A: Although adults, both males and females, were much fewer in number than children, one thing that was really noticeable, was the sound of very loud music cassettes. Music Centers were very much in evidence.

(Actual sounds of bazaar with music sounds 5-10 Secs)

Voice B: "Availability always breeds demands. In the last few years, the absolute ban on music has created this situation of maximum demand," said Mr Mohammad Sarwar, an owner of a Music Center, commenting on the booming music business in Kabul.

Voice A: "There is more freedom now and that makes this Eid different from the previous ones," said a retired army officer (Retired colonel) Mr. A. Qayum Afzali.

Voice B: And another citizen from Kabul, Sayed Tabaruk Shah Badakhshanee, said that since there is no fear of war, so people are mentally satisfied and enjoying their Eid celebrations.

Voice A: "I really enjoyed it, after five years I had the opportunity of playing the chicken eggs game," said Ahmad Munir, a twenty-two year old Kabuli. "This is a game and a custom," he said, commenting on his favorite hobby and proudly looking at dozens of eggs lined up in front of him. He was sitting beside a boiled eggs seller, surrounded by young men of his age. "I know all different types of boiled eggs, I am a master of the game I have the knowledge, I know the tricks and I love it. No one, absolutely no one, can easily defeat me."

Voice B: Jawad, a student from Ariana Afghan lycee, felt that for him the Eid was not being fully celebrated and the reason he had was: "Many citizens of Kabul have left the city because of recent fighting. They haven't returned yet. I am missing all those friends who I used to see during the past Eids. If they had returned, then this Eid would have been wonderfully celebrated. At least it's more peaceful now".

Voice A: Malalai, an educated Afghan lady said: "There are not many women out, and they don't show their faces, because they are not really sure if it's safe yet."

Voice B: But Farida, a ten-year-old girl said, "I am very happy this time, I can play with my friends without any fear."

Voice A: Khodai Dad, a taxi driver, although complaining that "there are less people now in Kabul," but he was happy at the rising value of the Afghan currency, stating that so far he has earned well.

Voice B: Ghulam Farooq, a city shopkeeper, also reflected similar views. He said that the rising price of the Afghani has benefited him, because he purchased Pakistani rupees, when the rupee was strong and now that the price of the Afghan currency has risen, he is selling it back in Afghanis.

Voice A: On the second day of Eid, it rained. Although this affected Eid celebrations slightly, still the music went on and the celebrations continued.

(Rising slowly sound of Afghan Music, kept initially under presenter's Voice)

Voice B: Now, with our best wishes for this Eid and all the future Eids, we say good-bye to you.

Voice A: Till next program, bye-bye

(Rising Afghan Music also used as a closing sig).
End

Several short months later, these humanitarian assistance radio broadcasts ended, their USAID funding terminated. The total cost of this effort with the potential to reach millions of poor Afghans with useful information was less than $150,000. Efforts were made internally, within USAID, to shift radio programming from an emergency focus to long-term development information. Obstacles to this fundamental shift included overall inadequate funding, earmarks and the legacy of USAID's traditional focus. The strategic choices that were made faced obstacles, both from these internal constraints and from the difficult Afghanistan environment. These choices were to have both remarkable success and associated risks.

Communication's Strategy Focuses on Local Media

USAID's Office of Transition Initiatives, OTI in USAID parlance, is the Office, which funded the IOM/VOA broadcasts at the Administrator's request. Once the humanitarian broadcasts came to an end, OTI made the choice to emphasize the development of local media, over the more immediate goal of reaching the population with current programming and information. While idealistic, this strategy is fraught with risk and has few immediate benefits; benefits that are acutely needed in the impoverished, unstable environment of Afghanistan. Unlike the IOM/VOA broadcasts mandated by the Administrator, OTI's subsequently funded "strategic" program, for the most part, will have to await both listeners and results, as meaningful development programming could be at the very least several years away, and that is, provided that the efforts at building local media are successful.

All together the totality of mass media efforts of the U.S. government in Afghanistan comprised less than $2 million—less than a quarter of one percent of the $840 million committed in aid by the U.S., since October 1, 2001.[1] This is a debatable strategy, in a largely inaccessible country, without secure roads, subject to banditry and on-going hostilities and, where the urban population constitutes a small minority. A year after the hostilities were largely over, and assistance had begun, there is still virtually no security outside the capital of Kabul and no access for aid workers to the rest of country beyond the city limits. Radio waves have access.

Missed Opportunity?

As a counterpart to its support of our war effort in Afghanistan, the U.S. Ambassador to Pakistan had promised a $60 million educational grant to help reform Pakistan's school system. The lack of effective schooling and the rise of the "Madras" religious schools were poor substitutes for a functioning school system. These were felt to be fueling the radicals' hold on the youth of Pakistan and leading to support for the Taliban and Al Qaeda, across the border to the west. Was there a better way to marry U.S.

self-interest in the war effort with long-term educational benefits for the youth of the region?

Unfortunately, educational reform in Pakistan, as elsewhere, is no simple matter of test scores, or even vouchers for Madras students, if such a thing were possible. The complex educational bureaucracy, millions of students, tens of thousands of teachers, all would need to mobilize behind any reform. How was this to be achieved? Modern technology did offer some possible solutions. Via satellite, digital radio broadcast could reach with one signal all the schools in Pakistan and Afghanistan. Dari, Pashto and Urdu were languages spoken throughout the region and formed the basis for the teaching of children. Since 2000, WorldSpace Radio had broadcast satellites in place, serving the entire south Asia region including Pakistan and Afghanistan. WorldSpace Satellite Radio, a private company with some Middle East backing, was based in Washington D.C, friendly to U.S. interests and friendly to development. Five percent of WorldSpace bandwidth is currently allocated for public interest programming on a grant, non-commercial basis.[2]

The Pentagon purchased several thousand WorldSpace radios for use in the schools. These fifty dollar radios can receive short wave, local AM and FM signals, as well as the WorldSpace digital satellite signals. To succeed, the Pentagon still needed educational programming in local languages and a network for distribution of the radios to local schools. If the radios could be placed in progressive schools, and provided with quality educational programming, poor teachers and poor schools that might resist reforms could be by-passed, or at least so reasoned the Pentagon. Parents, students and teachers could gravitate to the enhanced resource school using the educational material made available via the radio. Students would be connected to a modern learning experience. Recruiting the National Security Council (NSC) to help them with their pitch to USAID, the Pentagon approached USAID to manage this important program. USAID rejected the proposal for reasons—not entirely clear to these authors—conjectured to be those of time, funding availability and program requirements. Radio was once again the bridesmaid, at the marriage of development information and the poor, in spite of a very ample dowry in Afghan terms.

New Opportunities?

At the time this book goes to press, USAID's Office of Transition Initiative's strategy of developing local radio seems to be imminently more successful than the authors anticipated. In addition to the FM station in

Kabul, a network of 28 rural stations has been established under the tute-lage of Internews, an international NGO.[3] These local stations have proven very useful as a source of news about political candidates and election processes in the run-up to the elections this year. Issues of sustainability and ownership, underscored by the authors, remain, however. Outside of the Kabul station that is currently covering its operating costs from adver-tising and other resources, advertising in the rural areas is scarce to non-existent. If the commercial value of many of these stations is a subject for skepticism, their political value is not. Once the security blanket slowly lifts, these stations could once again become prey to governments and war-lords alike.

Other aspects of the Afghan airwaves have also evolved. Congress has funded Radio Free Afghanistan, providing more powerful transmitters and increased air time to VOA type shortwave broadcasts. While overall appropriations by the U.S. government for assistance of all types has in-creased dramatically, reaching over $4 billion, expenditures on communi-cation have remained small, no greater than 2-4% of the total. Information oriented programming for the poor remains the main shortcoming. Almost the entirety of U.S. health, agriculture and related information and assis-tance for the poor, with minor exceptions noted, is delivered through tradi-tional means of extension. The only mention of communication in the nu-merous congressional testimonies on the subject of U.S. assistance to Afghanistan concerns the restoration of telephone service in Kabul. An important subject, no doubt, but one which understates the power and reach of mass communication for the poor.

A constructive turn has, nevertheless, occurred in the battle to educate the next generation of young Afghans, heretofore, being fought, teacher by teacher—some qualified, many less so, in poor classrooms around the country. First Voice International, partnering with the non-profit Equal Access, has received funding for a distance learning program reaching 3,500 classrooms. Several years after the original program was suggested to USAID, with seed capital from the Silicon Valley hi-tech community, enhanced learning will finally reach the Afghan classroom. Hopefully this will be a happy ending, but not the only one, for the learning possibilities of young Afghans.

Other changes are also taking place as people realize the power of the air-waves. With on-going funding from the Hewlett Foundation and on the ground support from UNICEF, Equal Access, which was founded in 1999 in San Francisco as a non-profit organization and began its international out-reach only in 2001, is already putting together a number of programs for Afghanistan, in addition to the classroom oriented programs with First Voice. These programs, on topics of traditional development assistance, referred to as *Radio Danesh* or *Knowledge Radio,* are broadcast via the Internews network, the BBC and Radio and TV Afghanistan. All this is being done with a staff of eight local Afghan correspondents and a San Francisco headquarters staff of eight, miniscule by international aid standards. Equal Access has also opened offices and begun programming in Nepal, and will soon do so in India. Additional funding comes from a variety of sources including DFID, the UN Foundation, Aga Khan Foundation and a number of U.S. hi-tech start ups and investors, contributing in varying measure. USAID has provided a small amount of funding for the Nepal program. Sufficient resources to cover programming needs have still been a challenge for the start-up. An emphasis on communication by the major donors could help organizations like Equal Access achieve quality local programming on a sustainable basis. Donors also have a rich base of technical resources. Devoting a small portion of these to programming would enrich broadcast possibilities enormously. Efforts like that of Equal Access, though still nascent, have to be viewed as positive, in terms of both the radio and the future of Afghan development. After a slow start radio is reaching the Afghan population with useful information, only time will tell if this change from the more habitual, and less promising, approaches to assistance takes root. The poor are without a doubt tuned-in.

Notes

1. U.S. Dept. of State, "Fact Sheet Details Support for Rebuilding Afghanistan", January 9, 2003. <http://usinfo.state.gov/sa/Archive/2004/Jan/29-298274.html>. Some of USAID's programs, such as those in the health sector include funding for communication not captured here. Outside the health sector such funding and understanding of the importance of information and communication is rare.

2. On July 1, 2003, the WorldSpace Foundation (WSF) a non-profit partner of WorldSpace Corporation changed its name to First Voice International. It is a 501(c)(3) tax-exempt, nonprofit organization which is able to provide lower cost satellite broadcasting for use in development. It is called First Voice (1st Voice) today while the corporate broadcaster has kept its WorldSpace name.

3. While setting up these radio stations has been a remarkable feat this has been done exclusively through the purchase of transmitters by Internews with donor funding. With the exception of one commercial station the stations are community run, with little programming and air time, un-trained management, supported for the time being uniquely from the continuing infusion of donor funds with little hope of commercial sustainability. The stations will be able, however, to play a significant role in providing information locally during a transition period to a hopefully better endowed Afghan environment.

9
"Women and War"
—49 Stations Broadcast Around the World On
Women's Day—

Of all the powerful uses of the radio for development uncovered by the authors, that of the oral testimonies of over 200 women in 12 war torn countries gathered as part of the Panos "Women and Conflict" project was one of the most captivating.

Part of a growing recognition of the crucial role of women in the reconstruction and rehabilitation following war, the project sought to learn more about the impacts of war and civil strife on women. Working largely through local NGO partners, workshops were held discussing and developing the themes on which the women wished to focus. Interviews with the women were recorded on tape, transcribed word for word in the language of the interviewee and then translated into English. Native speakers from the women's own country with a more than passable knowledge of English were found among students abroad, tourists and immigrants to volunteer to read the women's testimonies for the English language broadcast. Through the accented English of the foreign-born readers, the producers of "Women and War" hoped to render the rhythm and accent of the women's experience in what would be, nevertheless, an intelligible English for a non-native English listening audience. Music and effects while closely budgeted were commissioned to accompany the women's voices.

On the 49 stations broadcasting the initial Women's Day March 8, 1996 program release, the women's testimonies reached over 26 countries via translations of the program into Bulgarian, Spanish, Sinhala, Tamil, Swahili, Tigrigna, Shona, Sesotho and German. The one-hour long program—broadcast either in its entirety or in 15 minute to half-hour segments—is a powerful testimony of the women's experience of war. The 15 minute sections were divided into four themes: (1) coping in chaos; (2) forced to flee; (3) changed lives, changed relationships; (4) picking up the pieces. The Women's Day broadcast alone reached several million people—12 of the 49 broadcasting stations reporting listener ship of over 2 million—at a total cost of 6 pence per 100 listeners.

The experience of listening to "Women and War" is a curiously unsettling but an enriching one. Most development radio transmits information; for example, how to accomplish daily tasks in a more efficient or more productive manner, or what low cost technologies might be available to facilitate a particular household chore or work related task. "Women and War" does none of this at least in a linear manner that is explicit to the listener. On the contrary, the listener must derive his or her own information, interpret the women's story, understand the horror of war, learn how to resist and survive or in some manner, if only to contemplate the power of life, and fashion a personal message from the women's discourse. Listener surveys indicate that this "implicitness" was one of the more popular aspects of the program.

The following selections gather the experience and testimony of "Women and War" in their own words; how they reacted; what they did in the face of differing experiences within the common thread of war. Can we learn from testimonials themselves without a narrative discourse?

Here are some reactions from radio stations around the world:

➤ "Generally informative and thought-provoking" - Caribbean Broadcasting Corporation.

➤ "More sound affects would have given the program the 'real' situation effect. In general the material was great. - Papua New Guinea NBC.

➤ "It was an outstanding, impressive and touching docudrama, avoiding dry political statements, emphasizing the human aspect. The reactions we got were very positive." - Radio DRS Switzerland.

➤ "The stories of the women were very interesting on paper, but I thought the dramatization was not always credible—It sometimes lacked emotion and feeling. The concept of the program was excellent. The program production was very good." -Namibian Broadcasting Corporation.

➤ "The fact that the testimonies were all factual promoted the women around us here to come out and speak" - Swaziland Broadcasting Service.

➤ "It was a job well done." - Radio Tanzania.

> "I found it very interesting…It would be good to do the same with people who have AIDS." -Seychelles Broadcasting Corporation.
> "Overall very gripping and excellent programs with high production values." - Radio Australia.

Judge for yourself as you hear the women speak.

Women and War

SFX signature tune fade and hold under narration

Introduction: Around the world, war continues to affect the lives of millions of people. But, the impact of war, and its aftermath, on the lives of women often goes unheard. During conflict, many women take on new roles and responsibilities, ensuring the survival of families and communities, even taking part in the fighting. When peace comes, women are crucial to recovery, rebuilding damaged homes and livelihoods, caring for injured partners and relatives as well as their children. In this four-part programme, we give voice to women's testimonies, as they relate their experiences of war.

Women and War Part 1 - Coping in the chaos.

SFX signature tune fade up and out

(Anon) Bosnia: In just a few years I have seen my country torn apart by war.

SFX machine gun fire

When the first barricades were set up and the shooting had begun, the citizens of Sarajevo were leaving town on a massive scale. The "people's" army was shooting at its own people. Shooting at people—unprepared, unarmed, unable to fight back. It lasted for days, weeks, months, I don't even know for how long. There were moments when I thought not a single bird would survive, not to mention a human being. I was dreadfully worried about my older son, who was already showing signs of great distress.

Soon we saw the first wounded, young people without eyes, limbs, shot in the head. On one night like that, I heard a scream from my son's room upstairs. I just stood there, paralyzed. Something had broken inside his

mind. It was too much. All that evil and distress around him. An ambu-
lance came and took him to the hospital. They said it was a nervous
breakdown. So, my husband decided to get him out of the hospital' and to
run far away from this town. It was possible to try and escape across the
airport runway, but nobody could guarantee your survival. One dark, rainy
night, my husband and older son left the town

SFX wind and rain fade under narration

(Sabina) Uganda:You can imagine how I felt for days afterwards, until I
found out that they'd succeeded. Thank God, they kept their heads, saved
themselves from this hell.

[with anger]

I didn't get a chance to escape. I was abducted and taken to the rebel
camp where I was left to stay in a hut with a man. At night, he kept ask-
ing me for sex, but I refused. We continued like this for a week, then I
had to give in as there was no way I could escape.

Here in Uganda, some said that those like me who were abducted wanted
it—this was not true. Why would a woman go in for all these kinds of suf-
ferings? When people ask if I supported the rebels I say, "I don't take
sides. I was with the rebels not out of my own choice, but because I was
abducted and now I'm glad that I came back—alive!" I don't even know
why the two sides want to fight. They are like co-wives fighting for their
husband's attention

SFX Bush Sounds fade up, then hold under narration

(Alisantorina) Uganda: During the fighting in Uganda, I began to hide in
the bush during the daytime and return home only at night to prepare
food and to sleep. We made small shelters near streams and valleys or
deep in the bush where we thought at least it would be difficult for them
to find us. Soldiers began to follow us by our footprints and if they found
anyone they would burn down the shelter together with you in it.

(An) Vietnam: I remember 30 years ago in Vietnam we had to hide as
well. We and our organisations dug tunnels—and life, movement, every-
thing happened under the ground.

SFX Tunnel/domestic sounds fade up then hold under narration

A lot of families were afraid of living in tunnels; they split up to live in two or three of them, so they would not all be killed at once. Women in Vietnam could only tight and serve the war if their children were safe. In some cases, it was compulsory to take the baby from its working mother so she could help the war effort.

SFX Bush sounds fade up then hold under narration

(Alisantorina) Uganda: In the bush you had to talk in whispers. If you did hear any noise, it meant there were Uganda soldiers nearby.

SFX Bush fade and lose

When eventually we moved to a refugee camp in another part of Uganda, the place was just too noisy for me—even the children jumped if you spoke to them, as they were not used to loud voices anymore. They still thought whispers were the order of the day.

(Jenneth) Uganda: We had to live in the bush, too— for almost a year. During all this time, it was a struggle, we rarely ate cooked food. It went to the extent of us giving the children soil to eat to quiet them when things were very bad.

SFX musical bridge fade up and under

(Kokila) Sri Lanka: With war, we have lost the peaceful life. That is a big loss. Tension, stress and grief. all these are Sri Lanka now. I lost my own house. Books of value we'd collected have been lost. Lands have been lost. When we were displaced we couldn't bring anything with us, we could only bring human relationships.

We never used to buy firewood, vegetables, coconut, fruits, all carne from our own land. Neighbours also used to share their produce. Now, we don't get this. All the relatives are scattered. We have to buy everything for money. When we think of it, we feel sad. But, comparing our lives with those who now live in the refugee camps, we feel we're much better off. Dur'n 51

(Anthoncian) Sri Lanka: I'd agree. Although life is hard, I'd sooner be in my own house than in a camp. But in Sri Lanka, it's difficult for me to run my home now. Nobody helps me. My husband died shortly after being ar-

rested, accused of being with the rebels. I have to stay indoors and stitch or do some handicraft and manage my family. My husband had two fishing boats, but we lost everything. I know there's supposed to be government compensation for widows like me, but I never got it.

SFX distant gunfire fade under narration

All the time we hear gunfire. We can't get out after dark. No freedom. Always frightened. We can't sleep at nights and can't live peacefully during the day. When the children go to school, we panic till they come back. When we all stay together, we are at ease. But everyday, there is some sort of tension. We don't know when we will be allowed to live peacefully again.

(Marie) Lebanon: Yes, war does bring hardship, but I must admit sometimes it was very exciting, living through all that shelling and surviving. You had a great rush of adrenaline. There was a time when the only people in our apartment building in Beirut were us and an old neighbour. Everyone else had left. We were determined not to be driven out by the Syrians. We often huddled in the kitchen. My daughter says it was exciting for her too. She remembers us sheltering under the table, making puppet plays.

All you think about is survival. I can understand how people kill. I never believe anyone who says, "I could never kill." There were times when I would have shot people if I'd had a gun. I don't think women are any different from men in that way.

(Xot) Vietnam: As far as I am concerned, although I am a woman, I was brave. In 1973, in the Vietnam War, we were fighting tanks. We put explosives in bunches of vegetables. We put the mine into a basket to make it explode on the road which the enemy tanks always came along.

[forceful]

In the day, we behaved like mothers and sisters. When night came, we went to destroy their look-out posts. We fought in unexpected ways. A beautiful make-up box was stuffed full of explosives, pushed into a handbag which we left where the soldiers were eating. Twenty minutes later, it would explode. Fighting that way unnerved the enemy, much more than the battle full of explosions.

SFX musical bridge fade up and hold under narration

(Carolina) El Salvador: I always wanted to join the fighting—to have a weapon. I never stopped to think I was going to die or anything like that. But, I was always afraid about being captured. I used to say I would prefer them to kill me rather than fall into the army's hands.

SFX fade up music and lose under narration

[with enthusiasm]

I used to like the uniform of blue jeans and beige shirt and the early weapons. When I joined the guerrilla I was 22 years old and I already knew how to handle all kinds of guns because my father used to own some. What I did want was to carry a machine gun and they let me. I had it for about seven months. We started from scratch and as the people started supporting us, things began coming together until we finally became an army for El Salvador.

I say all this because it is what I experienced personally and I loved it. I really wanted to become a guerrilla soldier because everything was done in the name of the people.

SFX fade up music to end naturally

(Agnes) Liberia: [with outrage] In Liberia, girls who trained to be soldiers went away for months. People didn't know what they'd be trained to do, until they came back with guns—we couldn't believe it! The women soldiers were very aggressive. If you were stopped at a checkpoint the way they treated you, if you were not strong, you would faint. Anything nice on you, they would take away, and give you the ragged clothes that they were wearing. And, they were very quick to kill. The least mistake you made, you were down.

Their aggression was mainly against other women. They'd strip you naked. They would shove a grenade somewhere up in your private parts. They would put their hands all where they're not supposed to go, saying they were looking for weapons. People were more afraid of them than the men, because they were so quick-tempered.

My dear, if I was one of them, I would definitely be ashamed because nobody expected a Liberian woman to be so brutal to her fellow Liberians.

They were very wicked, even towards babies and children. A woman is supposed to be somebody with a soft spot. Dur'n 1 '08

(Kokila) Sri Lanka: [with pride] Women should not become fighters—I used to think like that. But in the last 10 years, there has been an enormous change. Before the struggle started in Sri Lanka, our society was very conservative and rigid. Women had no place among men. They wouldn't even talk with their heads up. So who'd have thought that they would ever take up arms? But nowadays, we see young women in the battlefield fighting equally with the men. It's the need of the time. Now, women all over the world participate in armed struggles. So why not our women? Instead of dying screaming, being raped by an aggressor army, it is a relief to face the army with your own weapon.

SFX signature tune fade up and under narration

PAUSE ANNOUNCEMENT

You have been listening to the first part of the series Women and War. The series was financed by NOVIB, the Dutch NGO, and produced by World Radio for the Environment for the Panos Institute, who collected the testimonies and published the book Arms to Fight, Arms to Protect. We are grateful to the women whose testimonies you have heard.

SFX signature tune to end

Women and War Part 2

SFX signature tune, fade up and under narration

Introduction: Around the world, war continues to affect the lives of millions of people. But the impact of war, and its aftermath, on the lives of women often goes unheard. During conflict many women take on new roles and responsibilities, ensuring the survival of families and communities, even taking part in the fighting. When peace comes women are crucial to recovery, rebuilding damaged homes and livelihoods, caring for injured partners and relatives as well as their children. In this four-part programme we give voice to women's' testimonies, as they relate their experiences of war.

Women and War Part 2— Forced to flee. Dur'n 49

SFX Signature tune fade up and out

(Wadad) Lebanon: No one, no one can escape responsibility for conflict, nor its effects. I consider that everyone in my country participated in the war in the Lebanon, not just those who carried weapons. Even the person who sat at home, in his heart was happy for one side and shunning the other.

During the war I supported one side, I used to help in social things, cleaning-up campaigns, first aid. I had small children and I was afraid to do more. Adnan, my husband, was more active. [pause] He was kidnapped.

The few minutes after I expected his return became I don't know how many days before I truly realized what had happened. I began to check up with the authorities immediately. They said, "Poor Wadad, many others have complained before you." I wanted to know who these others were.

(Rita) Sri Lanka: My son was 22 when they took him away. He's one of the many in Sri Lanka who have "disappeared". I can still see him. I was with him when it happened. While we were coming back from the courthouse a white truck stopped. They held a gun to the chest of my son and took him. One of them held a pistol to my chest. My son. even after they drove off, was looking back to see if they'd shot me. I can still see him turning and looking at me. Dur'n 30

(Wadad) Lebanon; One day, I had an idea. There are many private radio stations, so I put a short notice on the air to the families of the kidnapped, calling them to meet. I was surprised at the numbers who turned up, hundreds.

The first thing in my head was that the people who were kidnapped have names. We started to make lists. We have the names of over 2000 people, and that's not all who are missing.

We put a lot of pressure on the government, and they set up a committee. We fought hard to be on this committee, but it was useless. The committee included the very people who were accused of ordering the kidnap pings.

(Manorani) Sri Lanka: Losing someone this way is a devastating sorrow because it is arbitrary—it's not like a person dying of an illness. And this terrible thing of the house being invaded, and your child pulled out of your arms at gunpoint. It's a denial of one's own right as a citizen.

Normally village women in Sri Lanka scream and cry, but those who have lost dear ones through abductions, disappearances and arrests—they have been denied that. Mostly there has been no funeral, no body to weep over. They've been deprived of showing sorrow. It's been suppressed. This is soul-destroying.

(Wadad) Lebanon: If someone's killed, it's easier than kidnapping when you don't know if he's alive or dead. You don't know how to deal with yourself. And what do you tell your children—do you give them hope that their father may come back? We used to reach a point where we just wanted to know. Even if there are only remains, we want the bones, something to hold onto.

We want to remove the traces of the war and forget the past, but you can't guarantee that this will be accepted by children who grew up without a father. Dur'n 29

Musical Bridge fade up and under narration

(Anon) Bosnia: We were all convinced that war wouldn't happen in Bosnia. Muslims, Croats and Serbs mixed. We lived in the same buildings, led the same lives—even married each other.

One evening the phone rang. It was my friend from the next town. She was shouting: "Run away, as soon as possible!"

My husband decided we should leave. It wasn't safe to drive a car. Anybody could stop you, take your car, rob you or kill you. When we got to the bus station, there was a large crowd. The bus couldn't leave because a line of army vehicles was passing by.

SFX convoy of army vehicles passing by fade up and under narration

I looked at the soldiers. I was thinking, thinking and watching. They were not young, but older and bearded, with weapons around their shoulders.

That was the first time I felt really frightened of that army. My husband and I are intellectuals, middle-class, middle-aged. How could we have been so naive? How come the example from Croatia did not tell us anything? With one suitcase and a little money we left town. My God! We thought we'd be back in a week! We didn't believe that the war could go on and on. Dur'n 36

(Ninnal) India: People talk of what has happened in Bosnia. but the Partition of India. into India and Pakistan—50 years ago—was the first mass movement of people in the name of religion. Millions of families found themselves on "the wrong side" of the new border. So they fled: Muslims to Pakistan; Hindus and Sikhs to India. We came over to this side— to India. My sister and my mother, we came over to escape from the panic, riots and the killing—just for 10 or 12 days, we thought—but we couldn't return, because they completely closed the border. My father was still on the other side in Pakistan. The local people looked at the refugees with great contempt saying "These refugees are a burden to us." They never wanted to help, except giving food when we arrived at the railway station. They didn't want us to settle there.

But, it is not a crime to become a refugee.

(Khadra) Somaliland: Of course it's not a crime to be a refugee—you try to stay in your own home as long as you can. The day the liberation fighters attacked Hargeisa, I was alone at home with my five children. We stayed there for six days, with shells and bullets everywhere. I finally had no choice, but to leave Somalia with my children.

(Eva) Croatia: With us, it was all so sudden.

SFX working in the fields, with army vehicles in the background and aero planes overhead fade up, then hold under narration

The Serbian tanks were on the road, the aero planes in the sky. We could see them attacking Vukovar as we were gathering the last crops in the fields.

SFX as before fade up and under

The explosions were so loud as the bombs fell, but we kept on working. I remember I was cooking tomatoes. There were hundreds of litres of tomato juice in bottles! That year there were so many tomatoes and onions, potatoes and beans, it was indescribable. It seems it always has to be that way—when evil or war are just around the comer.

When we were forced to flee we did not think we were leaving for ever, so I only took only a few things with me, including something to remind me of life at home. Among all the embroideries, I chose the last ones my mother had made—I couldn't leave them there.

(Khadra) Somaliland: As homeless people, we were unable to put our hands on any of the things we needed.

SFX sharing out food rations and refugee camp

Queuing up for rations took all day. Luckily, I had my mother to leave the children with. The agencies helping the refugees gave us gas and little stoves. But, we could not use them. The gas was very expensive for us. The agencies seemed unable to calculate how much gas families need. Like others, I gradually sold the gold I escaped with, so that the family could survive.

(Anon) Bosnia: The status of "'refugee" is given automatically when you cross the River Sava and Bosnia enter Croatia. My younger sister told me that as soon as they arrived in Croatia, her little boy got a high fever. They took him to a doctor. He wrote a diagnosis down on a card and that's when my sister saw for the first time the word "refugee" next to her name. She took it hard, almost harder than the child's illness.

(Anon) Nicaragua: When we first crossed the border from Nicaragua to Honduras, I felt that I was being torn apart, because leaving your country for a foreign land is like ripping out your soul. My mother stayed behind. Just a few days after we returned, she died. Because she said she was only waiting for her children to come home. As a refugee, in another country, they treat you very bad.

SFX children playing fade up then hold under narration

Our children were picked on . . . just for being Nicaraguan. They were mistreated in the schools. They told my little girl that Nicaraguans shouldn't open their mouths, that "the Nica" shouldn't participate. They were three hard years for us.

(Eva) Croatia: Here in a displacement centre in Zagreb, we're not a community anymore. Some of our relatives are here. My husband says it would be better for me to talk with people. But somehow, it's too much for me. People are greedy, wanting material things and money. We were very close once, living in the same neighbourhood in Bosnia, having coffee

together everyday. But, this life is different. Some of my neighbours are also here, but our relationships are terrible. Everybody is so selfish. Maybe it's the normal behaviour in a situation like ours.

But how can we ever live together again when we argue now about using the kitchen? There is so much rowing and swearing even over a packet of flour or sugar. They shout at the aid workers: "This man gets everything all the time!" But, all the things given to us now can't be compared with our property at home. I can't lose anything more now. Imagine! Fights about a litre of oil! Dur'n I'll

(Vidya) India: If someone was giving something out in the camp, we had to grab it. I find it difficult to cry and they find that odd about me. I told my relatives: "Look, I have work to do. I go here and there, I have children to bring up, so I will not cry."

[Indignant]

If I sit in a comer and cry, who'll feed these children. who'll look after them? My husband has been killed—slaughtered in the riots against the Sikhs, when Mrs. Gandhi was assassinated. At that time, this was the only reality—grab what you can! We had had no time to grieve.

SFX musical bridge fade up and under

(Zamzam) Somaliland: Becoming a refugee is awful. I felt completely disoriented—I had no sense of direction. It is something that you can never understand unless it happens to you.

(Mita) India: So I don't think any of us, even the best intentioned, have any idea of what the victims of conflict are feeling, what they need, who they need. Physical needs are met by the relief organizations and I think they are often met very well: food, clothing, blankets. They need so much more though.

I think we don't understand violence until it happens to us We did get some counselors, people who knew how to deal with depression, problems and grief. But I don't think even they were able to really understand.

SFX Signature tune fade up then hold under narration

PAUSE ANNOUNCEMENT

You have been listening to the second part of the series Women and War. The series was financed by NOVIB, the Dutch NGO, and produced by World Radio for the Environment for the Panos Institute, who collected the testimonies and published the book Arms to Fight, Arms to Protect. We are grateful to the women whose testimonies you have heard. Dur'n 22

SFX signature tune to end 1

Women and War Part 3

SFX signature tune fade up then hold under narration

Introduction: Around the world, war continues to affect the lives of millions of people. But the impact of war, and its aftermath, on the lives of women often goes unheard. During conflict, many women take on new roles and responsibilities, ensuring the survival of families and communities, even taking part in the fighting. When peace comes, women are crucial to recovery, rebuilding damaged homes and livelihoods, caring for injured partners and relatives as well as their children. In this four-part programme we give voice to women's' testimonies, as they relate their experiences of war.

Women and War Part 3 - Changed lives, changed relationships.

SFX signature tune fade up and out

Anon) Nicaragua: Now that the war is behind us—and I hope it never returns—I realize that the war has left a lot of casualties in Nicaragua, in terms of relationships. I married a calm and responsible man, and while he's still responsible, he's no longer calm. He's a person more given to violence than to tranquility, if I'm not around to calm him down. He's like a match being struck.

I think this is something that the war left with a lot of men and women. Men learned to use kicks and blows and, at times, they'd transfer these kicks and these blows to their relationships and partners. And even if sometimes they did not give the kick or the punch, they gave the blow with their vocabulary and their actions. In this sense, I think, the war worsened the behaviour of men, even more so for those who have always believed they are the Eighth Wonder of the World. "

(Shirley) Liberia: Before the war, a typical Liberian man would like to take care of his girlfriend the best he could. Now, since the war, some men can't afford to look after their girlfriends. The love is there, the will is there, but their hands are tied. It's just a silent understanding between men and women now. And let me tell you this: To be a refugee in Africa, on our own continent, is bad.

SFX refugee camp fade up then hold under narration

Here I am. No husband. Kids to look after. Nobody to assist. Being a single mother here in a refugee camp in Nigeria has made me very, very strong. I can make it without a man. Liberian men have more respect for women, as a result of our new found strength. We are still precious jewelry to them even though they have little to offer us.

(Agnes) Liberia: [with scorn] My sister, you women in the camps may think Liberian men see you as precious jewelry, but those of us who stayed in Liberia see things very differently. During the war, women were treated like chickens, you know, to buy and sell, our bodies were exchanged for food. The rebels were in charge of all the food in the country at that time. The women that had pride and respect for themselves would rather die from hunger. But, if you wanted to live, you had to make a deal with a rebel.

These days, the relationship between men and women is strictly financial. We believe in the barter system that started during the war. My dear, you get the pleasure of my body and I get the pleasure of your pocket. I trust no man. In Monrovia now, you don't trust nobody. If I say I have any true love for anybody, I'll be lying. If you tell me you love me, I'll tell you I love you, but I'm in your pocket.

War made me kind of independent. I don't care any more what people think about me. I please myself.

(Amina) Somaliland: In Somaliland, the war has changed women's lives a lot. Before, the number of women who worked was limited. War has forced them out of the house. The one who has children is working to provide for them, and the one who has none has to work for herself

(Shirley) Liberia: Wars open everybody's eyes. Even the babies being born are aware. We women are going to speak out for our rights. Even now,

we've made a start by setting up a women's group. Liberian women be-
fore, I must admit we were very lazy. Our attitude was, "Me, go to the
market and sell?!" But now, in this refugee camp in Nigeria I've seen very
well educated West African women—some with masters degrees—on the
move, I said, "When I get back to Liberia, I'm very sure that women are
going to sit in some of the ministries, heading the ministries."

(Amina) Somaliland: Jobs for men in Somaliland are very scarce. Women
are forced to resort to little jobs, but men want substantial work. One
woman brings a few clothes from Djibouti, another sits on a street selling
a little bit of food. Men do not want to do this kind of trade; they do not
seem to be able to cope with it.

(Gopi) India: Before the riots against the Sikh community in Delhi, our
men used to earn and us women would keep the house, but now it is all
on one person. We are all widows now. In the early days, when we were
alone, we used to feel very scared. But, gradually I have learnt how to
cope on my own.

SFX Typists at work fade up then hold under narration

In the beginning, my brother would take me and leave me at work. For a
few months, it was quite difficult, but my office people were very kind
from the start. Now, I like going to work—even one day at home hangs
heavy! Going out, meeting people, talking, all this helps to take away
some of what I feel inside. The unhappiness goes away.

SFX musical bridge fade up and under

(Zamzam) Somaliland: War may change women's roles in society, but
maintaining these gains is difficult, especially when women are still not
consulted, not able to make decisions, even about the things which con-
cern them alone.

[sarcastic]

Outside agencies look at what they have been told is the "culture" and
conclude, "In this country, we must listen to men." No matter if the man
spends all day chewing too much qat, he does not work, he does not go
out and has no idea how his wife and children are doing. He is the one
who will be allowed to make the decisions. So, I feel no matter how active
women are economically, it won't last, because they're locked out of the

decision-making. They are not the ones who will sit under a tree deciding if there should be a war or peace.

(Olga) Uganda: Here in Uganda, we too felt the war had nothing to do with us—we had no power to end it. But what we have found since the war—is strength in working in groups. A lot of us are widows because our husbands got killed. And of the men who survived the wars, a lot of them are not being of much use to their wives either—most of them have become drunkards. It seems like they have lost their way, there's no cattle for them to trade, hardly any jobs.

SFX women working together in fields fade up and under

Now we women are carrying out many collective activities, digging, different ways of generating income and constant discussions among ourselves. But, I wasn't educated to take on such responsibilities. My father was a strong believer in traditions. Like most people at that time, he thought it was useless educating girls, because he thought educated women become prostitutes. Dur'n 29

(Rose) Uganda: Now, I have come to realize that the whole society was wrong in such thinking in Uganda because experience shows that most men and boys have become useless, while the women are very responsible and supportive to their families and even to their parents and other relatives. While I tried to work hard, my husband was very lazy. When I tried to talk to him about what we could do together in order to pay school fees, he would complain I was trying to dominate him. I, then, started struggling on my own to support my children. After the fighting ceased, since the man continued in his [with humour] irresponsible life, I found there was no point in keeping him, so I left him.

(Anon) Nicaragua: The war created a lot of difficulties for my marriage, but I'm glad we've managed to stay together. But truly, during the time of war, it is hard to be a couple. I'd say our relationship was more of friendship. Obviously, after the war ended, we got over that. But women's roles had changed a bit: women who had never had any experience of work outside the home were forced to by the war. Dur'n 29

SFX women sharing out tools fade up then hold under narration

After the war, I must have seen more than half of the women around me continue with their new roles. They realized that they were not just an ob-

ject in the home, that they were not just mothers, not just wives serving their husband's food, taking care of the house, but that they could feel much more productive, participating in the community in other ways. Of course, some didn't want to or perhaps it wasn't because they didn't want to, but because they were so used to being submissive—the woman at home and the man in the street. I think that Nicaraguan society changed a lot with the war, because some of us woke up.

(Vidya) India: In earlier times, before the riots, before we became widows, we had never actually gone out without our husbands. Going to work was the first time we were out on our own. There were a couple of stray incidents in the office in the early days—but not now.

SFX Bus fade up then hold under narration

Yes, when we traveled in buses and were in with crowds, there were men who used to touch us and make us feel dirty. So when we came back from work, we used to sit and talk about it, and we would laugh and be serious and share what happened to us. . . . and that way, by sharing and support, you would conquer your own doubts and fear. And gain courage.

[humour]

Yes, we have shouted at people in buses, we have even hit them!

(Amina) Somaliland: Since the war began, women seem to be better at work than men. Men seem to have lost their direction, lost confidence in their abilities to maintain their families. If only men were working as hard as women, I think Somaliland would have made much progress by now.

(Marie) Lebanon): But in some ways, war is easier for women. Whatever the situation, even in shelters, we are busy, looking after the children, managing the house. Men, meanwhile, have lost their role, if they can't go out to work. When we were here, with relatives who had taken refuge with us from East Beirut, I wouldn't let anyone touch the dishes, for instance. We had very little water, and washing up with little water is difficult, but I was determined to keep control of everything. When we didn't have any bread, and there wasn't any electricity for the oven, I found a recipe for making bread in a frying pan; that seemed a very exciting achievement at the time. But maybe I wouldn't be saying all this if I and my family were still suffering. War is a different experience for different people.

SFX signature tune then bold under narration

The real experience of war is not the shelling, those are just moments. War is what happens afterwards, the years of suffering hopelessly with a disabled husband and no money, or struggling to rebuild when all your property has been destroyed.

SFX signature tune fade up and hold under narration

PAUSE ANNOUNCEMENT

You have been listening to the third part of the series Women and War. The series was financed by NOVIB, the Dutch NGO, and produced by World Radio for the Environment for the Panos Institute, who collected the testimonies and published the book Arms to Fight, Arms to Protect. We are grateful to the women whose testimonies you have heard. Dur'n 22

SFX signature tune to end .

Women and War part 4

SFX Signature tune fade the hold under narration

Introduction: Around the world, war continues to affect the lives of millions of people. But the impact of war, and its aftermath, on the lives of women often goes unheard. During conflict many women take on new roles and responsibilities, ensuring the survival of families and communities, even taking part in the fighting. When peace comes women are crucial to recovery, rebuilding damaged homes and livelihoods, caring for injured partners and relatives as well as their children. In this four-part programme we give voice to women's' testimonies, as they relate their experiences of war.

Women and War Part 4 - Picking up the pieces.

SFX signature tune fade up and out

(Laure) Lebanon: In the beginning, all the protests against the war came from women. So it was a women's movement, but we were always calling

on men as well. Above all, we insisted on including all religions; nothing was done without representatives from all of them.

People feel that it was "other people's war," and they say the government is responsible for peace. But, it is us, the citizens of Lebanon. We are responsible for the peace.

(Maria) Nicaragua: In Nicaragua, women have had a lot to do with the work of reconciliation. Nicaraguan society had reached a point where we believed that everything could be solved through fighting—we've had to change that. It begins with the smallest step, convincing the man of the house, convincing the son, the uncle, the cousin, that violence is not the solution.

(Laure) Lebanon: In wanting peace, we had to ask ourselves what we are doing towards it? How are we educating our children for peace? My husband and I are Catholics, but we gave our children Arab names which don't show their religious identity. Recently, someone came to talk with my grandchildren who are Christians. He said to Ziad, who is eight, "Do you have friends who are Muslims?" Ziad said, "I have never asked them. They are just like me . I don't know who is Christian and who is Muslim." I was proud of him for saying so.

So this is something that we can do within our family. But, outside the family women are absent from power—from politics, from unions. Women weren't among those who decided on the war. But, if we had been in the centres of power, what would we have decided? One mustn't be too optimistic.

(Manorani) Sri Lanka: But, I feel women should have been the pushers in the peace process. After all, we understand what conflict means to a family. Look at the wives and mothers on both sides in Sri Lanka—they all suffer. All women shed the same tears.

(Maria) Nicaragua: There are mothers who don't even know where their sons died, where they were captured, who took them. Whatever side they are on, they feel the same pain as I do—the pain of having lost your dearest possession—your son.

[with strength]

We cannot go on feeling hatred for another mother. We must give them our hands and help those who have most hurt us. If we want a dignified peace, if we want reconciliation, we cannot hold on to these hatreds.

SFX musical bridge fade up and under

(Manorani) Sri Lanka: "Women are the ultimate victims of political violence"—that's my battle cry. Take any war, the women have to bear the brunt of it and carry on, cope with the children, cope with the unemployed man who gets frustrated.

When my son was killed, I was so much better off than the women isolated in the villages. At least, I could talk about the tragedy and express my point of view. That kept my sanity. Since then, I've set up a group to help families on both sides. The need for counseling is not always seen from the outside. There could be many who secretly weep tears into their pillows.

You have to try not to get destroyed. I believe always give expression to grief, work through it. You can convert that emotion into something positive, make a life for yourself, building the old life into the present.

(Cannen) El Salvador: Yes, we must continue our struggle— not through arms, but through our voices, through our thoughts. It's been hard for us Salvadorans. It's been difficult to get people organized, particularly as far as the women are concerned.

I've learnt to speak out, you have to. After the war, we had been given land. At first, they didn't include me on the lists, it was only my husband who was included. One day, the man who was dealing with the land arrived, and I asked: "Who's on the list? You must include me, because my husband might be here today and gone tomorrow,

[with an air of triumph]

but I'll always be here with the children—I will be left with nothing. I am their mother." Eventually—they put my name down.

SFX musical bridge fade up and under

(Katarina) Croatia: I experienced the beginning of the war in Yugoslavia as a very painful awakening. For me, it was like receiving personal news

about my own responsibility, since my not speaking up for peace had probably contributed to the fact that today we have a society like this one. It was a painful experience.

The first phase I had to go through was facing the fear—a terrible fear of physical suffering, killing and disability. This fear nearly emptied the city, but those who remained built an incredibly solid community of resistance. When the heavy shelling stopped and people started corning back, those who had remained and had gone through terrible situations together found themselves frustrated, because they couldn't cope with the loss of that solidarity.

We've had to find out how to show our resistance towards the violence. It wasn't only the violence imposed on us from outside, it was also spreading among us, within our community. We wanted to break this spiral of hatred, revenge, and fear.

(Wadad) Lebanon: The damage is done in Lebanon, all that's happened to the country, in victims and ruins and twisting of minds. But, the more dangerous thing I fear is that we're building for a new war. This is a booby-trapped peace. It's not enough that I see beautiful skyscrapers, and a highway that extends from the sea to the Gulf, and bridges and tunnels and mobile phones. In the end, if we only rebuild the stone and sand and steel, if we don't rebuild the people first, what's going to happen to us? The reform of the people is much more important because eventually they'll be the ones who will rebuild the country. Let me feel I am a human being with my dignity and my rights, before they build buildings that my eyes cannot reach the top of.

(Jenneth) Uganda: Things are okay right now in Uganda and I am optimistic that this peace will continue. However, the children we are bringing up these days are disobedient. They are lovers of guns and violence. We, parents, have a big task to change this attitude of our children. Dur'n 17

SFX children playing fade up and under

(Easter) Uganda: It is children without parents, the orphans, that really suffer. They have a lot of mental torture and it's not very easy to handle them. Some of them roam about and are very violent; some live by stealing in order to survive.

(Agnes) Liberia: I'm damn scared for my sisters and my brothers who are young. I don't want them to turn out to be criminals. I'm scared that we won't have any good leaders in the future because it will be the same old people coming back into office. The only thing I will advise a Liberian girl to do is to go to school and learn enough that you won't have to listen to anybody telling you garbage, because after this war we are going to receive a lot of garbage. Dur'n 28

SFX children playing fade up and under

(Mita) India: It really is children that are so important. I worked to help the widows of men killed in the riots in Delhi. We felt that not one of the organizations there paid enough attention to the children. I just didn't want to leave them alone, whether they were from families of the attacked or the attackers, because they were all just as terrified and just as traumatized. There was this one child, Suresh, he become very violent. He wasn't from the Sikh community, but we found out he lived next to the drain, where all the men who'd been killed were thrown. Witnessing those bodies was too much for him.

(Thorn) Vietnam: You worry about the impact conflict has had on your children. For me, the greatest sadness is that I will never be a mother. Men who were wounded like me are still able to marry, and when they get ill, their wives and children can help. I, I am still single and I live with my old mother.

[with despair]

I have had several operations, but my injuries will not heal- the doctors can't remove all the pieces of the bomb. When I had to go back to hospital, I stayed there alone, because my mother is too old and my brothers have their own families. I only want to die, but how can I?

(Sabaah) Somaliland: My husband died fighting in the war in Somaliland. The memory of him touches me with a pain beyond imagination. But I tell myself be patient: we will realize the fruits of his sacrifice, the country will settle down and eventually good will triumph. I am always full of hope.

SFX musical bridge fade up and under

(Jenny) Nicaragua: You have to look to the future. My aspirations, in the first place, are for peace in Nicaragua. If there's a war, there's no future. Secondly, I'd like to find some way of improving myself as a woman. I think women should never say I'm too old to do this or that. We, women, must always go forwards, forwards. Why should we go backwards, or even sideways—we're not like crabs on a beach! Look, whether it's a man or a woman. the person who doesn't have aspirations is like the living dead. No, I say, you have to die fighting for something, learning something, finding ways of improving yourself.

SFX musical bridge fade up and under

(Esmeralda) El Salvador: I feel we have learned something about what living in this country is about—how some El Salvador people in El Salvador have more opportunities than others. I have also learned how to work, how not to be self-conscious. I have stopped being afraid. I have learned to speak out in front of people, to know more things, both about others as well as about myself. Because there are a lot of things one doesn't know, that one's ignorant about, superstitious. I know now what is true.

SFX musical bridge fade up and under

For the coming generations, it's important they understand what we've been through, so that they don't repeat what has taken place. So, may the new generation be more aware and may the gains of our generation be continued by them. If we forget history, we forget everything.

PAUSE ANNOUNCEMENT

You have been listening to the last part of the series Women and War.

(SFX music fade up under narration and hold)

The series was financed by NOVIB, the Dutch NGO, and produced by World Radio for the Environment for the Panos Institute, who collected the testimonies and published the book Arms to Fight, Arms to Protect. We are grateful to the women whose testimonies you have heard.

SFX music to end

10
Medicine by Radio
—The Story of How 40,000 African Women Learned To Prevent Diarrheal Dehydration on the Radio—

Radio Program: The Gambia, West Africa. 1981. Broadcast originally in Wolof.

Woman: I learned that one of the best ways to keep my babies happy and healthy is to remember the diet that stops dryness, breast milk, solid food for babies, and especially sugar and salt mixture which is made from three Julpearl bottles of water, one leveled bottle cap of salt, and 8 leveled bottle caps of sugar.

Woman 1: And with that you can help to keep your baby free from diarrhea and give yourself the very special prize of a healthy happy baby.

Woman: Thank you very much Fatou for telling me that.

Woman1: My pleasure Marianne. Good-bye!

Woman: Good-bye!

In 1924, Americans were learning how to bake cakes, cook meals, and measure ingredients by listening to radio shows like Betty Crocker, Gold Medal Flour, and Home Service Talks. In the America of 2004 these shows seem corny—replaced by rap music, TV infomercials. But radio's power to teach as well as entertain remains critical.

In Africa, 1981, the problem was not cake mix, but the survival of millions of infants. Children throughout the developing world experience 6-10 prolonged bouts of diarrhea in their first year of life. As children come off the protection of breast milk and begin to drink well water and eat solid foods, their digestive systems have no natural defenses against the myriad of attacking bacteria. Eighty percent of an infant's body is water. A child with diarrhea can become seriously dehydrated in a matter of hours. In a society where intravenous rehydration is rare, thousands, indeed millions, of children will die of diarrheal dehydration. A practical answer to diarrheal dehydration was found in Bangladesh in the 1950s. It was called ORS or oral rehydration solution; a balanced electrolyte solution of water, sugar, and salt, properly proportioned and given one teaspoon at a time. For the first time in human history, mothers would have the ability to prevent dehydration at home.

But "dehydration" was unknown to mothers throughout the world; they would have to learn that ORS cured a problem they did not know existed. Mothers also had to get the ratios of sugar, salt, and water right: too much salt and the child would die; too much sugar and the dehydration would increase. ORS was not a medical break-through unless mothers had the motivation and the skills to mix and give it to their child in a safe and timely manner.

The Gambia is one of Africa's smallest countries—640,000 people in 1981. Many readers may know The Gambia as the home of Kunta Kinte, the fictional star of *Roots,* Alex Haley's famous sojourn to uncover the origins of slavery in America. The Gambia is a small country surrounding a mighty river. For 50 miles into the heart of Africa, the narrow country hugs the Gambia river; straddling its waters for no more than 25 miles on either side.

The Gambia of 1981 was different from that of Kunta Kinte's Gambia of 1733. In 1981, there was electricity in the capital city, Banjul. There were western style Ministries of Education and Health and Police. In the village there was now a water pump, a small store with soap, aspirin, and perhaps a bottle of soda pop. In the home, there was radio: a single national radio station, plus two smaller commercial stations that broadcast mighty signals over the river-dominated country.

If there were changes in The Gambia since 1733—there were also things that had changed very little. Most Gambians still lived in villages— clusters of huts called "compounds" —that wound through unpaved streets more like patios between the crowded compounds. Within these family compounds, there was the same cacophony of cultures and language that also existed 200 years before. The Gambia was a society of three primary language groups: Fula, Mandinka, and Wolof, plus five or six smaller ones. It was also a polygamous society. A man might have 3 to 5 wives and marry women from different language groups. This meant that the wives might actually be unable to communicate with any of the other spouses.

There was a highly respected village chief, the gatekeeper of local culture and an arbiter of outside influence. Nothing serious could happen in a Gambian village without the chief's knowledge and permission that it was acceptable.

If mothers were to mix the sugar, salt, and water needed to make ORS correctly, they would need some standard measuring tool and mixing vessels. No Betty Crocker teaspoon was available here. Indeed, there were few standard objects of any kind. Even the widespread beer bottle found in many parts of Africa was uncommon in the traditional Islamic culture. Julpearl, a locally bottled, sweet soda pop was the bottled drink of choice and the only reliable measurement tool available.

In 1981, a program called Mass Media and Health Practices, was funded by USAID and managed by the Academy for Educational Development. It worked with the Ministry of Health in The Gambia to promote the effective and safe use of Oral Rehydration Solution (ORS) in villages throughout the country. A standard formula for ORS was developed using the Julpearl soda pop bottle and the Julpearl bottle cap as measurement and mixing tools. One liter of the solution is made using 3 Julpearl bottles of water, 8 Julpearl caps of sugar, and 1 Julpearl cap of salt.

But how could thousands of women learn such a complicated formula in only a few months? How would men in a male-dominated society give women the permission to learn such innovation? How would women get a chance to practice mixing the ORS so they could learn through practice as well as memory? How could women come to feel confident, at the moment their child comes down with diarrhea, to use a simple mixture of sugar, salt, and water for such a serious disease? Most important, how would it be possible to remember the strange, nonsensical proportions—3 bottles of water, 8 caps of sugar, and 1 cap of salt?

The answer to all questions was a program called the "Happy Baby Lottery." And radio was the heart of the answer.

On the radio:

Mother: When I went to the Happy Baby Lottery contest, this is what I did: I washed my hands, took a clean bowl, clean water and a clean Julpearl bottle. I measured 3 Julpearl bottles of water filled to the top, and poured it into the bowl, 8 leveled bottle caps of sugar, and poured it into the water, and 1 leveled bottle cap of salt, and poured it into the water. Then I mixed it until it dissolved. Then the judge asked me how to give the mixture to my child. I should give him all the mixture, that is, the 3 Julpearl bottles in 24 hours. I should wait a while and give it

*to him again. I should make a fresh mixture everyday. I am happy I
have won this radio cassette which I am going to use to listen to the
health radio program. I'll always invite the other women in our com-
pound to listen.*

The central idea of the "Happy Baby Lottery" was to provide an intense
period of radio education in ORS. It used graphic materials, radio messages, face-to-face instruction, and simple incentives (lottery prizes communities could win if their women could prepare the sugar salt solution) to
encourage mothers to take part in this educational process.

Tam tam...wollof!

*Announcer: Hello and welcome to the 24th edition of our health program
"datakandea"—The Happy Baby Lottery.*
Baby laughing . . . coughing . . .
*Announcer: Last Saturday night, the president's wife Lady Jennie Jaora,
announced in the last edition of this program, the names of the winners in the Happy Baby Lottery. Fifteen women won individual prizes of
radio cassette players, five villages won the community prizes of a bag
of rice and a bag of sugar.*
*Mother: You have brought us a bag of sugar and a bag of rice which we
appreciate very much but you have also given us something more
valuable than the bag of sugar and the bag of rice, that is the knowledge we have gained to mix the sugar and salt solution, and how to
administer the solution. You have given us this prize but it should have
been the reverse, because we have benefited a lot from the campaign.*

Specifically, the Lottery motivated mothers to seek out a colorful 8 x
11 handbill showing the Julpearl formula and to listen to a special series of
radio programs that explained how to interpret the handbill and how to use
it to mix and administer the solution. Four months of prior radio broadcasting had told mothers of the special danger of diarrhea, namely dehydration, and had introduced the sugar-salt solution as a way to prevent it.
A series of training workshops for 150 key health personnel throughout
the country had also been held to ensure that the campaign's radio messages would receive personal reinforcement from health workers in the
field.

tam tam...drum beat- calling people to listen

Woman: Hello Fatou! How are you?

Woman1: Hello Marianne! I am fine and you?

Woman: Fine thank you. Have you been listening to the radio lately?

Woman1: Do you mean have I been listening to the Happy Baby Lottery?

Woman: Yeah.

Woman1: Yes I have, it was very exciting, even though I did not win a prize.

Woman: I am sure you could have won a prize if the judge had come to our village Fatou. You know all about the sugar and salt mix that can save babies from diarrhea. And you also know all the five points about how to give them the mixture correctly.

Woman 1: I am sure Marianne, there are lots of mothers who know all these things and who did not even have a chance to win a prize.

Woman: I think that it's a pity. It would be good if everybody who knew these things could win a prize.

Woman1: But don't you think in a way everyone does win a prize?

Woman: Oh, I had not heard about it. How does everyone win a prize Fatou?

The Lottery worked as follows: an estimated 200,000 handbills or "mixing-pictures" as they were called, would be delivered by the Mass Media Project staff to approximately 20 health centers and dispensaries throughout the country. The local government health workers would give out a portion of these to mothers at the health centers. The rest would be delivered to a network of some 800 village volunteers, the "Red Flag Ladies", who had been trained by the health workers as village "diarrhea experts" following their own training at the Project's workshops.

On Radio:

Red Flag Lady: I showed them how to mix the sugar and salt solution with 3 Julperal bottles of water, 1 leveled bottle cap of salt, and 8 leveled bottle caps of sugar. All the women can now do it. We are very happy, because our babies are now safe from the dryness that goes with diarrhea.

An extensive publicity campaign about the Lottery began on Radio Gambia in four local languages—Wolof, Mandinka, Fula, and Serehule. It explained that the mixing-picture was to be used as a "ticket" for entering the Happy Baby lottery and encouraging all women to obtain one. Appealing to pride, men were told to be sure their wives got a ticket for their family and for their village. A series of radio programs interpreting the mixing-picture on the lottery ticket and explaining key points of giving the sugar-salt solution would be aired throughout the Lottery period at regularly scheduled times.

The distribution of the mixing-picture tickets would be followed by the Lottery's core activity once each week for four weeks. The names of 18 villages from all over the country would be drawn randomly and announced over the radio. Each of these villages would be visited by a contest judge, one of the local health workers. Every woman in the village who came to the contest with a mixing-picture in hand would be eligible to enter an initial drawing, conducted by a judge. The drawing would choose 20 women who would then have a chance to show their mixing knowledge in front of the whole village. Each of the 20 women who correctly demonstrated for the judge how to mix the sugar-salt solution would win a prize—a one-liter plastic cup. If she could also correctly answer at least three out of five questions about how to administer the solution, she could win a second prize as well—a bar of locally made soap. She would also become eligible for the Grand Prize Drawing: a special one-hour program, broadcast on Radio Gambia. At that time, the First Lady of Gambia would draw and announce the winners of 15 radio-cassette players from among the village contest winners. Five community prizes, consisting of a 50-kg bag of sugar and a 100-kg bag of rice each, also would be awarded to the villages that had participated most actively in the village contests. But what happened to villages that were never visited and women who didn't win a prize?

On the radio:

Woman 1: Well, the real prize that comes from having a mixing picture and using it to know how to mix the sugar and salt solution, is that you will always know how to help your baby get better if he gets diarrhea.
Woman: I don't think that that's the real prize. It's not a prize like a radio cassette player.
Woman: But Marianne, you must remember that God has given our children a very special gift, so the best way to thank God for the special gift of children is to keep them as happy and healthy as we can.

September and October were chosen for the lottery because it is a time when most of the rainy season's planting has been completed and women have some leisure time. It is also a time when rainy-season diarrhea is at its peak and the Lottery's educational message was most needed and could be expected to arouse high interest among the rural audience.

Radio taught women to mix the ORS solution through nightly broadcasts. Radio told them about "Red Flag Ladies" in their community, women who had trained and were given the red flag to fly above their homes. Women who could help them practice mixing the solution. It congratulated communities on their success and radio put the voice of a successful woman in every village to encourage even more women to use the water, sugar, and salt solution.

Africa 1981 – Radio Gambia broadcast:

Man: According to the Koran, the first thing that God says is that the Koran is very strong, and it contains the secrets of mankind, therefore nobody is allowed to touch the Koran if you are not clean. God said that before you pray to him, you should be clean first. And I think in this way, people are also preventing diseases. If a person is not clean, he is not accepted by God, and is not free from diseases. Cleanliness brings good health and builds up a good relationship between a person and God.

Stanford University's Institute for Communication Research studied 21 rural villages in The Gambia, concurrent with the project's implementation, to assess whether the 'Happy Baby Lottery' worked or failed. The Centers for Disease Control conducted a parallel investigation. The success of the 'Happy Baby Lottery" was measured by the numbers of mothers who: 1) heard the Lottery programs; 2) obtained and learned how to use the mixing-picture; and, 3) learned how to mix and give the sugar-salt solution as a result of the Lottery. The evaluation team reported that after less than a year of programming 60% of all mothers in the Gambia named the sugar-salt solution as the *"preferred treatment for diarrhea"* and 40% were able to cite correctly the Julpearl bottle and-cap formula. In 1981, no one in the Gambia had ever heard of rehydration much less believed ORS to be the preferred treatment for diarrhea. Once again radio combined with culturally sensitive, ingenious programming showed the way to large-scale success even in the most limited and difficult of conditions.

The second most important lesson of this effort occurred as an unexpected "natural" experiment. Because of the oil crisis of the late 80s, Radio Gambia had to cut back broadcasting drastically. The ORS message disappeared for months and at the end of a year many of the learning gains had been lost. As stressed throughout this book, even the most successful program rarely survives without constant reinforcement. The lesson of development is also the lesson of sustained messaging and the critical role radio can play in keeping an idea, a service, a new behavior alive and well.

11
So The World Turns
—The Insidious March of HIV-AIDS—

The neighborhood is quiet, night has fallen, there is no moon, people are watchful. At a dock in the port of Los Angeles, the watchman on patrol runs a radiation detector alongside a just arrived metal container. In the neighborhood, it is a prowler or in the worst case, a killer. In the United States, thirty thousand people die by homicide yearly. In the case of the port, our attentiveness to port security evokes the specter of terrorism, 3,000 people died in an act of terrorism visited on New York City and Washington D.C. on September 11, 2001. Our fears in the face of these two ever-present dangers are constant, our responses vigilant and costly in terms of social resources. But, how much more of an insidious killer lurks in the HIV virus?

Slightly more than twenty years after the first discovery of the virus' ravages, more than 65 million people have been infected; 25 million people have died of HIV-AIDS. Soon the virus will have accounted for more deaths than occurred during all of World War II. Every day more than 14,000 people are infected, that is more than four times the number of deaths at the WTC and Pentagon. Ninety-five (95%) percent of infections occur in developing countries. HIV-AIDS is now the leading cause of death in Africa and the fourth leading cause of death worldwide behind heart attacks, cancer and tuberculosis. War for all its horror hardly makes this list. Terrorism? Forget it. It is not a clear and present danger on this scorecard.

The distribution of HIV-AIDS around the world is uneven. In the U.S., some progress was made early on in containing the disease, but it now appears to have made a resurgence. The number of deaths in the U.S. peaked in 1993 at 40,000, almost as many in one year—two thirds of the total—as in the entire Vietnam War, but it is slowly regaining its peak level after several years of decline. Still by comparison with the developing world, its impact is less invasive, affecting one million people in the U.S. and Canada but only a small percent of the population.

The effect of HIV-AIDS on poor countries with fewer resources to address the problem, however, has been dramatic. In seven sub-Saharan African nations, more than twenty percent of the population is infected with HIV-AIDS. In South Africa, AIDS is so widespread that children now play a game called "funerals".[1] The pandemic has made significant inroads in South and South East Asia (7.2 million people infected), is growing in India (3.97 million) and China (1 million) and on a rapidly growing path in the former Soviet Union and Eastern Europe (1.2 million). Having made in-roads later in some of these countries, it has yet to reach the proportions it has achieved in Africa, but may soon do so if more is not done to stem the disease's progress.

More deadly than street crime or terrorism? Certainly, but not for all that has this grim reaper of families shown itself in the sights of our valiant political leadership. They appear to have left this battlefield to our public enemies, free from the patriotic and vitriolic rhetoric they reserve for more petty crimes.

The international community has begun to pay attention to this silent killer in our midst. As it has done so, it has turned to mass communications and the radio in a belated recognition of its power to reach the poor. Has it done so to the extent the problem warrants or at the level of attention paid to other perceived plagues of our time, crime or terrorism? We will let the reader judge this ultimately political question. However, while the politicians have dithered, communities have organized. They have used the means at their disposal to communicate among themselves about the dangers they face. And they have turned to their friends and partners to help them do so.

Population Communications International (PCI) has been assisting communities as they carry on discussions relating family choice to resources and community prerogatives for over two decades. In Africa, Asia, Latin America and the United States, PCI, with a handful of other organizations, has been in the forefront of public communication about communities and families.

A growing body of evidence shows what has been self-evident since the advent of the crisis, the effectiveness of the radio in making people aware of and helping them to address public health issues such as HIV-AIDS. In Mali, a study carried out by the US Demographic Health Survey in 1996 found that the radio was the principal source of HIV-AIDS information, outstripping friends, relatives and public health services. A Save the Children Survey of 2,000 individuals in the region around Mopti, also in Mali, confirmed these findings. A World Health Organization study carried out during the same time period found mass-media by far the cheapest way to carry out HIV-AIDS education.[2]

Here is an example of a PCI-assisted radio drama from Kenya Broadcasting Corporation, helping the Kenyan community discuss issues of adolescent sexuality, female circumcision, the status of women, drug abuse, family planning maternal and child health and, of course, awareness of HIV-AIDS. The episode includes one of the most dramatic moments in the HIV-AIDS engendered saga, the disclosure to one's beloved of an HIV positive test.

Imagine the learning power of this real human drama as it provides a caution to some and a guidepost to others. Imagine the power of being able to reach potentially 90% of a nation of 30 million on Monday and Wednesday evenings and with a rebroadcast Saturday afternoon. Such is the power of "Ushikwapo Shikamana" (Once Helped, Help Yourself!) on Kenyan radio. An episode follows:

USHIKWAPO SHIKAMANA EPISODE 268

Scene I:

Setting: At Chezi's home, Chezi soothing her granddaughter, as her husband Gogo and Mchikichi, a neighbor, enter.

Sound effect: child crying; noises made by domestic animals . . .

Gogo: (Confirming what he had said) Do you hear the child? As I told you, she cries all the time. She is a real pain!

Mchikichi: She cannot just cry for nothing. There must be a reason . . . something must be bothering her.

Gogo: What would bother her?

Mchikichi: It could be anything. Maybe she is experiencing some pains?

Gogo: She is as fit as a fiddle! She is just being stubborn.

Mchikichi: Tell me, what name did you give her?

Gogo: She is named Chezi, after my wife, but mmh . . . she cries too much!!

Mchikichi: Maybe she is rebelling against the name; that's why she cries incessantly

Gogo: (cutting him short; agitated) Then she must really be cheating herself . . . what other name would she want? Let her dare! Not in the house of Gogo wa Jabali. the custodian of culture and tradition. She must bear the name Chezi. for that is our tradition.

Mchikichi: Would she cease being your granddaughter if you called her by any other name?

Gogo: This is your weakness, Mchikichi. You want to pretend that you don't understand our culture?

Mchikichi: Gogo . . . Things change with time; it's time we discarded harmful cultural beliefs.

Gogo: Hold it! Which are these harmful beliefs? If they were harmful, would you be here now after being brought up on them?

Mchikichi: You believe I was brought up under those beliefs?

Gogo: You didn't know? It is a requirement that the child be named after somebody. That is our tradition here at Langoni. This is Chezi and if it was a boy, he would have been named Gogo. That is the essence of being a Mlangoni. It will never change.

Mchikichi: Then your child will have to beget many children if he is to name them after you, your wife then her mother and father . . . then the uncles, aunts even grandparents and most likely other relatives. Don't you think? ∴ . .

Gogo: (interjects) What's wrong with that? If she is fertile enough to give birth and name the whole clan, very good. That is the role of women . . . to give birth! (Child continues crying. Gogo raises voice and calls) Chezi! . . . Pangupangu's mother . . . what's wrong with your friend?

Chezi: (off mike) Heh! It's good you are back (brief silence - on mike) Let me tell you, since you left. the baby has been crying as if possessed.

Gogo: Why didn't you take her to the mother?

Chezi: Ah! Gogo. where do I trace the mother?

Mchikichi: You mean that the mother is away?

Gogo: What would she be doing here? Her work is over. She just deposited her child here and off she went to get another one.

Chezi: No Gogo, this child's mother has gone for studies; that is, she is in school now.

Mchikichi: You mean she was not married to Pangupangu?

Gogo: Since when? They were just buddies and this is the outcome. We, as grandparents, are now burdened with a girl child to bring up. The parents are nowhere to be seen: they are living the high life.

Chezi: When I gave birth to sons, you boasted all over Langoni that you had no daughter's who could get pregnant. Well, enjoy the fruits of your son!

Gogo: Despite this small problem, the home belongs to us men not the women. This is Gogo's home not Chezi's!

Mchikichi: By this do you mean that the child should be abandoned because it is a girl?

Gogo: Let her go to her maternal relatives; girls are just too expensive to bring up. They are not worh the pain.

Chezi: You are too late this time! This child will stay here and I will care for her as I trace the father to come and take up his responsibility.

Gogo: Don't delude yourself. Where will you trace him? What if he is living together with his woman after burdening us with upbringing their child?

Mchikichi: You really hit the nail on the head, my sister-in-law. Pangupangu must take his responsibility and not to hoist it on you. You are too old to care take care of infants.

Gogo: Very wrong Mchikichi. This is my grandchild and it is her right to be brought up here. For this home to be renown, and lively we must have grandchildren and great grandchildren living here.

Chezi: In other words. do you agree that this child lives here?

Scene II

Kanyageni - A slum area. Jaka has just arrived at Kinga's garage. A lot of panel beating is heard and running motors

Jaka: (surprised) Yes big man Kinga!

Kinga: (sounds happy but surprised) Ah! Jab! Welcome my brother. How is everything Jaka?

Jaka: Very fine and congratulations for the new garage!

Kinga: Thanks a lot but this is just the beginning. Business has not picked up yet.

Jaka: From what I have just seen, this is not a bad beginning, provided you do a professional job and the right time, all will be okay. Don't be over zealous and take in too much work at once, for this may lead to loss of confidence. Your clients will just disappear.

Kinga: That's very good advice. I will follow it to ensure that my business prospers.

Jaka: Are the mechanics in the workshop your employees?

Kinga: Some, but others are on contract. They give me a certain percentage of all the work they undertake here.

Jaka: You mean they do their own work in your garage and they remit a certain percentage?

Kinga: Yes. The main reason being that by doing this, I attract car owners here for their repairs.

Jaka: You have really aimed high, Kinga, and I truly believe that you will succeed tremendously.

Kinga: That's my dream. Jab. Why the unexpected visit? Is there anything wrong'?

Jaka: I am involved with the mill project and all the initial preparations are over. I come to place an order for the welding of the equipment.

Kinga: (surprised) Wow! You have planned to really change Langoni eh!

Jaka: I am just trying. The development and success of Langoni depends on the unity of Langoni people and their ability to embrace this project.

Kinga: Definitely! True! You are very right you can take a cow to the watering place but you can't force the it to drink the water.

Jaka: That is true. A cow can only take water when it wishes but not when forced.

Kinga: There is a difference. though. Langoni people are human beings with the intelligence to recognize their responsibilities. If they are helped they should also appreciate it by making a contribution. How many people have even thought of developing their home towns?

Jaka: I don't know, but there could be a few.

Kinga: Very few. Jaka, what you are doing needs personal commitment, both financial and physical. Development doesn't arise from just verbal praises and acclaims of one's home. People need put their words into action and yours is an explicit example of action, not empty words.

Jaka: (smiling) I see you are out to put me on a pedestal with too much expectations . . . (settles) Hold on a minute, where is Lulu? I didn't see her at the house. nor at the salon?

Kinga: (saddened) She has traveled to South Africa to set the stage for her niece's modeling endeavors.

Jaka: Pambo's?

Kinga: Yes, Pambo will be participating in the Miss Africa modeling competition.

Jaka: My goodness, you mean she has reached that level of competition?

Kinga: Oh, yes . . .

Jaka: So the loneliness has made you lose a lot of weight, eh?

Kinga: Not really . . . (silence) my weight loss is due to other causes my brother, other serious matters. I really do not know how to tell you. .

Jaka: Just do it. Feel free. I am very anxious and you know, a problem shared is a problem half solved.

Kinga: My problem is physical

Jaka: Physical? Please explain.

Kinga: From the medical examinations I have recently undergone, doctors tell me that I am infertile.

Jaka: (shocked) How? What is the cause?

Kinga: The doctor tells me that my spermatozoa are too weak to fertilize. Lulu cannot conceive due to my weakness.

Jaka: (surprised) What! Come again!

Kinga: My spermatozoa collapse before making contact with the egg and that is why I have failed in making Lulu pregnant.

Jaka: Mmh. What happens now?

Kinga: That is my big problem Now I can neither eat nor sleep. I am so shocked!

Jaka: That is truly a serious problem. Does Lulu know all this?

Kinga: Not yet . . . Jab, do you think Lulu will abandon me on learning that I am infertile? Do you think she will desert me?

Scene III

Ulimboni city. Sineno visits her lover Haiba at his residence. Slow music can be heard faintly. Other natural sounds like birds singing, cock crowing can be head intermittently.

Sineno: Darling, you really made me anxious when you left a message urgently asking me to see you.

Haiba: It is very important and urgent. I tried calling you on your cell phone without success. That is why I left you the message.

Sineno: Oh yah! I gave it to the driver to recharge it in the office.

Haiba: That is ok. I really wanted to see you.

Sineno: Go on, here I am, my love.

Haiba: Hold on. Just relax. Open this bottle of wine and take a drink as we talk. Sineno.

Sineno: (Anxiously) Mrnh! What is wrong? It is not like you to be generous with your wine stock. You would rather go out and buy one so as to save your precious stock!

Haiba: No sweat, there is always something new in this world.

Sineno: Just as I was to you

Haiba: All new things are welcome until their novelty wears off.

Sineno: (laughs) don't start your wise-cracks. You really amuse me (Laughs)

Haiba: Laughter is the best panacea for thoughts, loneliness and low mood swings. It enhances your self image and confidence and makes one feel up to facing the world.

Sineno: Thank you; but what do you mean? Are you still hunting? Looking for someone younger? Better?

Haiba: I am not in the market anymore. Not now; not for ever. I gave up the hunting game along time ago.

Sineno: (sighs) Aah. You of all people! Take care lest what you wish for becomes real!

Haiba: Go on dreaming. You will have a long wait. There is an end to everything and this is where the buck stops.

Sineno: I don't understand you, dear. What do you mean?

Haiba: You will definitely understand after I tell you why I needed to see you so urgently.

Sineno: (anxiously) Are you trying to tell me that our relationship is over?

Haiba: Not my words. Maybe, if that is what you want.

Sineno: Reason

Haiba: My next question exactly (silence). There is a beginning and an end to everything. However, the end to our relationship is not welcome. It is being forced on us.

Sineno: I knew this would happen. My fears and anxieties have materialized! You really cheated me into being your lover and after giving you my body, my love, my everything you discard me?

Haiba: That is not my aim and I didn't really want this to happen. It just happened. I am not in control any more.

Sineno: That is not true. . . . I will not waste more time listening to more lies. Goodbye, Haiba.

Haiba: Just a minute . . . I still love you more than anything else, Sineno,. But our future depends on what you decide. I . . .

Sineno: What I decide?

Haiba: Yes, over what I am going to tell you.

Sineno: Go ahead. I am all ears.

Haida: Do you remember last time we were together when I told you that I was going to see a doctor? !

Sineno: Yes I do.

Haiba: The examination results were very disturbing.

Sineno: In what way?

Haida: It was revealed that I have H.I.V.; that is, I am HIV positive.

Sineno: (A glass shatters. Silence)   What! Oh my God . . . (cries desperately). You mean you have AIDS, Haiba?

Haida: Not yet. I don't have AIDS; but I am H.I.V. positive.

Sineno: (Tearfully)   Why didn't you tell me before? You must have infected me! Oh my God . . . (Cries desperately)

Haiba: Crying will not solve anything, darling. You need to be examined to determine your status.

Sineno: (Cries intensely)   what stupidity led me into having unprotected sex? Haiba . . . why have you killed me? . . . Dh God what shall I do? . . .

End of Scene III

EPILOGUE

In Langoni, Mzee Gogo is erratic; he can't decide whether to take care of his grandchild—Pangupangu's daughter—or not. What is likely to happen to the child?

And in Kanyageni, Kinga continues worrying about this weak spermatozoa despite reassurance from the doctor that he can be assisted. What avenues will Kinga use to help himself? Meanwhile, Sineno regrets having unprotected sex with Haiba. My dear listener, are you as shocked as Sineno? Remember that there is no cure for AIDS!

Notes

1. Singhal and Rogers, *Combating AIDS*, 24-25.
2. Fardon and Furniss, *African Broadcast Cultures*, 98-99

12
Radio Advertisements
—The Radio Nag—

Man: I am Jones, a teacher, and I was told last week I am HIV positive.
Woman: I am Doreen, a mother of seven, and I have AIDS.
Man: I am Derick, a footballer, and I am HIV positive.
Woman: My name is Kathleen. My classmates would be surprised if they knew I have AIDS.
Man: My name's Hill. I am a doctor and it's two years since I found out that I have the human immunodeficiency virus.
Woman: I am Pam. I am employed with the Ministry of Health as a secretary. I am HIV positive.
Woman: My name is Joan. I am a prostitute. I have AIDS.
Woman: I am Alice. I'm in a family of five. I have four sisters, but I am the only one infected with the AIDS virus.

At the beginning of the AIDS epidemic, people believed that AIDS was someone else's problem. In Africa, it was believed that only prostitutes and their clients had AIDS. How to confront such dangerous confusion? In the radio spot "I am Jones," the simple repetition of eight serious voices—deadly serious—who recite their profession and that they are HIV positive begins to get the message across. The approach was created by a student as part of an international radio production workshop sponsored by the Radio Netherlands Training Centre. The voices were carefully crafted to sound like personal testimony and avoid the sense of actors reading a script.

Sound effect: school children talking

Professor: Let's see children, tell me ten words that end in "cida".
(TRANSLATION NOTE: AN ENDING OF MANY COMMON WORDS IN SPANISH, BUT "SIDA" IS ALSO THE WORD FOR AIDS.)
Child: Conocida.
Child #2: Descocida.
Child #3: Plagacida.
Child #4: Professor?
Professor: Yes.
Child #4: Infidelity.
Professor: But infidelity doesn't end with "sida."
Child #4: Yes it does, professor. My father says that people who aren't faithful to their partner can end up with "SIDA."
Announcer: Don't expose yourself. Fidelity to your partner is the best prevention. For more information, call 81-4019 from 11 a.m. to 7 p.m. You decide. Prevention or AIDS.

National Commission for the Prevention of AIDS, COMASIDA.

This AIDS spot is from El Salvador where a play on words in Spanish is used—the sounds "cida", which ends each word, is identical with the word "SIDA" which is Spanish for AIDS. The setting is a classroom where one child points out to the professor that while infidelity doesn't end with the sound "cida" it does end with the reality of "SIDA".

In this next spot from the Eastern Caribbean, the story of a married woman remembering conversations with her husband dramatizes for women the risk they run in trusting their husbands' fidelity.

Woman: I would say to my husband," we've got to be faithful in this relationship."
He said, "I know that."
I would say to him," you can't tell who has AIDS."
He said, "I know that."
I would say to him, "Don't sleep around."
He said, "I know that!"
One day his doctor said to him, "You have the AIDS virus." (PAUSE)
Now, he says nothing.
Announcer: Knowing about AIDS is not enough. Act on what you know. Respect yourself. Protect yourself. An AIDS-free you depends on you.
This message is from the Caribbean Family Planning Affiliation in collaboration with CAREC.

One of the biggest challenges for AIDS prevention is the embarrassment surrounding condoms. Adolescent boys are particularly embarrassed to ask for a condom —in India as much as in Indiana. Here's a spot that tries to make the young boy feel okay about asking, and gives him a tip on how to ask discreetly.

Sound effects: marketplace up and under
First Teenager: It's your turn today. You buy the condoms.
Second Teenager: Okay. (CLEARS HIS THROAT) Give me one of those.
Shopkeeper: A matchbox?
Second Teenager: No, no that!
Shopkeeper: This soap? . . .
Second Teenager: No, no . . . that thing there!
Shopkeeper: Oh, condoms! My boy, feeling shy won't help. If your are embarrassed to ask for a condom, write it down and I'll sell it to you. After all, it's a matter of life!

Announcer: Lubricated condoms—the protection against the fatal disease, AIDS.

Radio has many voices. Radio is the voice of news and the voice of song. Some radio voices are long and serious like community radio forums, others are long and emotional like the radio soap operas. The voice of radio can also be staccato, powerful, and repetitive, like the AIDS spots you've just seen.

Commercial spot announcements on radio are the mass media version of the household nag. They interrupt your favorite program to sell some crazy product you don't want. They are widespread, never-ending, and relentless. The radio spot is sometimes funny, sometimes serious. It knows it is interrupting and like a nag, it doesn't care. Indeed it works hard at breaking through the clutter of your mind and finding its way into your consciousness. It is always short, repeated often, and like the nag, there when you least expect it in order to remind you of something you didn't think you cared about.

The radio spot works because you can't escape it. Even if you hate it—you have to hear it. The basic rationale for the spot advertisements is the realization that people forget messages over time, no matter how powerful their first impact. In 1885, a German psychologist, Hermann Ebbinghaus found that[1]:

> ➤ People forget 60% of what they learn within a half day.
> ➤ The more times you repeat something the better they remember
> ➤ Forgetting occurs almost immediately after exposure, then levels off.

The more often you remind people to act, the better the chance that they will act. No matter how powerful and emotionally moving a radio special on AIDS might be, the next day or the next week, its power is depleted by memory loss and the constant pressure of new events and problems.

To understand the power of the radio spot you have to understand the concepts of reach and frequency and the power of "media exposure." In modern media marketing, the "media buy" is as powerful as the creativity of the message itself. *Reach*, as in "reach and frequency", is the number of targets (households, rural women with children under 5, etc.) who hear a message at least once. *Frequency* refers to the number of times the message is potentially seen or heard in a defined period of time. There are several well-known tools for maximizing reach and frequency with limited dollars. *Flighting*, for example, refers to broadcasting a large number of ads in a short period of time, like birds bundled together in a flock. *Pulsing* is the use of *flighting* over a long period of time, to reduce the costs of a media buy but provide intense exposure to audiences, enhancing their ability to remember the spot.

If you want people to use a condom, breast-feed a child, or learn about infant diarrhea, it is indispensable to understand the power of *exposure, reach and frequency*. If you're promoting voting rights in Eastern Europe, there are election dates you want people to remember. If you're trying to get mothers to recognize when their child has diarrhea, you will want to remind them of the signs of dehydration often. If you want people to use a condom, you must interrupt their safe and cozy worlds with powerful, short messages they hear over and over, but don't always want to hear. And you need to reach millions of people more than once.

Is such messaging "propaganda" or "benevolent social marketing"? Is its objective information, mediated community broadcasting, or the simple reflection of class consciousness? Messages may be one or all of these things at the same time. It is not our intent to decide here where your message falls in these categories. However, if your message is to be effective it must master the possibilities offered by the media to communicate. This is what development practitioners have largely failed to do.

With such possibilities within easy reach, it is not surprising that people have used radio spots for years to promote social change, improve public health, protect the environment, or to get out the vote. These civic-minded radio "nags" have a long and colorful history filled with variety, humor, and compelling emotional moments.

lalalala . . . woman singing happily . . .

Woman: finally, finally I finished with them!
Older Woman: woman! what are you talking about?!
Woman: about those damned ones that are trying to kill my kid.

Older Woman trying to object . . .

Woman: no! no! no! . . . I was just referring to bacterias. these are those little animals that you cannot see, but you can only see their effects.
Older Woman: their effects?!
Woman: yes, diarrhea, dysentery, they can even cause death.
Older Woman: and how do you do to get rid of them?
Woman: very easy! wash your hands before you eat, re-heat everything you eat, and boil all water you give your child. And if you follow all this perfectly, you will then be as happy as I am.

same lalalalala singing . . .

Very Serious Speaker with strong voice: we work towards a healthy community, Ministry of Public Health . . .

HIV-AIDS has not been the only target of the radio nag. A series of radio spots produced in Honduras in the late 1980s by Honduran broadcasters working with specialists from the Academy for Education Development (AED) focused on infant mortality. These spots worked like a continuous radio series, broadcast in short 30 – 60 second segments. They were broadcast in different rotations, repeated frequently over a year, and provide an intensive penetration of information and advice about the country's biggest killer of children, dehydration from diarrhea. It's an idea that would be interesting to consider again.

noise of strong water such as a flush . . .
Speaker: what makes our harvest get ruined?
More Serious speaker: the lack of water.
Speaker: what makes our newborns so skinny when they die of diarrhea?
More Serious Speaker: the lack of water. If you don't water it, the plant will die. If the little body loses its water, the little child will die.

Speaker: dehydration, in other words, the dryness in the kid's body that causes death.

loud music comes in the background . . .

More Serious Speaker: parents of family, do not let your kids die of the dryness caused by diarrhea. Prevent their body from losing the water that keeps them alive. They have to drink liquids when they have diarrhea.
Very Serious Speaker with strong voice: we work towards a healthy community, Ministry of Public Health .

Diarrheal dehydration is a complex business. It strikes the youngest child first and, therefore, mothers must be particularly careful whenever a child gets diarrhea. Because diarrhea is so common, most children have dozens of bouts with no real dehydration, leading moms to think it is not dangerous. Mothers can do several key things to help. First, they can breastfeed instead of giving contaminated food and water when the child is very young. Second, they can give lots of liquids to a child with diarrhea, especially liquids like rice water that has been thoroughly cooked. Third, they can watch for the earliest sign of dehydration—indeed, the concept and the word *dehydration* was foreign to most women in Honduras before this campaign. It was like teaching them that plaque exists before they would believe that they needed a plaque fighting toothpaste. Some of the spots focus on just teaching the word and its signs.

One of the most interesting roles of radio in this series was to confront a common myth about the cause of diarrhea without offending either local tradition or the medical community. Because diarrhea is such a common problem, there are many home remedies and folktales about how it is caused. One of the most common beliefs about diarrhea is that children are born with a sack in the lower part of their abdomen that is loaded with worms. While this is not true, worms are a common problem in children and de-worming medicine produces a visually dramatic exiting of worms when used in children. Over the years, worms became falsely associated with infant diarrhea. A powerful local belief focused on the cause of diarrhea being the "worms exiting their sack inside the child's stomach." Local home remedies were designed to "get the worms back in their sack." The AED team proposed doing a series of spots on how well cooked food would get the worms to go back in their sack. The medical authorities refused to endorse any such local myth. So, a spot was produced that allowed two fictitious worms Lombrofo and Lombriscio to talk to each other about what made them happy. This lighthearted treatment of the myth was fine with the medical community and mothers could put a new idea into a long held and respected traditional belief.

loud water noise such as a flush or a digesting stomach . . .

More Serious Speaker: What happens in the stomach of a sick child?
speaker X: Lombricio, so good to see you!
Lombricio: Lombrolfo, I did not think that we would never see each other again?! You gained weight!
Lombrolfo: same with you!
Lombricio: it's because this kid does not feed himself that well with all the dirt he eats.
Lombrolfo: He drinks water that is not boiled, eats badly cooked food that he likes a lot. Consequently, we have prospered much.
Lombricio: Yes, Lombrolfo we are so many now, that some of us had to go to find food outside.
Lombrolfo: the child sleeps now with bare eyes, and wakes up like a crazy person. His end is near

baby's cry, getting louder and louder . . .

Very Serious Speaker with strong voice: we work towards a healthy community, Ministry of Public Health . . .

Tag lines were created for each spot to emphasize the key message. For example:

Si sus nino tiene obradera, dele liquidos para que no muera
(If your child has the runs, then give him liquid so he won't die.)

Madre que pecho da, es madre de verdad
(A mother who breast-feeds is truly a mother)

Los ninos tiernos son mas delicados, deles mas cuidadoes
(Small infants are more delicate, give them more attention.)

crowd noises . . .

Woman: Doctor Salustiano, I am really worried about my son. Look how bad he seems with this diarrhea ?! His skin is all wrinkled and sucked in, with a sad look on his face.
Dr. Salustiano: Maria, what your kid has is dehydration.

Maria: dehy . . . what!?
Dr. Salustiano: dehydration.
Maria: and what is this?
Dr. Salustiano: dehydration happens when the body of the child loses the vital liquids he needs in order to live.
Maria: then, is dehydration dangerous?!
Dr. Salustiano: the child can die if you do not replace those liquids he is losing.

victorious music . . .

Speaker: if your kid has the runs, give him liquids so he does not die.
Very Serious Speaker with strong voice: we work towards a healthy community, Ministry of Public Health . . .

This nag campaign makes uses of various spokespersons that were shown by research to be important to different audiences. Some women for example trusted a physician—a Dr. Salustiano was created with a serious tone giving advice to mothers. Some women trusted older women and therefore a character called Dona Chela was created. The emotional tone of her messages was conversational and upbeat. She often congratulated women for doing the right thing, rather than scolding them for mistakes.

bip bip bips . . . noise like a telegraph, or old fashion news release on the radio . . .

Woman: the Ministry of Public Health wants to inform the public about the creation of a new oral rehydration room, created by the Maternal Child Hospital. The initiative for this room was taken so that Honduras can take advantage of technological progress. It now allows the mothers to use rehydration in order to replace the liquids lost by their child because of diarrhea. The personnel of the room, wants to let Honduran mothers know that they can prevent their child from becoming dehydrated by giving liquids to their kids when they have diarrhea.

bip bip bips . . . again . . .

Very Serious Speaker with strong voice: we work towards a healthy community, Ministry of Public Health . . .

News programs were shown to be highly credible. Therefore, several spots use a "breaking news" format to announce information about the rehydration centers and the leadership role of Honduras on child mortality in Central America.

water noise . . . baby crying . . .

Speaker: father of family, do not let your child die of diarrhea losing all the vital liquids from his body. If your child has the runs, give him liquids so he does not die.

water noises again . . .

Very Serious Speaker with strong voice: we work towards a healthy community, Ministry of Public Health . . .

Finally, you've seen how dramatic music and crying babies used emotions to break through the clutter of ordinary programming on radio. Spots also targeted fathers as well as mothers, a novel approach in a society where child rearing was a woman's responsibility. Many of these spots may sound a bit stale to you as a 21st century audience. However, in Honduras, in the early 1980s, these spots were powerful, repeated, ear-catching, and continuous.

These multiple themes and emotional approaches capture the multiple messages needed for effective diarrhea education. They gave radio an effective way to deal with a complex subject in short, nagging radio spots, while creating a year-long "soap opera" Hondurans came to love and trust. Their rhyming quality in Spanish was important to their memorableness. But most important was their construction as the "radio nag"—the constantly repeated, endlessly available reminder that only the spot message makes possible.

Notes

1. Hermann Ebbinghaus, *Memory: A Contribution to Experimental Psychology*, trans. Henry Ruger and Clara Bussenius, (New York: Dover, 1964), 52–79, http://psychclassics.yorku.ca/Ebbinghaus/>.(27 Jan. 2005).

13
"Soul Buddyz"
—Radio Consoles Children in South Africa—

South Africa is a country of 45 million people at the southern tip of the African continent. It is considered a middle-income country with per capita income totaling $9,400. Large disparities in income exist, unfortunately major pockets of poverty are a residue of the apartheid era. While South Africa accounts for only 10 percent of Africa's population, its economy produces one-fifth of Africa's production and its business people play an important role throughout the continent.

Because of its economic weight and the prestige of its former President, Nelson Mandela, who led the country out of apartheid to majority rule, South Africa plays an oversized diplomatic role throughout Africa in mediation of the continent's numerous ethnic and political conflicts.

There are 11 official languages including English and Afrikaans—a derivative of early Dutch. The largest isiZulu, is spoken by 23 % of the population. Two tragic fault lines sunder South Africa, currently teetering between being a beacon of tolerant diversity and economic development on the continent and being in real social turmoil.

The first, poverty, is a direct legacy of the apartheid era and difficult to address, even with continued economic growth. It affects more than half the population which lives below the poverty line and causes an ensuing high rate of violent crime. The second, HIV-AIDS, has stricken South Africa more profoundly than any other country of its size, with almost 20 percent of the population HIV positive. The misery and dislocation that the disease has caused to families, children, individuals and the society at large is difficult to fathom from a comfortable armchair somewhere far away from the wailing and burials, which are now a regular part of life in many places.

It is in this context that the Soul City Institute for Health and Development Communication was founded. "Soul City" as it is widely known is a non-profit organization founded in 1992 to promote public health. Ten years before Dr. Garth Japhet, MD was to begin the odyssey of "Soul City" as a young medical doctor assigned to a rural health clinic in South Africa's KwaZulu Natal Province. The dismal record in treating very treatable infant diarrhea, with ensuing mortality, was at the origin of Dr. Japhet's realization that lack of information and practice were at the root of much of South Africa's imminently preventable medical problems.[1]

Consumer health messages of the period consisted more in sloganeering than attractively designed informative pieces. This type of doctrinaire information in a politically wary community was easily discounted. Convinced that education packaged in an entertaining format was the way to reach masses of South Africa's underserved health information consumers, Garth began raising money for what was to become "Soul City". In 1992, he was joined by Dr. Shereen Usdin as an unpaid volunteer. Dr. Usdin co-editor of *Critical Health,* a journal on the impact of apartheid on health, had been personally profoundly influenced by viewing the American tele-drama "Roots." Like Dr. Japhet, she believed in the power of the media to affect people beneficially when used correctly.[2]

"Soul City" has grown from these simple origins to produce the most widely followed TV drama in South Africa as well as numerous other TV, radio and printed health centered broadcasts and publications. One of "Soul City's" principal interests are South Africa's children, a segment of South Africa's population particularly affected by the HIV-AIDS and general health crisis.

"Soul Buddyz" is a multi-media education/entertainment production of the Soul City Institute for Health and Development Communication (IHDC) targeted at children from 8 to 12 years of age. A number of organizations contribute to its funding and broadcast under the overall direction of Soul City IHDC and the South Africa BC Education. These include: British Petroleum, MTM, UNICEF, Radda Barnen, UNESCO, the Academy for Educational Development, the Open Society Foundation and the European Union. Funding for the second "Soul Buddyz" series was augmented by the likes of the Rockefeller Foundation, Nelson Mandela Children's Fund, DFID, Ireland Aid and the South African Department of Health. Along with the TV and radio broadcasts, "Soul Buddyz" prepares a "Life-skills Booklet" for Grade 7 and a "Parenting Booklet".

Needs and aspirations of children, ages 8 through 12, in poor communities are often neglected and "Soul Buddyz" fulfills emotional and educational needs which otherwise go unmet. The dramas are heart rendering for someone not confronted with the problems these children face as in the radio drama that follows:

Scene 1

(Nokeng Primary School—Lunch at Makhaya)

SANDILE:	*Are you feeling alright, buddyz?*
ALL:	*One Time!*
NOMA:	*Buddyz, how many bags of cans do we have?*
MPHO:	*Bags?*
TUMI:	*What are you talking about Noma?*
NOMA:	*Why are you all surprised? Sandile, how many . . . ?*
SANDILE:	*No, I also don't understand what bags you are talking about. Or do you mean the ones we are going to put the cans in*
TUMI:	*But you didn't tell us to look for bags too.*
NOMA:	*Okay guys, where have you been putting your tins? (pause)*
MPHO:	*. . . why are you also . . . please don't tell me you haven't collected cans guys.*
TUMI:	*No . . . but . . .*
NOMA:	*(angry) I told you to collect cans the last time, Tumi and you old me stories. . . .*
MPHO:	*But chomi mos . . .*
NOMA:	*Please don't tell me you haven't collected too, chomi please.*
MPHO:	*But collecting is not a big deal.*
NOMA:	*Guys, the last time I asked you nicely to collect the cans and you were all like "nywe will collect nywe wil collect!"*
TUMI:	*(giggling) But you can't say that Noma.*
SANDILE:	*Guys, Noma is right to be angry.*
TUMI:	*You can't say that Sandile. Noma can't be so angry as if the deadline has passed already.*
NOMA:	*But you know that if we waste time we may not win the competition. I have already heard that there is a group that has collected a lot of cans.*
MPHO:	*You're not serious.*
NOMA:	*I am. I don't know why if you did not want to enter this competition . . .*
SANDILE:	*Please Noma, don't be so angry. You know we all want to enter the competition.*
NOMA:	*So, where are the cans?*
TUMI:	*Don't worry Noma, we'll fix that.*
NOMA:	*When? How?*

MPHO: We'll make a plan my friend. Stop worrying or else you'll get highhigh.

(TUMI LAUGHS)

NOMA: I'm not your joke!

TUMI: *(giggling)* Sorry, but can you imagine yourself having heebeejeebees?

MPHO: What is heebeejeebees Tumi? You teasing Noma again!

TUMI: What? You started this.

SANDILE: Guys, Let's be serious please. *(pause)* I have a plan.

NOMA: Let's hear it Sandile.

SANDILE: At Re a Dula there's a lot of rubbish, tins,plastic and papers. People from the township dump their rubbish in our streets.

MPHO: That's not fair, why are they doing that?

SANDILE: I don't know and it makes me so angry.

NOMA: Some people just don't care about others' feelings.

TUMI: And that of trees you know Noma. *(laughs)*

MPHO: Tumi we are serious, what's wrong with you?

TUMI: Sorry Noma. Mpho can never come between us okay.

SANDILE: You are just playing and we are serious here. *(pause)* So Buddyz, I think we can collect tins from Re a Dula. I am telling you we will have bags and bags of cans.

NOMA: *(as if thinking)* Hm . . . that's a good idea Sandile. We won't just do tins.

MPHO: You mean we can pick up all the rubbish Noma.

NOMA: Yes, I think so, what do you think guys?

TUMI: Cool. As long as we don't hurt their feelings. *(GIGGLES)*

MPHO: Tumi!

NOMA: Forget him Mpho. I'm used to him.

SANDILE: We can pick up plastics and give them to mama for her hats and mats.

TUMI: Cool Sandile. And we leave your place very clean.

NOMA: What do you say buddyz?

ALL: One Time!

SANDILE: Cool! So we do that on Saturday.

TUMI: Sure!

NOMA: Re a Dula here we come!

ALL: One Time!

MPHO: Guys, we must tell Matlhodi that we're going to Re a Dula on Saturday.

NOMA: Eish. I feel sorry for Matlhodi. It means her father is sick again.

TUMI: It means we must go to her after school to inform her.
           Maybe her father won't be sick on Saturday.
SANDILE: Sure!
           (SCHOOL BELL)
NOMA: Buddyz, it's time up. We meet after school.
ALL: One time!
                     (STING)
SCENE 2

             (TOWNSHIP STREET AFTERNOON)

TUMI: Why are you walking alone? Where is Mpho and Sandile? Or
           aren't we going to Matlhodi's place anymore?
NOMA: We are. I think they are coming.
TUMI: And why are you angry?
NOMA: I am not angry Tumi. I'm just worried about my mother.
TUMI: What? Is Mama D sick?
NOMA: No. But you know her problem.
TUMI: You mean drinking problem?
NOMA: Yes Tumi. I'm just scared that papa will leave us. If he leaves
           us what's going to happen to me Tumi?
TUMI: Why do you think he'll leave you?
NOMA: Always when my mother is drunk, they argue, and then my
           mother will be swearing, and then . . . you know, she'll be
           telling him that I'm not his child and what.
TUMI: Are you serious Noma?
NOMA: I'm serious Tumi.
TUMI: So you think he'll pack and go.
NOMA: I'm scared of that, Tumi.
TUMI: But your father is a good man. I don't thin he can do that to
           you. And besides, he loves you.
NOMA: I know he loves me. But you see mama keeps telling him not
           to think that I'm his child.
TUMI: You know what, Noma, let's not think of bad things. Your
           father is a good person and he won't leave you.
NOMA: I pray for that you know Tumi.
TUMI: Oh Sandile is coming, where is Mpho now?
NOMA: Oh please Tumi, can't you see? Who is walking with Sandile?
TUMI: Eh son, I didn't see her.
NOMA: I'll get you triple lens spectacles.
TUMI: You're starting with me, Noma.
           (FX: RUNNING & GIGGLING)
                (BRIDGE MUSIC)

(MATLHODI'S PLACE)

MPHO: So we're going to Re a Dula on Saturday, my friend.

NOMA: We want to make sure that when we leave Re A Dula there's not a single paper in the streets.

SANDILE: You mean the place will be spotless?

NOMA: Sure!

TUMI: Plastics will make hats and mats, the other rubbish will be burnt and then cans . . . FNB here we come!

MATLHODI: That's a nice plan guys, I'm impressed.

TUMI: Sandile came up with the plan.

SANDILE: Is it necessary, Tumi?

MATLHODI: It's great Sandile! I want to join you.

(FOOTSTEPS)

Oh, you're up daddy?

NTATE TAOLO:

(weak) I just want some fresh air. But I feel much better. Hello kids.

ALL: Hi Ntate Taolo.

NTATE TAOLO:

I overhead you talking. I'm impressed.

MATLHODI: It's great daddy. We're increasing our chance to win and at the same time, we clean Sandile's area.

NTATE TAOLO:

That's really good. You are responsible kids.

NOMA: Thank you, sir. So, can Matlhodi help us on Saturday?

NTATE TAOLO:

No problem. I feel much better and I think she'll go to school tomorrow.

TUMI: Cool!

MPHO: Guys, where will we store our cans?

SANDILE: Ei son, we never thought of that.

NTATE TAOLO:

You can use my garage to store your cans.

NOMA: Really Ntate Taolo?

NTATE TAOLO:

Yes. I don't use it.

MATLHODI: Thanks, daddy.

NTATE TAOLO:

Let me leave you so I can go and rest.

NOMA: Thank you Ntate Taolo.

TUMI: Yo man . . . look who's coming?

SANDILE: The man and the man!

PHEMELO:	*(off mic) Are you feeling alright buddyz?*
ALL:	*One Time!*
AMANI:	*Jambo buddyz!*
ALL:	*Hola!*
TUMI:	*This is cool. We going to jiva yoyo!*
NOMA:	*Oho . . . as if he can jive.*
TUMI:	*Who, me? I'm the man.*
SANDILE:	*Guys, on Saturday we're going to Re a Dula to pickup cans.*
NOMA:	*Not only cans. We're going to clean the place and collect cans.*
AMANI:	*What is this Ba ya Dula?*
TUMI:	*Re a Dula, is where Sandile stays, my man.*
PHEMELO:	*Sure. Plus we also don't have enough cans.*
AMANI:	*And cleaning the place will be cool.*
MPHO:	*Yes, we'll be helping the people.*
AMANI:	*And we'll be taking care of the environment.*
MATLHODI:	*And volunteering our service, you see.*
PHEMELO:	*You are the best, buddyz.*
ALL:	*One Time.*
NOMA:	*And then, Ntate Taolo says we can use his garage to store our cans.*
PHEMELO:	*Sure, why don't we start cleaning the garage?*
SANDILE:	*You are right Phemelo. We can actually clean the whole yard.*
Noma:	*One time. Are we together, buddyz?*
MPHO:	*And you know we can actually help Matlhodi with her work here at home.*
NOMA:	*You are so right Mpho.*
TUMI:	*Sure. So she can be able to do her school work.*
MATLHODI:	*That's great, buddyz. Thanks*
ALL:	*Sure.*
TUMI:	*So buddyz, let's get to work.*
AMANI:	*But why don't we dance first and the clean after?*
PHEMELO:	*Sure guys let's have fun first.*
TUMI:	*Just play the music and we will dance while we working.* (they laugh)

(FX: ONE OF THE SOUL BUDDYZ SONGS AND THEY SING ALONG)

SCENE 4
(NOMA'S HOUSE EARLY EVENING – KITCHEN)
(MAMA DOL IS DRUNK)

MAMA DOL: *Hey you Madam Matlaopane, where were you this late?*
NOMA: *But, I wasn't late mama.*
MAMA DOL: *Hey, Don't answer back okay. (burps) You don't have*
                    manners, whose child are you?
NOMA: *But I told you mama that we were cleaning Matlhodi's yard.*
MAMA DOL: *Are you a municipal worker? (pause) Do you work for the*
                    municipality?
NOMA: *I don't work for the municipality, but we . . .*
MAMA DOL: *Don't make me mad! What is but . . . when you're talking to*
                    Mama Dol? Mama Dol doesn't want buts . . .
NOMA: *Can you go to sleep mama, so I can wash the dishes, please.*
MAMA DOL: *What? In my house? Over my dead and alive body my girl!*
                    This is my house and my property and I've said what I've
                    said!
NOMA: *Okay mama, but can you make way so I can wash the*
                    dishes.
MAMA DOL: *Look here . . . you were gallivanting with your loafing friends.*
                    I work and work here, but I have a daughter. What do you
                    do Noma? Tell me! What is it you're working on? What is
                    your work?
NOMA: *What you're doing is not okay mama. You know each day*
                    you shout at me. If you are not shouting at me, it's papa,
                    why?
MAMA DOL: *Don't put me on trial! I am not on trial, okay!*
NOMA: *Mama, please. (sighs) Can I ask . . .*
MAMA DOL   *Hey you!*
NOMA: *But what you're doing is not right, mama. I think . . . I think*
                    you must reduce your drinking because . . .
MAMA DOL: *Hei..hei..hei . . . Don't you insult me.*
NOMA: *I'm not insulting you, mama. (pause) You drink everyday and*
                    end up fighting with me and papa.
MAMA DOL: *Papa my foot! Listen you stupid girl . . . that man is not your*
                    father. Your father was killed by a train!
NOMA: *(almost pleading) You can't talk like that, mama, please.*
MAMA DOL: *But that is true. He is not your father?*
NOMA: *But you know mama, papa will get fed up with this. Can you*
                    imagine what will happen if he leaves?
MAMA DOL: *Why worry because he is my husband, not yours.*
NOMA: *I know mama, but . . .*
MAMA DOL: *Hey you! Who do you think you are?*
NOMA: *But mama . . .*

MAMA DOL: *Hey you. Shut up! Or do you want a slap to close that big mouth?*

NOMA: *No, mama.*

MAMA DOL: *So shut up okay! Or do you want me to show you . . .*

NOMA: *What are you doing mama?*
             (FX:PLATES BEING THROWN ALL OVER)

MAMA DOL: *These are my things and I'm breaking them!*

NOMA: *Mama, please!*

MAMA DOL: *Do you want me to show you?*

Notes

       ·1. Singhal and Rogers, *Combating AIDS*, 303.
       2. Singhal and Rogers, *Combating AIDS,* 305.

14
Miners' Radio
—Broadcasting in Front of the Muzzle of a Gun—

One of the most remarkable stories in the history of radio, indeed in all of human history, is that of "Radio Mineras", the "Miners' Radio" of the Bolivian highlands. Over five decades from 1947 until today, networks of community radio persisted against all odds in the high mountains of Bolivia, the miners' own community voice and rallying point.[1] The radios were tied together in "cadena minera" or "miners' chains" in times of political or natural crisis, linking themselves through rebroadcasts of each other's programs. When times were quieter, they operated independently. Financially constrained by the poverty of their communities, lacking journalistic and engineering skills, assaulted legally and physically by diverse governments in the Capital, the radios persisted, grew and thrived for a period spanning more than fifty years.

Origins of the various stations are somewhat lost in time but writers are consistent on the blood soaked efforts of these radios to survive in a political climate periodically deadly hostile to the poor. One story places the origin of the stations in Llallagua in the District of Siglo XX in 1952, at what was to become one of the most famous of the stations, La Voz del Minero. It was itself a successor to a smaller pirate station, Radio Sucre, founded in 1947 and was also the first radio station to be destroyed, in this instance, by the civil war of 1949.[2]

Sucre is the constitutional capital of Bolivia while La Paz, the administrative seat, is home to the government. Located high in the arid mountains like several Bolivian cities, Sucre was a wealthy mining center in the 17th century, its population on a par with London and Paris. Ancient peoples inhabited the region with sophisticated cultures dating to their first century settlement around Lake Titicaca. These early Kolla and Tiahuanco cultures gave way to an expansion of Incan civilization into the region in the 13th century. Spaniards conquered the area in the 16th century, the discovery of silver in 1544 following on the heels of Spanish settlements in El Chaco and Santa Cruz. The discovery brought a rapid increase in population with the establishment of cities in La Paz, Sucre and rapid development along the Cuzco-Potosi road. Today the population is mixed with a predominance of indigenous origin.

The silver mines discovered by the Spanish conquerors, made 17th century Sucre one of the wealthiest cities in the world. Today, Sucre has a population similar to that it enjoyed in the 17th century, 200,000, but it has lost its wealth and dynamism. Silver mining has given way to tin whose price has suffered on the world market. With the decline in silver and tin, the mines around Sucre and Potosi, another of the important mining cities, have suffered economically. Potosi's population has declined from rivaling that of Sucre in the heyday of Spanish silver mining to 10,000 today. If it were not for its role as ceremonial capital, Sucre may have followed this silver "boom town" scenario. However, we are at the beginning of our story of the stations, in 1949 with mines and communities poor but dynamic and part of a prosperous provincial economy. With life expectancy in the mines limited to 35 years at the time, there was good reason for the miners to organize and plenty to talk about on the radio.

Another version of the radio's origins places the first station in the mining district of Catavi in 1949.[3] What all can agree is that over the next fifteen years, stations sprang up throughout the mining districts of the mountains, supported and in-turn supporting, the powerful union movements of the mines. Some radio stations used union halls, some had limited outside support. Communities contributed cash or in-kind to their stations, sometimes as a percent of a miner's salary levied along with his union dues and sometimes as volunteer assistance offered to help maintain the station or prepare broadcast material.

Another aspect of the miners' radios on which observers are agreed is that the stations' personnel: anchors, journalists, engineers and accountants were all drawn almost exclusively from the community. Outside support, to the extent that there was any at all, figured as a minor factor in the radios' growth and dynamism. By 1956, the stations had grown to 19 in number.[4]

In spite of their limited resources and their isolation in the mountainous and poor regions of the Bolivian highlands, the miners' radio stations were seen as a threat in distant La Paz the Capital. Every time right wing nationalist governments protecting the interests of the wealthy came to power, the left leaning miners' unions and especially their radio messages were perceived as mortal enemies of the regime. In 1967, Bolivian Air Force planes attacked the stations during a period of military rule. Ascendancy of the military and their anti-democratic tendencies generally posed the greatest threat to the stations.

Miners' radio survived the attack as they were to do again and again. Either they used armed resistance successfully or when they were shut down forcibly, and off the air, by rebuilding as soon as the times changed and authoritarian control from La Paz relaxed. By 1970, 26 radio stations in all were in operation as part of the miners' network.[5]

The miners' stations routinely broadcast the time, union news, personal messages, music, cultural programs, poetry readings, women's magazines and live programs from the union hall auditoriums, at least from the one at La Voz del Minero on Saturdays.[6] In time of threat or natural disaster, stations relayed each other's news transmissions passing along the signature of the original broadcast station along with the message.

Canadian Oblate fathers started Pio XII, another highland radio station located next to the church near La Voz.[7] It started broadcasting in 1959, with the mission from Pius XII to "eliminate alcoholism, silicosis and communism". Professional broadcasters produced high quality programming and there was considerable competition with the miners' radio stations which argued contentiously with much of Pio XII's political message.

In 1967, shocked by the military's massacre of workers, women and children, Pio XII did a political and ideological about-face. It was then crushed by the military but resuscitated later as a fully miners' community station.

Beginning in 1959, Radio Nacional also served as a pilot or relay station for the miners' chain. It had 16-18 employees broadcasting 14 hours a day, including some credits and advertising although these represented a small percentage of broadcast time. Radio Uncia was another community station, which unlike the union owned stations, was owned by the residents of Uncia who were shareholders in the radio corporation.

In spite of the politically radical posture of many of the unions affiliated with or owning the miners' radio stations, ideological disputes seem not to have overly hindered the stations' broadcast vocation. The biggest ideological threat to the stations clearly came from without not from within. Within the stations, community mediation of different political tendencies and messages generally prevailed. In January 1975, the army invaded the mining towns and occupied the radio stations. The miners went on a strike that threatened to become national. This time, a commission sent from La Paz settled the dispute and returned the stations to the miners[8].

In July 1980, army units led by General Luis Garcia Meza sought to extend control to the miners' communities that their coup d'etat had gained over the cities two weeks earlier. Control of the radio would cut out the dissidents tongue, therefore radio control was an important tactical goal of the coup d'etatists. Numbering about 20 stations, the miners' stations relayed messages, one to another in the Potosi and Oruro highlands; the miners' network continued to transmit in spite of the orders emanating from the military junta. Radio Viloco held out until August 6, 19 days after the coup. Radio Nacional Huanuni broadcast for three days under siege from a massive bunker-like building, built in part by the radio with the periodic forays of the military in mind. The Jesuit owned Radio Fides was particularly targeted. Tank fire and machine guns demolished the station and killed the broadcaster Luis Espinel.[9]

A broadcast made in La Paz in response to the coup was relayed over 15 miners' stations:

> *The troops are approximately five kilometers from Siete and very near to Santa Ana . . . therefore we are preparing to defend ourselves... The number of arrests grows to 31, who have been brought to the city of Tupiza according to reports which have arrived at our newsroom . . . This is Radio Animas for all of the South of the country.* [10]

Another relayed broadcast rallied the women:

> *Women of Catavi, come to our station to defend it! We know very well that "Radio 21 de Diciembre" is part of our homes, part of our husbands' salaries . . . We have to unite ourselves as never before. Come as fast as possible to defend our radio station.*[11]

One of the last stations to fall, Radio Animas, transmitted together with Radio Pio XII and Radio Nacional Huanuni up to the last minute when guns silenced the broadcasts. Over the static of the tapes of the last transmission, one hears:

> *[Repeat of news from La Paz] The army is now about five kilometers from Siete Suyos very near to Santa Ana, so we are pre-*

*paring to defend ourselves . . . We know about 31 people detained
who have been sent to Tupiza. This is Radio Animas for all the
south of the country . . . [local]We are living critical moments, we
are all mobilized, even our women have contributed to preparing
the defense Companeros, we will hold out until the ultimate conse-
quence, because this is our mission* [12]

A year later the coup d'etatists and General Garcia were out of
power, their reputation irrevocably sullied by their bloody suppression of
the miners and their radios.

Notes

1. Written source material on the miners' radio stations of Bolivia is limited. This section relies heavily on three sources:

Gumucio Dagron, *Making Waves*, "Miners Radio Stations," 43-48.

Don Moore, "Bolivia: Radio Under the Gun," *Monitoring Times*, June 1994, <http://www.swl.net/patepluma/south/bolivia/miners.html>.(23 Dec. 2003)

Alan O'Connor, "The Miners' Radio Stations in Bolivia: A Culture of Resistance," *Journal of Communication*, 40 (1990): 102-110. .

Principal Spanish language sources include:

Gridvia Kúncar and Fernando Lozada. "Las Voces del Coraje," *Chasqui,* April 1984, 52-57.

Fernando Lozada and Gridvia Kúncar, "Bolivia: Las Radios Mineras, Voces del Coraje," in *Communicación Alternativa y Cambio Social,* ed. Máximo Simpson Grinberg, (Mexico: Permiàa Editora, 1986).

2. O'Connor, "Miners' Radio Stations," 104.

3. Gumucio Dagron, *Making Waves*, 44.

4. O'Connor, "Miner's Radio Stations," 105.

5. Gumucio Dagron, *Making Waves*, 44.

6. This section and the discussion of the various stations relies heavily on O'Connor, "Miners' Radio Stations," 105-106

7. Moore, "Bolivia: Radio Under the Gun". See also: Michiel Schaay, "A History of Bolivian Radio," *Review of International Broadcasting* (Dec. 1980), <http://donmoore.tripod.com/south/bolivia/cp_bdxc.htm>.(22 Dec. 2003).

8. Schaay, "History of Bolivian Radio."

9. Moore, "Bolivia: Radio Under the Gun."

10. O'Connor, "Miners' Radio Stations," 107.

11. Moore, "Bolivia: Radio Under the Gun."

12. Gumucio Dagron, *Making Waves,* 43-44.

15
Talking Back to the Radio
— African Children Learning English, Radio Language Program Kenya—

It is 9:30 AM and the children have already begun to "talk back" to the radio. The crowded classroom in Kenya's highlands barely holds the forty active second graders. On the table sits a battery-operated radio, by today's standards of wind-up and solar technology, quite primitive. But, at precisely 9:30 AM every morning, children in classrooms throughout the country are speaking in unison wishing the radio announcer in a lilting East African, "good moooorning, Safiri".

"Good morning, children," says the radio voice. The children in the class-room respond enthusiastically and wait for the next cue from the radio. They are learning English by radio, and it is time for instruction to begin.
"I hear David and Anna are going to the coast," says Safiri, one of the ra-dio characters.
"Yes, they're going to visit their grandparents," says Tina, another charac-ter.
"Children," Safiri asks, "why are David and Anna going to the coast?"
"To visit their grandparents," the students respond loudly, in English.

The children are animated and eager although they have walked a long way from isolated rural homes to reach their school. Their modest classroom has been built by the community and is typically a dirt-floored room lit only by sunlight through small windows or the open doorway. A few handmade posters and some drawings decorate the walls. Prominent on the teacher's desk is a radio. The children sit crowded together three or four to a bench at rough desks and listen for the next question.

Tina says, "Child, where are David and Anna going?"

At the signal of a bell on the radio, the classroom teacher points to one child who stands and answers:

"To the coast."

Tina reinforces the correct answer:

"To the coast."

For several minutes, the students continue listening and speaking in English with the radio characters. They have come to know and love them during their three years of radio instruction. During the remainder of the 30-minute English lesson, the children also read silently and answer comprehension questions posed by the radio. They read aloud, with the radio repeating the same sentences to confirm correct pronunciation and intonation. Under the direction of the radio characters, the children begin a writing exercise that they finish with the classroom teacher's help after the broadcast.

"Teacher," directs Safiri on the radio, "point to sentence one on the blackboard." The classroom teacher points. *"Children,"* Safiri continues, *"read sentence one, aloud."*

"Although I was tired, I couldn't sleep," the children read as the teacher points to each word.

The teacher, untrained and of limited English-speaking ability, works with the radio instruction, encouraging and helping during the broadcast and in follow-up complementary lessons. The teacher is confident and comfortable with the activities suggested by the radio.

"Although I was tired, I couldn't sleep," repeats Safiri. *"Good reading, children. Now let's look at Worksheet number ten."*

At the end of the 30-minute lesson, only English has been spoken. For thirty intensive and fun-filled minutes, Kenyan students have been immersed in a language as foreign to them as Swahili is to children in

America or Europe. The designers of the program, with a bit of 60s romanticism, called radio a "door into another world."

Across the country, another group of second graders are in a similar classroom; the only light entering their classroom is from an open doorway. It reflects onto a well-used blackboard and a few nubs of chalk. No textbook or materials are in sight. A dedicated but inexperienced teacher is lecturing on English grammar while speaking Swahili; the children are attentive, but silent throughout most of the one-hour class.

These two snapshots were taken twenty years ago during one of the earliest international experiments with interactive instructional radio. Five years before, a similar experiment in pre-Sandinista Nicaragua had shown that carefully developed radio programming could improve math test scores in the most underachieving schools throughout the country. The Nicaraguan program beamed some 600 radio lessons to 10,000 rural primary school students. More than 20,000 adults also listened to the daily broadcasts. Students in radio classes were compared to control group students that did not receive the radio lessons. Radio students showed a major gain in mathematical knowledge over non-radio students in their first year alone (65.4% for radio students compared to 38.9% for control students).

Radio Math, as the first experiment was called, used a form of *distributive learning* whereby students learned the four basic math functions—adding, subtracting, multiplying, and dividing at once; rather than the traditional linear format, adding first, than subtraction, etc. Distributive learning had shown that children learned abstract math best by doing—by moving used bottles caps on desktops to add or subtract, and by "talking back" to the radio—answering questions, practicing skills, participating fully in the hour-long class.

The next great test of interactive instructional radio took place in Kenya, a country where English was the language of academic survival even though few children spoke it at home. In the 1980s, children who could not pass the national English test by Standard (grade) 4 could not go on to Kenyan schools where all instruction and all textbooks were in English only. This was the setting where Safiri, one of Kenya's most popular radio   characters,   took   control   of   the   traditional   classroom.

Safiri: Children, today I'm going to tell you a story about Sara and Rono.
Tina: But first let's practice the words "somebody" and "nobody."
Safiri: Last night Sara and Rono were asleep. It was dark.
*   Sara woke up. She said . . .*
Sara: Rono! Wake up!! There's somebody in the room!

Safiri: Rono woke up. He lit the lamp.
                    (Sound of match striking.)
Rono: No, Sara. There's nobody in the room.
Sara: Then, what is it?
Rono: It's a cat!
                    (Sound of cat meowing.)
Tina: Now, children . . . let's talk about the story.

This is a good example of what the designers called "radio as a door." The actors as characters can walk in and out of the classroom, taking the children with them. This helps avoid imitating the traditional methods of their classroom teacher. It respects the creative potential of the scriptwriters and frees them to be creative while staying on the instructional target.

The program in Kenya's schools was known as the Radio Language Arts Program (RLAP). It was developed by a team of professionals from the Kenyan Institute of Education, the Voice of Kenya Radio, the Academy for Educational Development and the Center for Applied Linguistics. The Kenyan government and USAID financed it as one in a long series of major experiments to show how mass media can foster national development.

The results were impressive, although not as impressive as the earlier Radio Math project. Radio students studying English showed a marked improvement over the non-radio students in both listening and reading comprehension, as measured by grade one achievement tests (58% for radio students versus 30% for control students). Gains in English language speaking and writing were much lower than listening and reading, but radio students still did better than controls.

How did RLAP work? Table 15.1 shows the RLA production board. This is a detailed battle plan for producing effective radio programs on time and on target. From preparing lesson plans, writing segments, drafting scripts, through production and final revisions to future broadcasts, there is a ten-day schedule which guides all decision-making. What makes RLA work is the systematic interaction of instruction, student response and creative production. The nineteen steps were a battle plan for success.

These programs were produced with care and an understanding of how children learn English. As the designers understood, an important part of all learning is reinforcement and the best reinforcement occurs immediately. But how does the radio know what the children say? It can talk, but it can't listen. Teachers with low English skills cannot help much. The radio therefore, gave students correct answer to problems as often as possible without assuming that the teacher was participating. If the student gives the right response, then the radio reinforces it.

Table 15.1 Radio Language Arts Production Board
(- - 8 day sample schedule - -)

September	10	11	12	13	14	17	18	19
1. Lesson plans prepared					III/13			
2. Segments written					III/12			
3. Draft Scripts reviewed			III/11					
4. Segments revised	III/10						III/11	
5. Content records updated					III/9			
6. Teacher's materials written				III/8			III/9	
7. Teacher's materials reviewed & revised					III/8			
8. Formative evaluation materials written			III/8					III/9
9. Formative evaluation materials reviewed					III/8			
10. Scripts to actors	III/8				III/9			
11. Pre-production completed	III/8					III/9		
12. Production completed		III/8		III/8	III/8			III/9
13. Production reviewed & post-production completed				III/8	III/8	III/8		III/9
14. Printing completed						III/7		
15. Tapes & scripts copied and filed						III/7		
16. Distribution completed		III/3						

September	10	11	12	13	14	17	18	19
17. Broadcast			III/2				III/3	
18. Formative evaluation						II/14		
analysis completed						III/1		
19. Revisions completed to					II/12			
lessons broadcast					13			

{Roman numerals–lesson no., Arabic numerals–program segment no.}

If the student gives no answer or a wrong answer, the radio corrects it. Here is an example of oral reinforcement; notice, Safiri pauses to allow the students to answer and then uses either Sarah or Rono, the radio characters, to give the correct answer.

Sara: Look, Rono, I can touch the top shelf!
Rono: You're tall, Sara!
Safiri: Children, is Sara tall?
        (Pause 3 seconds for pupil response.)
Rono: "Yes, she is." Again.
        (Pause 2 seconds for pupil response.)
Sara: Rono, try to touch the top shelf. (teasing)
Rono: I can't, Sara. I'm too short.
Safiri: Children, is Rono short or tall?
        (Pause 3 seconds for pupil response)
Sara: "He's short." Again.
        (Pause 2 seconds for pupil response.)

Unlike math, English has many correct responses. Question: "Is Rono short or tall?" Possible answers: "He is short". "He's short". "Short." "I think he is short." or "Short, of course." As the child learns more and more English, these multiple right answers occur more often. The RLA team used classroom observation to detect whether a single reinforcing answer given by the radio was confusing to children. The observations showed that children managed the radio response intelligently. Sometimes the children changed their already correct response to imitate the radio, and other times they simply kept their already chosen pattern.

Let's take a look at a long block of programming to really understand how this amazing system works. This is a section excerpted directly from scripts in *Teaching English by Radio: Interactive Radio in Kenya.* [1]

Drama Theme 3, Under and Hold

Safiri: Children, today I'm going to tell you a story about Sara and Rono.
Tina: But first let's practice the words "somebody" and "nobody."

Drama Theme to End

Instruction begins with the use of a classroom pupil-participant, "Juma," to help review the meaning of the words "somebody" and "nobody" and allied structures.

Rono: Juma, come to the front.
(FX Travel Music 5)
Sara: Juma, stand in the corner at the front of the room.
PPR: (Pause for Pupil Response – "Pupils")

Sara and Rono model target material.

Rono: Sara, there's somebody in the corner, isn't there? 6. Sara: Yes.
Rono: Who is it?
Sara: It's Juma.

Then the class repeats the first modeled utterance while Rono carries out the appropriate meaning-giving action-standing in the corner.

Rono: Children, say, "There's somebody in the corner."
Pupils
Rono: There's somebody in the corner. Again.
Pupils

Juma comes back to the center of the room and the process is repeated with the contrasting utterance, *"There's nobody in the corner."*

Sara: Now, Juma, come out of the corner. Stand in the front of the room, in the middle.
Rono: Teacher, please help Juma.
Pupils
Rono: Now there's nobody in the corner.

Sara: *Children, say, "There's nobody in the corner."*
Pupils
Sara: *There's nobody in the corner. Again.*
Pupils
         Juma is sent back to his desk.

Rono: *Good, Juma. Sit down.*
                         (FX Travel Music)

The class' attention is directed to the blackboard, where the teacher has written and boxed a cluster of vocabulary items: the words "light," "dark," "light/lit," and "lamp." The teacher will point to these words as appropriate.

Sara: *Now, children, look at the words in the box on the blackboard.*
Pupils
Rono: *Look at the word "light."*
Pupils
Sara: *Children, say, "light."*
Pupils
Sara: *Light. Again.*
Pupils
Rono: *Sara, is it light during the day?*
Sara: *Yes, it is.*
Rono: *Is it light now?*
Sara: *Yes, Rono. It's daytime now.*
Rono: *Children, say, "It's light during the day."*
Pupils
Rono: *It's light during the day. Again.*
Pupils
Sara: *Children, look at the second word in the box . . . the word "dark."*
Pupils
Rono: *Children, say, "Dark."*
Pupils
Rono: *Dark. Again.*
Pupils
At this point a guitar chord, a two-line exchange between Tina and Safiri, and student repetition of the target structure from the exchange form a transition into a familiar song.

                (Guitar: Strum C Major Chord)
Tina: *Safiri, is it dark now?*

Safiri: No, Tina. It isn't dark now. It's dark at night.
Rono: Children, say, "It's dark at night."
Pupils
Rono: It's dark at night. Again.
Pupils
Tina: Yes . . . It's dark at night . . . (A little dreamily) . . . and I'm sleepy.
*   (Maybe a small yawn.)*
*   (Xylophone Intro:"Sleep Song")*
Tina: (singing) At night it is dark and I'm sleepy, There is darkness all
*   around. At night it is dark and I'm sleepy And the rain falls softly*
*   down.*
*   (Xylophone: "Sleepy Song" Refrain Under Line 12)*
Safiri: Children, sing with Tina.
Tina: (singing) At night it is dark and I'm sleepy, There is darkness all
*   around. At night it is dark and I'm sleepy And the rain falls softly*
*   down.*
*   (Xylophone: Refrain Around Again)*
Tina: (singing) At night it is dark and I'm sleepy, There is darkness all
*   around. At night it is dark and I'm sleepy And the rain falls softly*
*   down.*
*   (Xylophone Outro)*

Now attention returns to the remaining items on the blackboard.

Rono: Now, children, look at the words "light" and "lit"
*   in the box, and look at the word "lamp."*

Light/lit is new. Students have encountered "lamp" in reading, but it's likely many will not recognize it. The teacher is asked to provide mother tongue translations.

Sara: Teacher, please point at these words and explain them to the chil-
*   dren in mother tongue.*
*   (FX Drum and Ring Music 8)*

A repetition drill is used to reinforce the presentation of the irregular *light/lit*.

Rono: Thank you, teacher.
Sara: Children, let's drill.
Rono: Children, say, "He lights the lamp."

Pupils
Rono: He lights the lamp.
Pupils
Rono: He lit the lamp.
Pupils
Rono: He lit the lamp.
Pupils
Rono: He lights the lamp every night.
Pupils
Rono: He lights the lamp every night.
Pupils
Rono: He lit the lamp last night.
Pupils
Rono: He lit the lamp last night.
Pupils
Rono: He lights the lamp every night.
Pupils
Rono: He lit the lamp last night.
Pupils
Rono: He lights the lamp every night.
Pupils
Rono: He lit the lamp last night.
Pupils ·
Rono: He lights the lamp every night.
Pupils
Rono: He lit the lamp last night.
Pupils
Sara: Good drill, children.

The day's study to this point is now summarized in the form of a dramatized story.

Drama Theme 3, Under and Hold
Safiri: Children, I'm going to tell you a story. Listen carefully.
Drama Theme to End
Safiri: Last night Sara and Rono were asleep. It was dark. Sara woke up. She said . . .
Sara: Rono! Wake up! There's somebody in the room! (Tense, excited whisper-She thinks there's an intruder in her house)
Safiri: Rono woke up. He lit the lamp.
FX Match Striking
Rono: No, Sara. There's nobody in the room.

Sara: Then, what is it? (Still worried)
       FX Cat Meow
Rono: It's a cat!
*Sara: It's a cat! (Laughingly, relieved as they discover together what's in
        the room)*

A brief modeled discussion of the story follows.

Tina: Now, children . . . let's talk about the story.
Tina: Last night Sara woke up. Safiri, what did Sara say.
Safiri: She said, "Rono, wake up."
Tina: And then she said, "There's somebody in the room."
Safiri: Children, say, "She said, 'Rono, wake up.' "
Pupils
Safiri: She said, "Rono, wake up." Again.
Pupils
Tina: That's right, children.
Safiri: Rono woke up. Tina, then what did he do?
Tina: He lit the lamp.
Safiri: Children, say, "He lit the lamp."
Pupils
Safiri: That's right! He lit the lamp.

The modeled discussion is finished with an unmodeled comprehension question.

Tina: Children . . . what was in the room?
Pupils
Tina: That's right! A cat.
Safiri: Children, what was in the room?
Pupils
Tina: That's right! There was a cat in the room!

And the block ends.

Safiri: Good work, children.

Writing for RLA was a challenge. Writers had to follow the instructional map and be creative too. Working as a team, creating lively believ-
able characters, ensuring continuity from one segment to another, adding
musical as well as verbal cues, incorporating songs and games, as well as

pattern drills and reinforcement was the challenge. Programs were written in blocks and then larger segments. "PPRs" (pause for pupil response), were critical to every program. Questions and answers were mixed with conversations, vignettes, worksheets, and games.

"Talking back radio" needs a lot of smart thinking, planning, and teamwork. It is not for the faint of heart or those only intuitively creative. It requires discipline as well as imagination. And it works.

Several other countries have used, adopted, and adapted interactive radio instruction (IRI) to meet their own national needs over the years since RLA ended in Kenya. Countries as diverse as South Africa, the Dominican Republic and Thailand, have shown that the basic IRI approach can improve student test scores even when teachers are poorly trained and under-supported. New theory has been incorporated over the years. What we know now is:

➢ Children learn best by doing.
➢ IRI activates kids in the classroom.
➢ IRI can be standardized across an entire educational system without massive improvement in teachers or textbooks.
➢ IRI is adaptable to a wide variety of school systems and curriculums.

David: *I'm a good swimmer, Anna!*
Anna: *But I'm not!*
David: *Oh, come on, Anna . . . Onyango is very good at sailing the boat . . . and he'll be careful.*
Anna: *All right, David. (A reluctant little voice —she really doesn't want to).*

Drama Theme No. Three: End Fast on Relative Minor
Safiri: *Children . . . is Anna going to ride in the boat?*
Pupils
Safiri: *Yes, she is . . . that's right . . . .*
Guitar: *Strum AM or AM7*
Safiri: *. . . but she doesn't want to . . .*

Drama Theme No. Two: Under Line 28 and Hold
Safiri: *Tomorrow, children, I'll tell you what happened when David and Anna went for a ride in the boat.*

Drama Theme No. Two: End Fast and Firmly on Dominant Chord

Tomorrow children I'll tell you what happened when David and Anna went for a ride in the boat.

Let's imagine that the boat used by David and Anna is a radio and tomorrow is now. Radio can do more than advocate, entertain, and provide spot announcements or community lotteries. Radio can deliver science-based education in math and English that children all over the world need today if they are going to compete as entrepreneurs and citizens tomorrow.

The Radio Math, RLA, and other IRI experiences show that solid, science-based radio can improve the quality of education in a wide variety of countries and cultures. Coupled with this IRI experiences provide lessons on the vital role of parents, peer support systems among teachers and a focus on quality education. In African schools, where teachers are being lost everyday to AIDS, radio in the classroom can and should be a priority investment. The training of new teachers can benefit from RLA's lessons on how to create student participation. It need not be a choice, but a cooperative campaign among all educators to make learning smarter, more fun, and totally active.

Notes

1. Philip R. Christensen, *Teaching English by Radio: Interactive Radio in Kenya*, (Washington, D.C.: Academy for Educational Development, 1986).

16
Today's Radio

We interrupted our history of radio after reporting a steady decline in development radio programming. This was especially disturbing when seen in relation to the size of the population of poor and radio's increasing availability in poor areas. This is not the end of the story, however.

A number of technological and social changes have been occurring, making the radio's reach ever more ubiquitous. On the programming side a fundamental reawakening is beginning to occur.

First, let's take the technological and social changes. Surreptitiously, without the drama of the advent of the Internet, broad and fundamental changes in radio technology have been occurring. A simple but very noticeable change is the progressive reduction in broadcast costs. Part of the great revolution taking place in electronics, radio has participated in a reduction of costs for all aspects of broadcast transmission. The basic costs of setting up a station have declined dramatically. A fully operative community FM station can now be set up for the cost of from $10,000 to $15,000 and can reach an area of 50 miles in radius. Compare this cost to the four to five times this amount ten years ago and perhaps ten times this current cost when one goes back twenty years. The expansion of radio to include the FM band in the 1970s lowered costs, improved reception and opened the air for new stations.

On the opposite end of the broadcast spectrum, a low-level transmitter of several watts can be bought for several hundred dollars. Such a set-up, costing $600-$750, can reach a small community, a village, college campus or neighborhood with community oriented broadcasts. It is one of the least expensive ways for a community to organize. A far cry from satellite technology, community radios can serve multiple goals: political, entertainment, developmental or simply as a way to stay in touch through a birthday greeting, graduation salutation, announcement of a birth or death. Having plenty of air, time quality informational broadcasts on subjects of interest would be a welcome addition to these stations' broadcast schedules.

Lower transmission costs and greater transmission power mean the possibility of covering greater distances and more people at equivalent cost. Transmitters still need electrical power and their demands are significant. By way of example, the UK achieves 98% territorial coverage for the BBC with 150 transmitting stations in-full relays. In Africa, only South Africa has achieved near national coverage. The South African Broadcast Corporation (SABC) uses a system of FM stations with VHF signals to repeat the national broadcasts. A national network of AM stations is less costly than an FM one, but the solution is not ideal. Daytime transmission is limited and interference is widespread at night. Shortwave transmission is the least costly form of transmission over great distances, but problems of reception and interference persist. The advent of digital shortwave, a very recent development not widely exploited, could once again revolutionize radio transmission as is already happening with digital satellite transmission.[1] Within Africa in addition to South Africa; Ghana, Guinea, Zambia and Zimbabwe have plans for national FM coverage. In Asia, Malaysia has national coverage for Radio Television Malaysia (RTM) radio broadcasts, as is probably the case for several other Asian countries for which information is unavailable.[2]

The cost of radios has also declined, an important consideration for the poor. Small transistors, made in China, can readily be bought on third world markets for $5 dollars U.S. They work! The biggest cost associated with these radios turns out to be the batteries. Radios that are environmentally friendly also exist and have become less costly and more versatile.

The South Africa-based non-profit Freeplay Foundation works in more than a dozen developing countries to distribute self-powered radios that never require disposable batteries or electricity. The Freeplay *Lifeline* radio, developed specifically for use in the development sector, uses both wind-up and solar power. Designed with input from orphaned children in three African countries, the *Lifeline* was built for harsh climates and rugged conditions and can play for 18 hours at a time when fully charged. These radios cost about $50. To date, the Freeplay Foundation has provided more than 300,000 radios, conservatively providing radio access to more than 5 million people when family and group listening is taken into account. *Lifeline* radios were distributed to AIDS orphans in Africa, who often cannot attend school and enjoy only a minimal adult presence in their lives.

Radio penetration still far exceeds that of newspapers, television or PCs in both low and middle-income countries. Illiteracy and cost inhibit many of the poor from access to these more sophisticated and costly media. The table below clearly illustrates the dominant penetration of radio for a wide selection of low and middle-income countries.

Table 16.1: Penetration of Different Communication Media, 1996, 1997 selected low and middle-income countries.

Country/Media	—numbers of people per one media unit—			
	Newspapers	Televisions	PCs	Radios
Albania	29	43	- -	4
Algeria	26	15	238	4
Argentina	8	3.5	26	1.5
Bolivia	18	9	- -	1.5
Brazil	25	3	38	2
Cameroon	143	12	667	6
China	- -	4	167	5^3
Costa Rica	11	2.5	- -	4
Ethiopia	500	200	- -	5
Ghana	71	9	625	4
India	- -	14	476	10
Jordan	22	23	115	3.5
Kenya	111	53	435	9
Malaysia	6	6	22	2
Mali	1000	100	1600	20
Mexico	10	4	27	3
Morocco	38	6	400	4
Nigeria	42	16	196	5
Peru	23	7	83	3.5
Philippines	12	9	73	6
Senegal	200	24	88	7
South Africa	33	8	24	3
Sri Lanka	34	11	244	5
Turkey	9	3	48	6
Uganda	500	38	714	8
Uruguay	9	4	45	2

Source: World Bank, *Entering the 21st Century, World Development Report,* 1999/2000Table 19, 1996 & 1997 data, page 266.

Only Turkey, Costa Rica and China show higher penetration for another form of media than radio, in this case television exceeds radio penetration slightly. In all other countries, radio penetration greatly exceeds all other forms of media penetration. In China, the lower penetration of radio is accounted for by the failure of the statistical data to adequately account for the outreach provided by radio speakers in public places. If this very common form of radio access in China were accounted for adequately, penetration rates there would increase dramatically. Elsewhere, the numbers do not tell the whole story either, for unlike newspapers and to some extent PCs, radio listening is a social affair in families and villages, meaning that one radio can and does reach many more individuals than the simple per capita ownership figures would suggest.

On the other side of the equation, the cost of radio programming can be much less than those for other forms of media. Radio's simplicity when compared to television is self-evident. The Internet has also facilitated radio programming by making it possible to download prepared text or fully broadcast radio audio. The Food and Agriculture Organization of the U.N. (FAO) and a Canadian non-governmental organization the Developing Countries Farm Radio Network provide prepared radio scripts on various topics of interest to farmers in developing countries over the Internet. These scripts can be reworked for local programming and broadcast free of any additional charges by local stations. When newsprint or the Internet are used to provide information the user costs assessed to the provider involve overhead above and beyond content in order to reach each additional recipient. This is much less true of the radio. Once radio's relatively small fixed costs are accounted for, access is free to all those within range. And the range of radio has increased dramatically.

We are on the cusp of another major breakthrough in radio technology. WorldSpace satellites began broadcasting radio programming over 40 "L" band channels to Africa in October 1999 and Asia in March 2000. Now broadcasting to Africa, South Asia, the Middle East and parts of Europe, there are two WorldSpace satellites, *AsiaStar* and *AfriStar,* each with three digital beams—east, west and south—capable of broadcasting more than 40 channels each. The digital coding of the information, as opposed to analog, assures the integrity of the signal over 14 million square miles, literally capable of reaching billions of people. Special digital receivers cost little more than $70, have the size of ordinary radios and are also capable of receiving AM, FM and short wave signals. The radios have another interesting feature; with the addition of a small not very costly modem, the radios can be hooked to a PC and download dedicated text broadcast via satellite radio.

A number of major broadcast networks as CNN and National Public Radio, as well as the BBC and other foreign based networks, have signed on to WorldSpace and are broadcasting regularly to owners of digital radios. WorldSpace's commercial strategy which differed initially from the recently rolled out digital satellite radio in the U.S., has now moved to a subscription basis. As with XM Radio and Sirius, their U.S. counterparts, owners of WorldSpace radios now pay a fee to receive monthly broadcasting. An Ameri-Star satellite broadcasting to Latin America is soon to join the WorldSpace constellation. There are, as of yet, no WorldSpace plans to broadcast to North America.

The numerous WorldSpace channels carry a variety of commercial broadcasts. There is a leisure station, knowledge station, health and civic. WorldSpace has devoted 5% of its bandwidth to non-commercial broadcasts of public interest managed by the independent, non-profit "First Voice International."[4] First Voice broadcasts are carried free of listener charges on the WorldSpace system. Part of the schedule on Africa Learning Channel, First Voice's broadcast channel to Africa, includes programs such as: storytelling for children, HIV-AIDs *("AIDS Treatment, "AIDS Prevention"* and *"Children Affected by AIDS"*), agriculture, nutrition, health, the environment *("The Politics of Water")* , small business *("Sound Business Advice"* and *"Micro-enterprise and the Environment"),* conflict resolution *("Innovative Solutions Promote Peace")* and civic society *("The UN NGO Millenium Forum"* and *"The Status of Women").*

In Sudan, UNICEF signed an agreement with the then WorldSpace Foundation—now First Voice International—to provide teacher training via the WorldSpace radio. First Voice broadcasts over the WorldSpace system reach most of the areas affected by the December 2004 *tsunami* and are providing a steady stream of programming to the affected areas with the potential of helping them rebuild. The broad low cost coverage of the WorldSpace satellite system provides the potential to serve as the base for a regional early-warning system. While beginning to expand its programming, the power of digital radio has not yet caught on with foreign aid donors and the Foundation has struggled its first years to find quality public interest programming. With the breakthrough of digital satellite together with the still unexploited possibilities of digital shortwave, which offers a less radical break in broadcast patterns, today's radio is on the horizon of another sunrise in the globalization of communications.

Notes

1. Fardon and Furniss, *African Broadcast Cultures*, 28-29.
2. McDaniel, *Broadcasting in the Malay World*, 105.
3. Does not include wired speaker units in public places.
4. In July 2003 the non-profit partner of WorldSpace Corp., the World-Space Foundation, changed its name to First Voice International, <http://www.firstvoiceint.org/> (28 January 2005) .

Bibliography

Adelman, H., A. Suhrke, and B. Jones. *The International Response to Conflict and Genocide: Lessons from the Rwanda Experience*, study #2: *Early Warning and Conflict Management.* Odense, Denmark: Steering Committee of the Joint Committee of Emergency Assistance to Rwanda, March, 1966. <http://www.metafro.be/grandslacs/ grand-slacsdir500/0742.pdf> (3 Dec. 2002).

Afrik'Netpress. What News, 29 January 2003.

Behrman, Daniel. *When The Mountains Move, Technical Assistance and the Changing Face of Latin America.* Paris: UNESCO, 1954.

Bosch, Andrea. "Interactive Radio Instruction: Twenty-Three Years of Improving Educational Quality." (Working paper in Education Technology Technical Note Series, World Bank, vol. 2, no. 1, 1997).

Brunero, Angelo. "A History of Telegraphy." Translated by Andrea Valori. <http://www.acmi.net> (28 Dec. 2004).

Cassirer, H.R. "Radio in an African Context: A Description of Senegal's Pilot Project." in Spain, Jamison, and McAnany, *Radio for Education and Development.*

Caesar, Caius Julius. *Caesar: The Gallic War.* Translated by H.J. Edwards, Loeb Classical Library no. 72. Cambridge, Mass.: University of Harvard Press, 1917.

Christensen, Philip A. *Teaching English by Radio: Interactive Radio in Kenya.* Washington, D.C.: Academy for Educational Development, 1986.

Damle, Y.B. "Communication of Modern Ideas and Knowledge in Indian Villages." *Public Opinion Quarterly* 20 (1956): 257-70.

Deutschmann, Paul J. "The Mass Media in an Underdeveloped Village." *Journalism Quarterly* 40 (1963 Winter): 27-35.

Djankov, S., Caralee McLiesh, Tatiana Nenova, and Andrei Shleifer. "Media Ownership and Prosperity." in *The Right to Tell: The Role of Mass Media in Economic Development.* Washington D.C.:World Bank Institute 2002. <http://www1.worldbank.org/publications/pdfs/15203front-mat. pdf>.

Dock, Alan and John Helwig. "Interactive Radio Instruction: Impact, Sustainability, and Future Directions." (Working paper in Education and Technology Technical Note Series, World Bank, vol. 4, no. 1, 1999).

Ebbinghaus, Hermann. *Memory, A Contribution to Experimental Psychology,* translators, Henry Ruger and Clara Bussenius, (New York, New York: Dover Publications, 1964).

Encarta. "Edison, Thomas Alva." <http://www.Encarta.msn.com/ encyclopedia_761563582/Edison_Thomas_Alva.html> (2 Dec. 2002),

Entering the 21ˢᵗ Century, World Development Report 1999/2000. New York: Published for the World Bank, Oxford University Press, 2000.

Fardon, Richard and Graham Furniss, eds. *African Broadcast Cultures.* Westport, Conn.: Praeger, 2000.

Fox, Elizabeth. *Latin American Broadcasting: From Tango to Telenovela.* Lutton, U.K.: University of Lutton Press, 1997.

Fox, Elizabeth, ed. *Media and Politics in Latin America: The Struggle for Democracy.* London: Sage, 1988.

Freire, Paulo. *Pedagogy of the Oppressed.* new rev. 20th anniversary ed. Translated by Myra Bergman Ramos. NewYork: Continuum, 1993.

Georges, Joseph and Isabelle Fortin. "A New Dawn for Freedom of Speech Radio: Radio Soleil." Chap. 9 in Girard, ed. *A Passion for Radio.*

Girard, Bruce, ed. *A Passion for Radio, Radio Waves and Community.* n.p.: Communica, 2001, <http://www.commuinca.org/passion/contents. htm.> (3 March 2003).

Goodwin, Doris Kearns. *No Ordinary Time.* New York: Simon & Schuster, 1994.Gregory, Bruce N. *The Broadcasting Service, An Administrative History.* Washington D.C.: USIA Special Monograph Series, No. 1, 1970.

Gumucio Dagron, Alfonso. *Making Waves.* New York: Report to the Rockefeller Foundation, 2001. <http://www.communicationforsocial-change.org/pdf/making_ waves.pdf.> (5 March 2003).

Hall, Budd L. and C. Zikambona. *Mtu Ni Afya: An Evaluation.* Dar es Salaam, Tanzania: Institute of Adult Education Studies, No. 12, 1974.

Hirabayashi, G.K., and M.F. El Katib. "Communication and Political Awareness in the Villages of Egypt." *Public Opinion Quarterly* 22 (1958): 357-63.

Ilboudo, Jean-Pierre. "Rural Radio: Role and Use Over the Past Three Decades." Paper presented to The First International Workshop on Rural Radio, Rome, May 2001).<http://www.fao.org/documents/ show_cdr. asp? url_file=/docrep/003/x6721e/x6721e02.htm.>.

Kinyanjui, P. E. "In-Service Training of Teachers through Radio and Correspon-dence in Kenya." in Spain, Jamison, and McAnany, *Radio for Education and Development.*

Kúncar, Gridvia & Fernando Lozada. "Las Voces del Coraje." *Chasqui,* (April 1984): 52-57.

Lee, Aaron. "The Development of Sound Broadcasting in Mainland China During The Mao Era (1949 - 1976)." Master's Thesis, University of California Press, 1971.

Lerner, Daniel. *The Passing of Traditional Society.* Glencoe, IL: Free Press, 1958.

Liu, Alan P. L. *Radio Broadcasting in Communist China.* 2nd ed. (Cambridge UNESCO, 1964), cited in: Markham, *Voices of the Red Giants.*

Liu, Alan P.L. *Communication and National Integration in Communist China.* Berkeley: University of California Press, 1971.

Lozada, Fernando and Kúncar, Gridvia C. "Bolivia: Las Radios Mineras, Voces del Coraje." In *Comunicación Alternativa y Cambio Social,* ed. Máximo Simpson Grinberg, Mexico: Premià Editora, 1986.

Markham, James W. *Voices of the Red Giants: Communications in Russia and China.* Ames: Iowa University Press, 1967.

McAnany, Emile. *Radio's Role in Development: Five Strategies of Use.* (Information Bulletin number Four). Washington D.C.: Clearinghouse on Development Communication, 1976.

McDaniel, Drew O. *Broadcasting in the Malay World, Radio, Television and Video in Brunei, Indonesia, Malaysia and Singapore.* Norwood, NJ: Ablex Publishing, 1994.

Miller, J. "History of American Broadcasting." <http://www.members. aol.com/jeff560/jeff.html> (2 Dec. 2002).

Moore, Don. "Reaching the Villages: Radio in Tanzania." *Journal of the North American Shortwave Association* (1996). <http://swl.net/patepluma/genbroad/tanzania.html.>(29 Dec. 2004).

O'Connor, Alan. "The Miners' Radio Stations in Bolivia: A Culture of Resistance."*Journal of Communication* 40 (1990): 102-110.

Pekerti, R. and R. Musa. "Wait a While My Love, An Indonesian Popular Song With a Family Planning Message." *JOICFP Integration* 21 (Oct. 1989): 41-43.

Rogers, Everett, M. *The Diffusion of Innovations*. 4th ed. New York: Free
    Press, 1995.
Rogers, E. M., J. R. Braun and M. A. Vermillion. "Radio Forums: A Strat-
    egy for Rural Development." in Spain, Jamison, and McAnany, *Radio
    for Education and Development*.
Sahlman, Rachel. "Spectrum Biographies—Thomas Alva Edison."
    <http://www. incwell.com/Biographies/Edison.html> (29 Dec. 2004).
Schmelkes de Sotelo, Sylvia. "The Radio Schools of the Tarahumara, Mex-
    ico: An Evaluation." in Spain, Jamison and McAnany, *Radio for Edu-
    cation and Development*.
Schramm, Wilbur. *Mass Media and National Development, The Role of
    Information in the Developing Countries*. Stanford, CA: Stanford
    Press, 1964.
Schramm, W. and R.F. Carter. "Scales for Describing National Com-
    munication Systems." Unpublished manuscript, Institute for Commu-
    nications Research, Stanford University, Stanford, Cal., 1959.
Siculus, Diodorus. *Library of World History*, Loeb Classical Library. Cam-
    bridge, Mass.:Harvard University Press, 1939.Vol. X.
Singhal, Arvind and Everett M. Rogers. *Combating AIDS: Communication
    Strategies in Action*. London: Sage, 2003.
Singhal, Arvind and E.M. Rogers. *Entertainment-Education: A Communi-
    cations Strategy for Social Change*. Mahwah, N.J.: Lawrence Erlbaum
    Associates, 1999.
Singhal, A. and E. M. Rogers. *India's Communication Revolution—From
    Bullock Carts to Cyber Marts*. New Delhi: Sage Publications, 2001.
Spain, P.L. "The Mexico Radio Primaria Project." in Spain, Jamison, and
    McAnany, *Radio for Education and Development*.
Spain, P.L., D. T. Jamison, and E. G. McAnany. "Voices for Development:
    The Tanzanian National Radio Study Campaigns." in Spain, Jamison,
    and McAnany, *Radio for Education and Development*.
Spain, P.L., D. T. Jamison, and E. G. McAnany, (eds.). *Radio for Educa-
    tion and Development: Case Studies*. Washington D.C.: World Bank,
    May, 1977.
Stark, Phyllis. "A History of Radio Broadcasting."*Billboard* (Nov. 1,
    1994).
Theroux, J. and J. Gunter. "Open Broadcast Educational Radio: Three
    Paradigms." in Spain, Jamison, and McAnany, *Radio for Education
    and Development*.UNESCO, *Features* no. 424 (Sept. 20, 1963): 12-14.
UNESCO. *Mass Media in the Developing Countries*. Paris: Clearing House
    of the Department of Mass Communication of UNESCO, 1961.

Valenzuela, Eduardo. "New Voices." Chap. 15 in Girard, *A Passion for Radio.*

Washburn, Philo C. *Broadcasting Propaganda, International Radio Broadcasting and the Construction of Political Reality.* Westport, Conn.: Praeger, 1992.

Wen Chi-tse. "People's Broadcasting During the Last 10 Years." *New China Monthly,* no. 72, (Sept. 1955): 232, in Chinese; in Lee, *The Development of Sound Broadcasting.*

White, Robert A. "Mass Communication and the Popular Promotion Strategy of Rural Development in Honduras." in Spain, Jamison, and McAnany, *Radio for Education and Development.*

White, Thomas. "United States Early Radio History." <http:// earlyradiohistory.us> (28 Dec. 2004).

World Bank, *Entering the 21st Century, World Development Report 1999/2000.* New York: Published for the World Bank, Oxford University Press, 2000.

Yu, Frederick T.C. *Mass Persuasion in Communist China.* New York: Praeger, 1964.

INDEX

Numbers in sans serif italics refer to scripts

Stephen Sposato is an economist with the United States Agency for International Development (USAID). He has nearly 25 years of experience in international economics and development. He has been specializing in development communication issues for the last five years, with an emphasis on radio. A native of Mount Vernon, New York, Stephen has lived or worked in Africa, Eastern Europe, the former Soviet Union and Asia. After completing his studies at Georgetown University's School of Foreign Service, Stephen went to White Mountain, Alaska, as a VISTA volunteer in a remote Eskimo village. He then went abroad to do graduate work in Belgium graduating from the University of Louvain where he obtained a Masters in Economics, Finance and Trade and from the Rijksuniversiteit-Ghent, where he obtained a Masters in Development

Stephen's attachment to sound, information and radio has a long career, first as a boy hearing of the post-war imports of capacitors, then as an entrepreneur in Europe. As a small business entrepreneur in Belgium and Paris, Stephen began what must have been one of the first monthly news programs on audio cassette "The American Scene," bringing news from home to Americans abroad and European students learning English. He was also founder of a small business in the heart of Paris "L'Atelier du Pre," an art and furniture shop. Stephen speaks Dutch and French. His African wife and he have one son, Marius Ismael.

William A. Smith, Ed. D., is Executive Vice President at the Academy for Educational Development the largest and most experienced nonprofit in applying modern communication to social change and development. Bill has focused much of his work since 1970 on the use of radio as a means to give voice to people in communities around the world. He has helped prepare health and instructional material for radio broadcast in both Africa and South America. He directed the world's first program to combine radio and a national lottery to reduce infant diarrhea in The Gambia, West Africa. He helped rural people in Ecuador use radio to publicize the discrimination they suffered at the hands of local officials and supervised the world's first attempt to use radio as the primary means of teaching English in classrooms in Africa

Bill's interest in radio stems from his work as one of America's leading social marketers. He is co-founder of the Social Marketing Institute, a columnist and editorial board member of the Social Marketing Quarterly and has published dozens of articles on radio, social marketing and social change.

Bill's career began in South America in the Peace Corps where he lived and worked for almost a decade. He has a doctoral degree from the University of Massachusetts in education with an emphasis on gaming and simulation theory. Bill and his wife Ginger have two children.